Scientific Foundations of Clinical Assessment

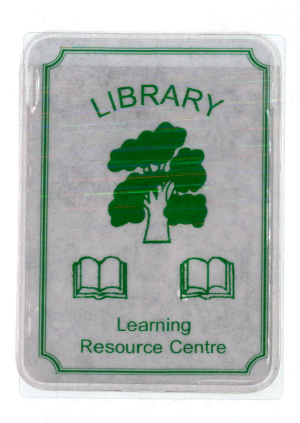

FOUNDATIONS OF CLINICAL SCIENCE AND PRACTICE

Series Editors:

Scott O. Lilienfeld, PhD
William T. O'Donohue, PhD

This series is designed to provide a user-friendly and engaging collection of brief books covering the fundamentals to a scientific approach to clinical psychology. It is based on the premise that science is the best path to the growth of knowledge about the myriad of problems in the field, such as the best way to measure a construct, and the most effective manner of treating a clinical problem. The quality of our field has been compromised for too long by a neglect of the value and the contributions of science. This series, by providing brief and accessible expositions of a scientific approach to the key elements of clinical psychology and allied disciplines, is meant to be a corrective. A more complete understanding of each of the dimensions of a scientific approach will move the field toward a more sound and thoroughgoing relationship with science—and in this way benefit clinical practice, research, and teaching. Consisting of brief manuscripts written by leading authorities, this book series will appeal to practitioners, researchers, instructors, and all others interested in studying the diagnosis, causes, treatment, and prevention of mental illness.

VOLUMES IN THIS SERIES

Scientific Foundations of Clinical Assessment
Stephen Haynes, Greg Smith, John Hunsley

Scientific Foundations of Clinical Assessment

STEPHEN N. HAYNES,
GREGORY T. SMITH, & JOHN D. HUNSLEY

Routledge
Taylor & Francis Group
New York   London

Routledge
Taylor & Francis Group
270 Madison Avenue
New York, NY 10016

Routledge
Taylor & Francis Group
27 Church Road
Hove, East Sussex BN3 2FA

Printed in the United States of America on acid-free paper
10 9 8 7 6 5 4 3 2 1

International Standard Book Number: 978-0-415-87650-6 (Hardback) 978-0-415-87651-3 (Paperback)

Library of Congress Cataloging-in-Publication Data

Haynes, Stephen N.
    Scientific foundations of clinical assessment / Stephen N. Haynes, Greg Smith,
John Hunsley.
        p. cm. -- (Foundations of clinical science and practice)
    Includes bibliographical references and index.
    ISBN 978-0-415-87650-6 (hardback) -- ISBN 978-0-415-87651-3 (paperback)
    1. Psychological tests--Methodology. 2. Psychodiagnostics--Methodology. I.
Smith, Greg. II. Hunsley, John, 1959- III. Title.

BF176.H396 2011
150.28'7--dc22   2010043259

Visit the Taylor & Francis Web site at
http://www.taylorandfrancis.com

and the Routledge Web site at
http://www.routledgementalhealth.com

Dedications

To Megumi
To Di, Corey, Jamie, and Daryn
To Catherine, for her love, friendship, and support

Contents

Editors' Introduction

As the great psychologist E.L. Thorndike (1926, p. 38) wrote, "If anything exists, it exists in some amount. If it exists in some amount, it can be measured." Measurement is a crucial component of science, including psychological science. Without measurement, scientific pursuits are impossible. Measurement allows us to determine the existence of entities (as the telescope revealed the existence of moons and planets and the microscope the existence of germs and cells). Measurement also allows the interested observer to capture quantity and magnitude—a thermometer, for example, captures the body's temperature. Finally, as clinicians, we are interested in the measurement of change—did my client's suicidal intent decrease from the last session? In the behavioral health professions, including clinical psychology, counseling psychology, psychiatry, and social work, we measure psychological and behavioral phenomena in many different ways: we interview, we observe, we obtain information from collateral contacts, we review records, and we test. We also measure many different constructs with these methods—each diagnostic criterion in the DSM calls for a measurement ("depressed mood or lost of interest or pleasure;" and we also measure other "meta" constructs like client's motivation to change and the client's truthfulness, etc). The average clinician may need to measure hundreds of constructs to rule in or rule out different clinical conclusions.

All measurement contains error. A key question, and a question thoroughly explored in this book, is how we can reduce errors in our measurements to minimize mistaken and potentially harmful clinical conclusions. The heart of a scientific approach recognizes the error term of measurement and makes assessment decisions with this error term in mind. In this respect, a scientific approach to assessment embraces humility, as it acknowledges the ubiquity of error in our observations and inferences and the need to delineate it and if possible compensate for it. An unscientific approach, in contrast, largely ignores such error, often pretending that it either does not exist or is unimportant.

We believe that this superb book will go a long way toward remedying the measurement problems that plague our field. Too often in practice, constructs are tossed around as if they can be, or have been, measured ("inner child"), or are simple when they are in fact complex ("best interest of the child" in custody decisions). Too often, tests are administered and used to draw inferences for which there is no evidential support or when there is evidence that they actually draw error to our clinical inferences (e.g., the negative incremental validity of the Rorschach Inkblot Test in making certain clinical decisions). Much of our measurement rests on the unstructured clinical interview despite the fact that much is unknown about its psychometric properties. The present book is a remedy to these common mistakes and others.

If we as clinical scientists have expertise to sell to the public, one key component of that expertise is surely a sophisticated approach to measurement. When measurement mistakes are made, we not only fail in our professional duties but we can inadvertently harm others. The error of concluding that someone is not suicidal when he or she actually is could be fatal. Sophisticated knowledge of measurement is also a prerequisite to conducting competent research to fill in key gaps in our knowledge of mental illness and its treatment and prevention.

Professors Haynes, Smith, and Hunsley are well known scholars of psychological assessment. In this book, they provide a fascinating and user-friendly tour of the intellectual landscape of a scientific approach to clinical assessment. Their basic premise is that there is an intellectual context to clinical assessment—unfortunately assessment is not so simple that all we need to do is ask our clients to complete a test and draw accurate conclusions. One needs to understand this test's conceptual and methodological underpinnings, along with its strengths and limitations and with a keen awareness of our own strengths and limitations as information processors. The authors' elegant treatment of the complexity of the intellectual context of measurement in clinical psychology allows readers to grasp this essential information in ways that are both useful and engaging.

REFERENCE

Thorndike, E.L. (1926). *The measurement of intelligence*. New York: Teacher's College.

Preface

Measurement is the systematic process of assigning numbers to properties or attributes of people, objects, or events. Measurement is at the heart of every science for, without measurement, meaningful research, both basic and applied, is impossible. Clinical assessment entails a plan to (a) collect measures and ancillary clinical information, (b) integrate these data in a meaningful and valid manner, and (c) generate service options based on this integration. Thus, assessment is at the heart of every health care service. Without assessment, especially assessment based on scientific principles and findings, health care services are, at best, ill considered or ill informed and, at worst, potentially dangerous to those receiving the services.

With these realities in mind, we had two main goals in writing this book. The first was to provide readers with a solid science-based framework for understanding psychological measurement and clinical assessment. The second goal was to provide guidance in using this framework to interpret clinical assessment research and to make good clinical assessment decisions, such as selecting the best instruments and measures for the task at hand, applying them in the most appropriate manner, and interpreting the obtained assessment data in a scientifically informed fashion. We believe that clients are at risk for receiving less-than-optimal services when clinicians fail to follow a science-based approach to clinical assessment.

To this end, as much as possible, we tried to avoid jargon and strove for simplicity over complexity in the presentation of the material. To demonstrate the relevance of psychometric principles and assessment research to clinical work, we included many clinical examples to illustrate our points. Text boxes, found in each chapter, provide extended presentations of the application of these principles and research to clinical work. The end of each chapter includes a summary of the key issues covered, often along with recommendations or suggestions for how these issues should influence your clinical assessment work. We also include additional sources at the end of each chapter. Moreover, to aid in the understanding of key measurement and assessment concepts, we included a glossary that we believe to be the most extensive and detailed ever provided in a clinical assessment volume.

The chapters were designed so that they build on material presented in preceding chapters, and when useful in explaining measurement or assessment concepts, we draw attention to critical material presented in other chapters. The first chapter provides an overview of what is to follow in the book, emphasizing the relations among clinical measurement, assessment, research, and clinical services and the importance of a science-based approach to clinical assessment. Chapters 2 and 3, with a focus on reliability and validity, provide details on the psychometric foundations of clinical assessment. Building on this, Chapters 4 and 5 provide detailed information on how psychometric data and evidence of clinical utility can inform diagnostic and other clinical decisions. Chapter 6 discusses a much-used analytic strategy in clinical assessment: factor analysis. With all this in mind, Chapter 7 emphasizes that all psychometric evidence is conditional inasmuch as data derived from specific samples and contexts may not be broadly generalizable. Appropriate recognition of this basic fact is crucial for using assessment data in a scientifically justifiable way. Chapter 8 emphasizes additional statistical procedures commonly used in assessment research, including analysis of variance, multiple regression, and methods for estimating the size and importance of associations observed among psychological variables. Knowledge of these procedures is crucial for understanding the research literature *and* appropriately applying research findings to clinical assessment activities. Finally, in the concluding chapter, we examine the potential of multisource assessment data to overcome the inevitable limitations associated with clinical data obtained from a single source.

Throughout the book, we emphasize the role of scientific evidence in conducting pretreatment assessments, developing diagnostic and clinical case formulations, and assessing treatment process and outcome. Given the nature of the book, this volume is best used to complement, rather than replace, texts that focus on specific assessment methods (i.e., interviews, self-report rating scales) or on procedures for conducting clinical assessments (i.e., addressing issues of informed consent, mandatory reporting obligations, report writing). Although many of the issues covered in the book are relevant to forensic, educational, personnel selection, and other assessment activities, we do not directly address these areas, concentrating instead on clinical assessment activities that encompass both health and mental health domains.

In closing, we would like to thank William O'Donohue and Scott Lilienfeld for initiating this book as part of their series on clinical science for Taylor & Francis and for providing valuable feedback during its preparation.

1

Introduction to the Scientific Foundations of Clinical Assessment

The Fundamental Relations Among Clinical Assessment, Measurement, and Clinical Science

INTRODUCTION

Clinical assessment provides essential information to help identify a client's behavior problems and treatment goals, to determine if the client's behavior problems are consistent with diagnostic criteria, to specify the variables that affect those problems and goals, to select and design the best intervention strategies for the client, to evaluate potential risk to the client and others, and to evaluate the intervention process and outcome. There are many approaches to clinical assessment; in this book, we advocate an important guiding principle: Clinical assessment will provide information that is most valid and useful when it is based on *principles of clinical science*. In this chapter, we introduce the basic concepts and methods associated with the scientific foundations of clinical assessment. Subsequent chapters consider these concepts and methods in greater detail.

CLINICAL ASSESSMENT AS ONE APPLICATION OF PSYCHOLOGICAL ASSESSMENT

*Psychological assessment** is the systematic measurement of a person's behavior[†] and variables associated with variance in behaviors as well as the inferences and judgments based on those measurements. Psychological assessment includes the entire assessment process: specific measurement instruments; assessment methods; assessment strategies; the targets of the assessment (e.g., behavior problems, causal and correlated variables, and contexts for behavior); and the assessor's ultimate judgments (e.g., diagnosis, case formulations, estimates of treatment outcome) based on the assessment data. Psychological assessment is applied in many domains, such as forensic assessment, educational evaluation and placement, personnel selection, cognitive assessment, and neuropsychological evaluation.

Clinical assessment is a specific application of psychological assessment in which the goal is to help the clinician answer questions that arise in a clinical context. Questions addressed in clinical assessment can include the following: (a) What are a client's concerns, behavior problems, and treatment goals? (b) Which variables affect the onset, intensity, severity, and duration of a client's problems? (c) How do the client's problems affect his or her daily living and persons in the client's environment? (d) Which interventions might be most effective in reducing the client's[‡] behavior problems, enhancing his or her quality of life and happiness, and achieving treatment goals? (e) What are the outcomes of a client's treatment and which variables affect those outcomes? and (f) How can treatment gains be maintained over time and in the face of challenges the client might face? The ultimate goals of clinical assessment are the selection, design, implementation, and evaluation

---

[*] Terms in italics are defined in the Glossary.
[†] We use the term behavior broadly to refer to a persons actions (e.g., a child's attention to tasks in a classroom, the statements made during a couple's argument); emotions (e.g., anger, sadness); thoughts and cognitive processes (e.g., the expectation that one will be more sociable with alcohol use, ruminations about a life stressor when one goes to bed at night); and physiological responses (e.g., asthma attacks experienced by an adolescent, a client's elevated blood pressure in response to interpersonal conflict).
[‡] The terms client and patient are used interchangeably throughout this book. These terms reflect different usages across countries and clinical settings and do not reflect differences in the collaborative relationship between a clinician and client/patient. Client is often more broadly applied to refer to the main focus of assessment. A client can include, for example, a single child or adult, couple, family, classroom, psychiatric unit, treatment program, or institution.

of treatments that reduce clients' behavior problems and help them achieve their anticipated treatment goals.

As we elaborate throughout, the guiding principle of this book is that clinical assessment is most effective when based on principles of scientific inquiry and inference.* Clinical assessment strategies should provide measures that are precise, sensitive to change, minimally inferential, and well validated for a particular assessment purpose and person; have well-documented sources of true and error variance; and can be appropriately interpreted by the clinician. Failure to follow a science-based approach to clinical assessment can harm clients in that it can adversely affect clinical judgments and diminish the outcome of intervention efforts with a client.

MEASUREMENT AND CLINICAL ASSESSMENT

Measurement is the foundation of clinical assessment and clinical science. Science-based measurement strategies enable us to improve our understanding of behavior and the factors that affect it. Without the ability to precisely measure phenomena such as mood, physical activity, blood sugar levels, or delusional thoughts, we could not precisely identify and monitor a client's behavior problems, goal attainment, or the variables that affect them, and we could not evaluate the effects of interventions to modify them.

In nomothetic research applications, measurement is necessary to identify and understand variables associated with individual differences, such as why some adolescents but not others start using drugs and why some patients experiencing chronic pain are impaired in their daily living whereas others with the same subjective pain level are able to continue with their lives in a normal manner. Precise measurement is also necessary to understand how and why behavior changes over time, settings, and contexts. Why are some children more likely to be physically aggressive in one setting than another? Which contexts increase the likelihood of panic attacks?

Data from well-designed clinical research provide important foundations of the clinical assessment process. These data help the clinician decide which assessment strategies might provide the most useful data with a particular client, which sources of error might be associated with the assessment process and its outcome, which signs and symptoms to look for in the assessment process, how a client's multiple behavior problems might be interrelated, and which variables might affect a client's

---

* An excellent discussion of the applications, history, assets, limitations, and controversies relevant to the "scientific method," with dozens of relevant examples and references, can be found at http://en.wikipedia.org/wiki/Scientific_method. See especially Kuhn, Thomas S., *The Structure of Scientific Revolutions*, University of Chicago Press, Chicago, 1962; 2nd edition 1970; 3rd edition 1996.

problems, goals, and treatment outcome. Thus, an important principle of clinical assessment is that *the clinician must be well grounded in the scientific findings relevant to the focus of the assessment*. Clinicians who are unfamiliar with the psychopathology and treatment research relevant to their client place their client at risk and may violate guidelines for ethical practice that are in place in many professional associations.

With this clinical science background to guide clinical assessment strategies, the clinician often supplements these nomothetic-based strategies with additional individualized assessments (i.e., *idiographic assessment*[*]) with clients to specify unique aspects of a client's problems and treatment goals and the variables and *functional relations*[†] related to them. The information derived in this clinical assessment process affects the ultimate clinical judgments stemming from the assessment. To be most useful, clinical *assessment strategies* should provide valid, accurate, relevant, and comprehensive measures of the variables of interest.

The scientific foundations of clinical assessment include four domains discussed throughout this book: (a) the nature of behavior problems and of the causal variables that affect them; (b) treatment research; (c) *psychometrics*, the study of the psychometric characteristics of measures; and (d) the clinical judgments that are derived from the information obtained during the clinical assessment process.

THE IMPORTANCE OF CLINICAL ASSESSMENT DATA

Several important judgments that are made during clinical assessment are outlined in Text Box 1.1 (see also Text Box 5.2). Each category of judgment involves multiple-component judgments. For example, diagnosis involves multiple-component judgments such as identifying a client's behavior problem signs and symptoms; establishing their rate, severity, duration, and time course; identifying factors associated with their onset; and matching signs and symptoms to inclusion and exclusion criteria within a formal diagnostic system. Clinical case formulation involves judgments such as specifying behavior problems, the functional relations among behavior problems, and the arrays of causal variables that affect them. Measurement is the foundation of each judgment: Invalid measures will diminish the validity of the judgment and, ultimately, diminish the quality of services to a client.

---

[*] Idiographic assessment involves psychological assessment instruments, methods, and strategies designed for an individual respondent. Idiographic assessment can involve an individualized assessment strategy, case formulation, elements selected from a nomothetically based assessment, or elements within a standardized assessment template (see discussion in Haynes, Mumma, & Pinson, 2009).

[†] Two variables have a functional relation when some dimension (e.g., rate, magnitude, length, age) of one variable is associated with (i.e., covaries with) some dimension of another (see Figure 1.1 for an illustration).

TEXT BOX 1.1   SEVERAL CATEGORIES OF
JUDGMENTS MADE IN CLINICAL ASSESSMENT

- **Diagnosis:** The process of assigning a psychiatric label to a person based on the degree to which the person's signs and symptoms conform to standardized diagnostic criteria
- **Professional Referral and Consultation:** Determining the need to seek assessment or treatment services from other professionals
- **Problem Identification and Specification:** The identification of a person's behavior problems and the specification of their rate, intensity, duration, and time course
- **Clinical Case Formulation:** The identification of important, controllable, causal, and noncausal functional relations applicable to specified behaviors for an individual
- **Intervention Design, Selection, and Modification:** The design or selection of the best intervention, given the characteristics of the client's behavior problems, the variables that affect them, and treatment goals
- **Treatment Outcome Evaluation:** Evaluating the immediate, intermediate, and ultimate effects of an intervention with a client and the variables that affect intervention outcome
- **Risk Assessment:** Estimating the likelihood that a client will harm him- or herself or others; the chance of recidivism following treatment
- **Identifying Variables Associated With Treatment Maintenance and Relapse:** The identification of variables that are likely to affect the maintenance of gains made in treatment or are likely to lead to relapse

For the judgments illustrated in Text Box 1.1 to be most beneficial to clients, the measurement strategies used in clinical assessment, and the resulting data, must be valid and appropriate in three ways. First, they must be valid indicators of the state of a variable when measured, such as the intensity of a client's depressed mood or the frequency of a child's aggressive behavior. Second, they must be valid indicators of changes in a variable, such as changes in the duration or severity of a client's depressed mood as a function of treatment or changes across time and settings in the frequency of a client's aggressive acts. Third, they must be relevant for detecting important functional relations for a client's behavior problems or treatment goals, such as the situations associated with a client's panic attacks or the relations between the responses by parents and a child's development of verbal communication skills.

TEXT BOX 1.2   COMMON ERRORS IN CLINICAL ASSESSMENT STRATEGIES

As we discuss further in this chapter and throughout the book, clinicians often use assessment strategies that fail to provide the most valid and useful data for clinical decision making. Furthermore, as also discussed further in the chapter, clinical judgment errors can occur even when the clinician gathers data using the best science-based assessment strategies.

In terms of assessment strategy errors, the clinician can

- Use assessment instruments that are readily available, such as those that can be copied from books on clinical assessment, rather than instruments that are most appropriate for the client
- Use assessment instruments that provide information that is insufficiently precise to guide clinical decisions (see discussion of other clinical judgment errors later in this chapter)
- Interpret assessment results (e.g., from interviews, personality tests, or projective tests) in a subjective manner, inconsistent with scientifically based strategies
- Use the same assessment instruments with all clients, regardless of their presenting problems, characteristics, and goals
- Use assessment instruments that have been developed and validated with samples that differ substantially (e.g., in age, economic status, sex, ethnic background) from the client
- Presume that an assessment instrument provides a valid measure of the construct simply because the construct is identified in the instrument's title

As we discuss in later chapters, we promote a *functional approach to clinical assessment*. That is, the most valid and useful measures and assessment strategies for an assessment occasion can vary depending on the goals of clinical assessment, the phenomena measured, and the characteristics of the client. There are common errors in clinical assessment strategies; these are given in Text Box 1.2.

The following sections and chapters further discuss the scientific foundations of clinical assessment. Because terms are often used differently among assessment scholars, Text Box 1.3 provides definitions of several frequently used clinical assessment terms. To aid in the use of this book, we provide many other definitions in the Glossary.

As we discuss in other chapters, the relevance of different psychometric indices varies across methods. For example, *internal consistency*

TEXT BOX 1.3   DEFINITIONS OF BASIC MEASUREMENT TERMS

- **Assessment Strategy:** The overall plan of action for deriving assessment measures. It involves a particular set of assessment methods, instruments, instructions to client, time-sampling parameters, and the context of assessment (e.g., in the clinic, home, or school).
- **Assessment Method:** A class of procedures for deriving measures of the behavior or other aspects of a person, events, aspects of the environment, or functional relations among variables (e.g., self-report questionnaires or analog behavioral observations).
- **Assessment Instrument:** A specific procedure for deriving measures of the actions, thoughts, or emotions of a person; events and aspects of the environment; or functional relations among variables on a specific assessment occasion (e.g., a specific self-report depression questionnaire; a specific checklist of child behavior problems).
- **Functional Relation:** A functional relation exists when two variables have shared variance: Some dimension (e.g., rate, magnitude, length, age) of one variable is associated with some dimension of another. Variables are functionally related when they demonstrate a mathematical relation. Functional relations can be causal or noncausal.
- **Measure (or Score):** (a) A number that represents the variable being measured. (b) The number obtained from a measurement process or assessment instrument (e.g., a blood pressure reading obtained with a sphygmomanometer, a scale score obtained from a personality assessment instrument; note that many assessment instrument provide multiple measures).
- **Measurement:** The process of assigning a numerical value to a variable dimension so that relations of the numbers reflect true relations among the measured variables (e.g., the process of estimating a child's rate of aggressive behaviors on the playground by external or participant observers).

(Chapter 2) is an important psychometric concept when generating a score from multiple self-report items but is less important for direct observation of discrete behaviors. Despite differences in the relevance of individual psychometric indices of measures derived in clinical assessment, the validity of judgments made during the clinical assessment process and advances in clinical assessment all depend on the adoption of a science-based approach to measurement, psychopathology, treatment research, and clinical judgments.

HOW RESEARCH ON THE NATURE OF BEHAVIOR PROBLEMS AND THEIR CAUSES AFFECTS CLINICAL ASSESSMENT

Our science-based approach to clinical assessment is guided, in part, by what research has revealed about behavior problems and their causes. Table 1.1 presents an overview of some findings in psychopathology and their implications for clinical assessment.

To elaborate on just a couple of the concepts from Table 1.1, we note that clinical assessment strategies are guided by the results of hundreds of studies that have documented that clients often have multiple behavior problems (i.e., evidence high rates of comorbidity). For example, persons diagnosed with schizophrenia, substance abuse, bipolar disorders, and personality disorders have a high likelihood of concurrently experiencing additional behavior disorders (see discussions of the concepts of comorbidity and the functional relations that underlie the covariances among behavior problems in Haynes & Kaholokula, 2007; Krueger & Markon, 2006; Lilienfeld, Waldman, & Israel, 1994). Most children diagnosed with schizophrenia have at least one co-occurring behavior problem (Ross, Heinlein, & Tregellas, 2006), and many persons who frequently use inhaled substances (e.g., amyl nitrate and nitrous oxide) also exhibit personality disorders (Wu & Howard, 2007). Further, each behavior problem can involve multiple response systems (e.g., cognitive, emotional, physical activity) along multiple dimensions (e.g., rate, severity, duration). Further still, a client's behavior problem response systems, and dimension of those response systems, can change across time and contexts and can vary in importance across persons (see reviews in Andrasek, 2006).

Research on comorbidity has important implications for the strategies and focus of clinical assessment and for clinical judgments based on the assessment data. Observe in Figure 1.1 how judgments about the most effective treatment focus would differ, depending on the different functional relations among a client's multiple behavior problems identified during the assessment process.

For a client whose behavior problems are interrelated in a manner similar to Functional Relations (a), the most beneficial treatment target would be the client's marital conflict because it also serves as a causal variable for the client's self-injury and depressed mood. In contrast, for a client whose behavior problems are interrelated similar to Functional Relations (b), the most beneficial treatment target would be helping the client reduce or adjust to his or her life stressors. Functional

TABLE 1.1   The Effect on Clinical Assessment Strategies of Research on Behavior Problems and Their Causes

Concept	Example	Sample Effects on Clinical Assessment
Persons seeking behavioral health services often have multiple problems.	Persons with bipolar disorders often present with concurrent substance use and personality disorders.	Initial intake and treatment outcome assessment strategies should be broadly focused to detect multiple problems (see discussion of clinical utility and clinical judgment in Chapters 4 and 5).
The multiple behavior problems of a client can have important functional interrelations.	The mood of a client diagnosed with a major affective disorder can be influenced by his or her interpersonal conflicts, pain, or use of alcohol.	In clinical case formulations with clients with multiple behavior problems, it is important to estimate the causal relations among the behavior problems.
Behavior problems have multiple aspects and response modes (e.g., cognitive, physical actions, emotional).	A client's mood disorders can involve multiple cognitive, behavioral, and emotional aspects and response modes.	The degree to which an instrument provides measures of the important aspects and response modes of a behavior problem affects its content and construct validity (see Chapter 3).
Persons with the same behavior problem can differ in the most important aspect and response mode of that problem.	Persons with social anxiety can differ in the degree to which they avoid social situations, avoid performance situations, experience subjective distress, and experience anticipatory anxiety.	Diagnosis is often insufficient to characterize a client's behavior problems, and individualized (idiographic) assessment can sometimes provide more precise data on behavior problems, causal variables, and treatment outcome.

(continued on next page)

TABLE 1.1 (continued)   The Effect on Clinical Assessment Strategies
of Research on Behavior Problems and Their Causes

Concept	Example	Sample Effects on Clinical Assessment
Behavior problems can be characterized along multiple dimensions, such as rate, duration, and severity, which can differ in importance across clients. Causal variables and treatments can differ in their effects across dimensions.	Panic attacks can be characterized on the basis of their rate, severity, and duration. For some clients, the most important dimension is the frequency of panic attacks. and for others the severity or duration of panic attacks can be the most important dimension.	Clinical assessment should include measures of the multiple dimensions of behavior problems, and assessment methods and instruments differ in the degree to which they capture different dimensions of behavior problems.
The aspects and dimensions of behavior problems can change across time and settings.	The type and frequency of an adolescent's use of alcohol or drugs can change across time and as a function of the social contexts.	Repeated measurement across time and settings, with measures that are sensitive to change, are necessary to capture the time and setting specificity of a client's behavior problem.
The causal variables for a client's behavior problems can be distal or proximal, differ in their degree of modifiability, and differ in their strength of effect.	Childhood exposure to domestic violence, conflicts with a domestic partner, and insufficient problem-solving skills can all serve as causes of self-injury but differ in importance and modifiability.	Pretreatment clinical assessment strategies are most useful when they identify the most important and modifiable causal variables for a client's behavior problem.
Behavior problems can be conditional.	A child may be more aggressive, oppositional, or communicative in one setting than in another.	Clinical assessment strategies that attend to differences in behavior across settings can often be helpful in identifying the operation of causal variables and in evaluation of the setting generalization of treatment effects.

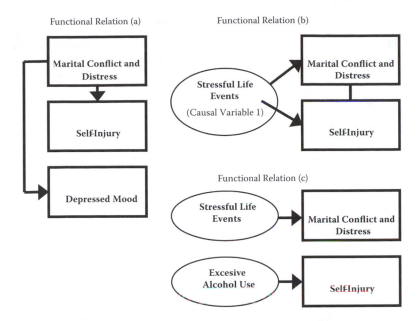

Figure 1.1   Three forms of functional relations (comorbidity) among behavior problems (Adapted from Kaholokula, Bello, Nacapoy, & Haynes (2009). In D. Richard & S. Huprich (Eds.), *Clinical psychology: Assessment, treatment, and research*, pp. 113–142).

Relations (c) illustrates how multiple behavior problems can each be a result of different causal variables (the behavior problems can appear to be functionally related if their respective causal variables are functionally related): In this case, life stressors, alcohol use, or both would be relevant intervention targets, depending on their relative strength of relation and the relative importance of the behavior problems. Note especially how the causal diagrams in Figure 1.1 illustrate the importance of clinical assessment strategies that not only describe behavior problems but also attempt to explain them—to identify the functional relations relevant to those behavior problems. The consequence of a clinician's failure to understand the research literature on comorbidity is clear. A clinician who fails to evaluate the possibility of multiple behavior problems and their interrelations is likely to generate an erroneous diagnosis, clinical case formulation, and intervention program for a client.

Kaholokula et al. (2009) discussed the importance of clinical assessment strategies that provide measures that are sensitive to change over time. *Sensitivity to change* is an essential psychometric aspect of measurement if the goal is to monitor treatment effects or to identify the variables

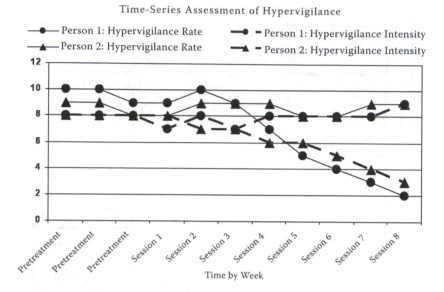

Figure 1.2 Time course data of two dimensions of hypervigilance (rate, intensity) for two persons diagnosed with PTSD before and during treatment (Adapted from Haynes, Kaholokula, & Yoshioka (2008). In A. M. Nezu & C. Nezu (Eds.), *Evidenced-based outcome research: A practical guide to conducting RCTs for psychosocial interventions*, pp. 67–94).

that affect a client's behavior problems. As we discuss in Chapter 4, measures can differ in the degree to which they accurately track true change in the measured constructs. To illustrate the importance of sensitivity to change (and the multiple dimensions and individual differences in behavior problems), Kaholokula and colleagues illustrated a possible time course of two dimensions of hypervigilance (rate and intensity) for two persons being treated for posttraumatic stress disorder (PTSD) (see Figure 1.2).

In this example, the rate and intensity of hypervigilance (measured when the persons were in crowded settings) were initially about the same for both persons. However, Person 1 experienced a drop in vigilance rate but not intensity with treatment, whereas Person 2 experienced the opposite change. In this scenario, the clinical judgment would be that the treatment was having different effects on the two dimensions for each person, and a modification of the treatment strategy might be warranted, depending on the importance of each dimension for each client.

Note also how a composite measure of PTSD that aggregated multiple items across response systems or dimensions would provide information that was less specific, less sensitive to change, and less clinically useful for evaluating the effects of treatment (see Chapter 9 and Smith, McCarthy, & Zapolski, 2009). For some goals, such as clinical case formulation and treatment outcome evaluation, clinical assessment can provide more useful information when focused on more precise (i.e., accurate, specific, and sensitive) lower-order variables (e.g., specific behaviors and thoughts) rather than, or in addition to, higher-order variables, which are aggregates of multiple facets and dimensions of a construct (e.g., summary measures of "depression" and "social phobia"). For other goals, such as diagnosis or screening, composite measures would be more useful. A frequent error by clinicians is to base important clinical judgments on easily available composite measures (e.g., from computer-generated scale scores of personality inventories), which aggregate numerous clinically significant behaviors, thoughts, and emotions. The key to best practices in assessment is to be aware of research that can inform the choice of whether to focus on lower-order variables or composite measures.

THE IMPACT OF TREATMENT RESEARCH ON CLINICAL ASSESSMENT

The relations between assessment strategies and treatment research were discussed in three chapters (Fernandez-Ballésteros & Botella, 2008; Haynes, Kaholokula, & Yoshida, 2008; Widiger, 2008) in Nezu and Nezu's (2008) volume on treatment research. Consider the importance of questions addressed in treatment research and how the answers depend on the quality of measures used in the research:

1. How effective is a treatment, and what is its relative effectiveness compared to other treatments?
2. Which components of a treatment most strongly affect the outcome, and what explains the treatment effects (i.e., what are the *treatment mechanisms* that account for changes in clients' behavior)?
3. What is the time course of treatment effects (e.g., how rapidly do treatment-related changes occur)?
4. What are the relative costs and benefits of a treatment?
5. How well do treatment effects generalize across participants, and what is the transportability of a treatment across applied settings?
6. How long do treatment benefits last and what variables affect treatment maintenance and relapse?
7. How do individual differences among clients affect treatment outcome, and what are the incremental benefits of basing treatment on individualized case formulations?
8. What is the clinical significance, or importance, of changes associated with a treatment?
9. Does the treatment affect some aspects of a behavior problem or goal more than others?

The interface between treatment research and measurement is obvious: Precise measurement is required for these questions to be addressed. These treatment-related questions guide the selection of the most clinically useful assessment strategies.

Treatment research guides many aspects of a scientific approach to clinical assessment strategies, methods, instruments, measures, and the judgments derived during the assessment process. For example, a major goal of treatment research is to estimate the effects of a treatment for a client. This goal invokes the deceptively complex mandate that clinical assessment strategies and measures must be *sensitive to changes* in the targeted phenomena. Some clinicians use minimal assessment strategies by obtaining only pre- and posttreatment measures of the depression, anxiety, pain, antisocial, self-injurious behaviors or other primary treatment targets. This strategy provides some data on ultimate outcome and is preferable to the assessment strategy followed by many clinicians of no systematic treatment outcome assessment efforts, but it does not help the clinician to sensitively monitor treatment effects, whereas doing so is essential for many purposes, such as the early detection of treatment failure. The results of many treatment outcome studies have much to say about how the clinician can best evaluate the effects of an intervention. For example, frequent monitoring of a client's progress during therapy can help in the early identification of clients who are unresponsive to a treatment, suggest that a refinement of the treatment program may be needed, and help to reduce the chance of ultimate treatment failure (see discussions in Kazdin, 1993; Lambert, Hansen, & Finch, 2001; Mash & Hunsley, 1993; Persons & Mikami, 2002).

Many assessment instruments that are used in treatment outcome evaluation are not well constructed to measure change. For example, Froyd, Lambert, and Froyd (1996) noted that the Minnesota Multiphasic Personality Inventory (MMPI) is frequently used to measure treatment outcome but is excessively lengthy and expensive, and many of its items are insensitive to change. Vermeersch et al. (2004) outlined several aspects of an assessment instrument that can reduce its ability to provide measures that are sensitive to change. First, an instrument could include elements that are not relevant to the phenomenon or persons assessed. Consider an instrument that purports to measure depression that also includes items that measure anxiety. Measures from the instrument would have diminished *discriminant validity*, which means, in this case, that changes in the measure over time could reflect changes in anxiety rather than depressed mood, and changes in mood could be masked by changes in anxiety. Similarly, an instrument could fail to include (or disproportionately include) elements that tap important aspects of a measured phenomenon. Consider the impact on measures from an instrument that purports to measure depression but does not include items on the client's feelings of energy or fatigue: Treatment-related changes in these components of depression would not be reflected in changes in the measure. In summary, the *content validity* of an instrument (i.e., the degree to which its elements are relevant to and representative of the targeted construct) is fundamental to sensitivity to change.

Content validity is a necessary but insufficient aspect of an assessment instrument to ensure that measures derived from it are sensitive to change. Sensitivity to change can also be affected by the response format of an instrument. For example, consider the differences between a questionnaire that uses a small number of categories or a restricted scale (e.g., yes-no or 0–2) and one that uses a more extended response format:

1. Are you satisfied with your marriage: ___ yes ___no

versus

2. To what degree are you satisfied with your marriage:

    ___ very unsatisfied ___ unsatisfied ___ satisfied ___ very satisfied

The second response format, compared to the first, is more likely to detect shifts in marital satisfaction across time.

The time frame of the inquiry can also affect sensitivity to change. Generally, longer time frames, or unspecified time frames, are less sensitive to change than shorter time frames. Consider the differences in likely sensitivity to change between these time frames:

1. Are you satisfied with your marriage?
2. In the last month, how satisfied have you been with your marriage?
3. In the last week, how satisfied have you been with your marriage?

It should be evident that if the clinician wants to detect changes in marital satisfaction associated with therapy, the last time frame would be most useful. Vermeersch et al. (2004) outlined additional aspects of assessment instruments that can affect sensitivity to change. For example, some items and measures can have ceiling or floor affects that limit the range of values in which a measure is sensitive to change (see discussion of this issue in the context of item response theory in this chapter). This example also illustrates the conditional nature of validity evidence (Chapter 7) in that "sensitivity to change" would be a less-relevant consideration if the measure were used as a brief screen for clients entering an outpatient behavioral or mental health center.

As we illustrated, sensitivity to change is also affected by the clinician's *assessment strategy*. Judgments about the effects of therapy that are sensitive to change mandate that assessment occur frequently (see Figure 1.2 for an example). For example, without frequent measurement and the use of sensitive measures, failing therapies are less likely to be quickly identified.

We have concentrated our discussion of the impact of treatment research on the importance of using measurement strategies that are sensitive to change. However, other aspects of treatment research are also important for the scientific foundations of clinical assessment: (a) The effects of a treatment can differ across the components of a behavior problem, highlighting the importance of using measures that provide valid indices of all components (i.e., good *content* and *construct validity* (Chapters 3, 6, and 8) and that have been subjected to appropriate *factor analysis* (Chapter 6). (b) The clinical significance of treatment-related changes can best be estimated using highly *reliable measures* (see discussion of reliability and *reliable change indices* in Chapter 2). (c) Judgments about treatment outcome can be erroneous or biased when based on a single source (e.g., a single informant or instrument), emphasizing the importance of *multisource assessment* (see Chapter 9). (d) Inferences about the effectiveness of a treatment depend on the degree to which the treatment was appropriately delivered, emphasizing the importance of assessing independent (treatment delivery accuracy) as well as dependent (change in problem behavior) variables in treatment research.

PSYCHOMETRIC FOUNDATIONS OF CLINICAL ASSESSMENT

We began this chapter by emphasizing that science-based measurement strategies are the foundations of good clinical judgment, and that a clinician's failure to implement science-based assessment strategies places a client at risk for diminished benefits. We reflected on several ways that psychopathology and treatment research provide important foundations for a science-based approach to measurement and clinical assessment. *Psychometrics** provides further methodological and conceptual bases for a science-based approach to clinical assessment. Psychometrics is the evaluative processes applied to data from psychological assessment instruments and to the judgments based on those data: It is the science of measurement and psychological assessment. Psychometric evidence discussed throughout this book, such as validity, reliability, item response characteristics, and factor structure, provide information to the clinician about the quality of clinical assessment data, help the clinician acquire the best data, and guide the clinician in interpreting the data (see an overview of psychometrics in Furr and Bacharach, 2008, and a discussion of the evolution of psychometric concepts and methods in Bechtold, 1951).

---

* The term psychometry is derived from the Greek words psyche ("soul") and metron ("measure") and was first used by Joseph R. Buchanan in 1842. In other disciplines, psychometry, in contrast to psychometrics, sometimes refers to the study of paranormal abilities (http://psychometricanalysis.blogspot.com/2006/03/psychometry-brief-history.html).

Psychometrics contributes to clinical assessment in two ways: (a) It includes principles and methods to guide the development and refinement of clinical assessment instruments, and (b) it includes principles and methods to help the clinician obtain and evaluate evidence about the quality of clinical assessment measures. The ultimate goals of psychometrics are to guide the construction, selection, application, and interpretation of measures that are optimally valid indices of the attributes of people and events they are designed to measure.

As we discuss in Text Box 1.4, the "validity" of a measure is the primary focus of all approaches to psychometrics. However, validity is a complex and evolving construct that can be approached in several ways. When applied to clinical assessment, *validity* most often refers to the degree to which a measure reflects the phenomena it purports to measure. Stated differently, validity is the degree to which changes on a dimension of an attribute produce changes in a measure of that attribute dimension (e.g., Borsboom, Mellenbergh, & van Heerden, 2004; Messick, 1995; Nunnally & Bernstein, 1994).*

As noted in Item 4 in Text Box 1.4, psychometric evidence about the validity of a measure comes in many forms. Table 1.2 presents definitions and examples of some types of validity evidence that are especially relevant for clinical assessment. The Glossary defines additional types of validity evidence.

As we discus in Chapters 2 and 3, evidence about the validity of a measure can be gathered through several analytic strategies. The most commonly used are often referred to as *classical test theory* (CTT), *item response theory* (IRT), and *generalizability theory* (GT).

1. *Classical test theory* (CTT or *classical true score theory*) is the most frequent strategy used in the development and evaluation of clinical assessment instruments. In this paradigm, scores from an instrument are considered to reflect both true variance in the measured construct and error variance associated with the instrument or assessment process:

$$O = T + E,$$

   where O is the observed score, T is the true score, and E is the total error associated with the measurement. The goal of many validation procedures such as those in Table 1.2 is to estimate the proportion of variance in a measure than can be considered "true" versus "error."

---

* Borsboom et al. (2004) also discuss the validity in the context of logical positivist, realist, postmodernist, constructivist, metaphysical, empiricist, and ontological perspectives.

TEXT BOX 1.4   THE EVOLVING CONCEPTS AND CONDITIONAL NATURE OF VALIDITY

In an article published in *Psychological Review*, Borsboom et al. (2004) traced the increasing breadth and fuzzy boundaries associated with the concept *validity*. They noted how an original, narrow, and commonly accepted definition of validity of a measure, such as the one offered in the preceding paragraph, has evolved to incorporate a broader array of evidence, particularly decisions based on the measure. For example, many educational scholars objected to how some IQ and achievement test results were being used to place a disproportionate number of ethnic minority children in restrictive learning environments. As a result, the concept of validity began to include not only the degree to which a measure reflected the attribute measured but also the social consequences of the judgments and decisions that were based on it (see also discussions by Messick, 1998).

While acknowledging the ethical, social, and political importance of judgments based on assessment data (see Chapters 4 and 5), we emphasize throughout this book the more restrictive approach to validity encouraged by Borsboom et al. (2004) and adopted by many contemporary psychometric scholars. How measures are used, decisions and judgments based on measures, and their social implications are important concerns but are, we believe, independent of the validity of the measure on which those decisions are based. In other words, bad decisions can be based on valid data.

However, as we discuss in subsequent chapters, there are several important caveats associated with this narrower definition of validity that underscore the relevance of the broader view of validity. These caveats address the *functional approach to validation and the conditional nature of validity evidence*:

1. Validity is not an invariant trait of an assessment instrument; an instrument can provide multiple measures that can differ in their validity and as a function of assessment contexts, as noted next.
2. A measure can be more valid for some than for other assessment purposes (e.g., diagnosis vs. treatment outcome evaluation).
3. Because attributes of a construct can vary across populations, a measure can be more valid for some than for other populations or dimensions of individual differences (e.g., ethnicity, age, sex, and severity of a behavior problem).
4. Evidence for the validity of a measure can come through many operations, such as convergent and criterion validation, discriminant validation, discriminative validation, content validation, reliability evaluation, and item performance characteristics. The evidence for validity of a measure can differ across these sources of evidence.

TABLE 1.2 Common Forms of Validity Evidence

Type of Evidence	Definition	Example
Content validity	The degree to which elements of an assessment instrument are relevant to and representative of the targeted construct	The degree to which the items on a self-report questionnaire of depression are relevant to that construct and appropriately capture all components of depression
Convergent validity	The degree to which the data from the assessment instrument are coherently related to other measures of the same construct as well as to other variables that they are expected, on theoretical grounds, to be related	The degree to which a self-report measure of social anxiety is related to other self-report or observer ratings of social anxiety
Discriminant validity	The degree to which data from an assessment instrument are not unduly related to other exemplars of other constructs	The degree to which a measure of childhood aggression does not reflect physical activity or oppositional behavior
Discriminative validity	The degree to which measures from an assessment instrument can differentiate individuals in groups formed from independent criteria and known to vary on the measured construct	The degree to which a score from a marital satisfaction inventory can differentiate individuals who are and who are not seeking counseling because of marital distress
Ecological validity	The generalizability of measures, and judgments from measures, to the populations, contexts, purposes, or situations that are of primary interest of the assessment	The degree to which responses to a stressor presented in a laboratory are similar to responses of the respondents to a stressor that occurs in their natural environment[a]
Internal consistency	The degree of consistency of the multiple items or elements within an assessment instrument that are used to form a composite measure	The degree of intercorrelation among multiple items selected to form a composite measure of obsessive thinking

(continued on next page)

TABLE 1.2 (continued)   Common Forms of Validity Evidence

Type of Evidence	Definition	Example
Positive and negative predictive power	The positive and negative "hit rate" for a score; true positive rate/(true positive + false positive rate or true negative rate/(true negative rate + false negative rate)	The degree to which persons identified on the basis of a measure as having or not having an eating disorder truly have or do not have the disorder (for positive predictive power and negative predictive power)
Sensitivity	The proportion of positive cases so identified on the basis of a measure from a particular assessment instrument	The proportion of children in a school diagnosed with a conduct disorder who are so identified on the basis of a teacher rating form
Temporal stability	The degree of linear relation of a measure obtained across occasions from the same individuals under similar conditions	The degree of correlation between two measures of sleep disturbance obtained from the same sample using the same assessment strategy at two points in time

[a] As discussed in Blanton and Jaccard (2006) and Kazdin (2008), ecological validity of measures can have another meaning: the degree to which changes on a standardized measure (e.g., a 3-point change in a measure of mood or anxiety) translate to changes in functioning in everyday life.

2. *Item response theory* (i.e., latent trait theory) was developed to address some of the limitations of classical test theory and is most often used to examine the performance of individual items across levels of a latent construct. IRT is a prevalent measurement model in cognitive and computerized adaptive assessment but has recently also been applied in the development and evaluation of clinical assessment instruments. The performance of individual items across levels of a construct is often illustrated with *item characteristic curves*, examples of which can be found in all basic texts on testing. Mathematical equations are used to estimate the amount of a latent trait that is possessed by an individual, based

on information about the difficulty, discrimination (the ability of an item to discriminate across persons who differ on levels of the measured trait), and probability of correct guessing, from a group of items. Although large samples are required to estimate item performance characteristics, IRT paradigms have several advantages over CTT paradigms: (a) They allow different sets of items to be used on different assessment occasions; (b) different sets of items can be selected based on a client's level on the measured construct (e.g., low vs. high level of depressed mood); (c) *differential item functioning* across groups can be examined as a method of identifying equivalence and bias of items; and (d) measures of the same construct from different instruments can be equated. Item discrimination is indicated by an *information function*—indicating which items are most likely to discriminate at various levels of the measured construct. A chapter by Gorin and Embretson (2008) provides an overview of the underlying assumptions and methods of IRT, with a particular emphasis on Rasch models (used especially for dichotomously scored items).

3. *Generalizability theory* examines the relative contribution of multiple sources of variance in obtained scores by using multivariate analysis statistical techniques. For example, one can estimate how much variability in obtained measures from repeated interviews of clients is due to the occasion of measurement (i.e., measures from the initial vs. repeated interviews), the interviewer conducting the assessment, the setting, and other factors. In a generalizability study, data on a measure are collected within the assessment facets of interest (e.g., to estimate variance associated with different observers, at different times, in different settings). Through this strategy, variances associated with each facet can be examined, which can help identify sources of error and of stability in measures. *Reliability coefficients*, called G coefficients, are then calculated by dividing true variances by the sum of true and error variances (Suen & Rzasa, 2004).

The three measurement models differ in analytic strategy, level of focus (e.g., attending to performance at the item level vs. the composite measure level), and applicability across assessment methods. However, they have the same goals: to construct measures that provide the most valid data possible and to evaluate the validity of assessment data so that the clinician can make the best judgments regarding his or her client. Clinical judgments are the ultimate product of clinical assessment. We introduce basic concepts of clinical judgment next and address them in greater detail in Chapters 4 and 5.

Psychometric evidence can also be misinterpreted. Text Box 1.5 lists some common errors in interpreting psychometric evidence.

TEXT BOX 1.5   COMMON ERRORS IN INTERPRETING PSYCHOMETRIC EVIDENCE FOR CLINICAL ASSESSMENT MEASURES

Psychometric evidence is multifaceted and often challenging to understand. Furthermore, the relevance of different forms of evidence varies across the behaviors and events that are measured *and* the goals of assessment. The following are several errors that clinicians can make in considering the psychometric evidence for a measure in clinical assessment:

- Assuming that a reliability index for a measure indicates its validity. Indices of internal consistency, such as Cronbach's alpha, indicate the degree of interrelationships among items, not the degree to which those items provide a valid measure of the targeted phenomenon.
- Assuming that a validity index for a measure is generalizable across other validity indices for that measure. For example, a measure that has demonstrated a high degree of discriminative validity may not demonstrate a high degree of convergent or discriminant validity.
- Assuming that validity evidence for a measure from prior research is always applicable to a current assessment occasion. A strong indication of validity may have been obtained with a sample that differs in important ways (e.g., age, ethnicity, economic status, language abilities) from the client or current sample. The likely generalizability of the prior validity evidence to the current assessment occasion must be carefully considered.
- Disregarding conflicting evidence of internal structure of an instrument. Often, factor structures identified during the original development of an instrument fail to satisfactorily replicate in subsequent studies. An unreliable factor structure indicates either problems with the content of the measure or that important differences in performance of the measure occur across populations.
- Assuming that supportive validity evidence from one measure of an instrument is applicable to other measures from that instrument. Often, a clinical assessment instrument can provide multiple measures that can differ in their degree of validity.
- A bias for one form of validity. In selecting clinical assessment instruments, a clinician can emphasize the importance, for example, of convergent validity more than discriminant validity. The importance of different forms of validity evidence varies, depending on the goals of assessment (see Chapter 7).

RESEARCH ON CLINICAL JUDGMENT
AND DECISION MAKING

The previous sections of this chapter introduced the scientific foundations of clinical assessment methods and strategies. We presented the concepts and perspectives that advise the clinician how to obtain the most valid and useful data in the clinical assessment process. The last step in the clinical assessment process is for the clinician to draw inferences from these data; to make judgments about diagnosis, case formulation, treatment selection, the effects of treatment; and to identify variables that might affect relapse and treatment maintenance (see Text Box 1.1). This is a challenging decision-making process subject to many potential errors in the clinician's assessment strategy, as discussed in the following section. Several science-based principles and a vast array of research findings on clinical judgment, also discussed in Chapters 4 and 5, guide this process.

We do not artificially separate or presume a conflict, as some do (e.g., Zeldow, 2009), between clinical and actuarial or statistically based clinical judgments. That being said, there is compelling evidence, across a wide range of clinical assessment contexts, that the use of empirically derived statistical decision rules yields more accurate predictions than do strategies based on the intuitive combination of assessment data (Ægisdóttir et al., 2006; Grove et al., 2000). Of course, among the myriad assessment tasks clinicians face, relatively few have established evidence-based decision rules that can be employed. Nevertheless, many clinicians are disinclined to use such rules when available (Vrieze & Grove, 2009), possibly because there is limited coverage of decision-making issues and procedures in most professional training programs (Harding, 2007).

Whether based on valid evidence or not, the clinician must ultimately make decisions about the services a client will receive. As do many others (e.g., Kazdin, 2008; Kihlstrom, 2006; Lilienfeld et al., 2003), we presume that judgments are most likely to be valid and beneficial to the client when based on sound clinical assessment evidence and when the clinical assessment and judgment process is guided by scientific principles.

We also recognize that, within our emphasis on clinical science, in many assessment contexts there is limited evidence to guide the clinical judgment process. In such instances, it is particularly important that decisions be informed by sound scientific reasoning and relevant research. Therefore, to introduce the reader to the literature on clinical judgment, we briefly discuss principles and research on clinical judgment. Many of these are consistent with the principles introduced in earlier sections of this chapter and are further emphasized throughout the book, especially in Chapters 4 and 5.

A Clinical Science Orientation to Assessment

Valid judgments in clinical assessment mandate that the clinician adopt a clinical science orientation, for example:

1. The selection of the best assessment instruments to use with a client necessitates that the clinician be knowledgeable concerning research on the psychometric evidence pertinent to those instruments;
2. Decisions about assessment strategies and foci with a client necessitate that the clinician be familiar with evidence about comorbidities and causal relations that can affect the client's behavior problems and treatment goals;
3. Decisions about the best treatment strategy for a client necessitate that the clinician acquire valid data about the client, be knowledgeable about evidence on the effectiveness of available treatments, and understand how well the mechanism of action for an intervention matches the individual characteristics of the client;* and
4. Judgments about a client's diagnosis require that the clinician understand base rates of behavior disorders and limitations of diagnostic instruments and the predictive efficacy of the obtained measures.

An iterative, hypothesis-testing, decision-making strategy is an important part of a clinical science orientation to assessment. Intrinsic to the clinical assessment process, the clinician develops hypotheses about the client's goals, problems, causal variables, and possible intervention strategies.† In the "testing" component of this strategy, the clinician acquires additional data on these foci and is open to refinement and potential disconfirmation of these hypotheses (see scientist-practitioner, problem-solving, and hypothesis-testing approaches to clinical decision making described by Nezu, Nezu, & Lombardo, 2004).

This approach is consistent with evidence-based practice (EBP) in clinical decision making: an emphasis on clinical decisions that are informed by evidence about assessment strategies, behavior problems, interventions, clinical expertise, and patient needs, values, and preferences (see discussion of EBP in treatment by Kazdin, 2008, and Hunsley & Mash, 2008b). It should be evident that, without an evidence-based strategy, clinical judgments are more likely to reflect the biases of the clinician and the clinician's judgment shortcuts (see page 26) than the characteristics of the clinical case.

---

* See Kazdin (2008) for a review of sources of information and issues relevant to evidence-based treatments and suggestions for narrowing the research-practice split.
† Several systems have been proposed for organizing multisource clinical assessment data into clinical case formulations. For discussions of systems developed by Marsha Linehan, Jaqueline Persons, Stephen Haynes, and others, see Eells (2007), Sturmey (2009) and Haynes et al. (in press).

TEXT BOX 1.6   VALIDITY OF A MEASURE AND THE VALIDITY OF THE CONSTRUCT IT IS SUPPOSED TO MEASURE

Sechrest (2005) discussed the challenges of measurement validation in the social sciences posed by the complexity of the constructs that are measured. To illustrate, he examined a seemingly well-validated measure of a seemingly useful construct: the measurement of blood pressure with a sphygmomanometer (measures are provided in terms of millimeters of mercury). After hundreds of years of clinical applications and research, it would seem that a measure of blood pressure with a sphygmomanometer could easily be validated by comparing it to consensually identified criteria for blood pressure. But, "blood pressure" is a complex latent construct. And what, Sechrest asked, is a measure of blood pressure supposed to measure? What is its meaning?

We measure blood pressure not because it has any inherent meaning itself but because we presume it is associated with disease—stroke, heart disease, and kidney disease. But, what facet of blood pressure has meaning: systolic blood pressure, diastolic blood pressure, the difference between the two, the lability of blood pressure across time or contexts, maximum blood pressure, or average blood pressure?

So, the validity evidence for a blood pressure reading depends on how we define the construct of blood pressure—what aspect of it has meaning. And, perhaps different aspects have different meanings (i.e., predict diseases with different degrees of accuracy). Further, and of particular relevance to our discussion of multisource measurement, the validity of measures of blood pressure depends on how they are acquired. Do we measure blood pressure in a physician's office, at home, during sleep versus awake, after resting for a while or not, after precluding the intake of caffeinated beverages or not, sitting up, laying down, standing up, during a stress test, with an arm occlusion cuff, with an ankle cuff? These are important considerations because the values we obtain in these different measurement contexts can be very different and evidence low levels of correlation.

Which of these aspects of blood pressure and which of these methods of measurement help us predict or monitor the diseases in which we are most interested? For validity evaluation of something seemingly simple like blood pressure, and based on this limited presentation of facets and variables, we now have a 7 × 14 (depending how one counts) potential cells for validity evaluation. And, we

(continued on next page)

have not discussed technical aspects that have been shown to affect blood pressure readings, such as the size of the occlusion cuff, microphone placement over arteries, microphone sensitivity, speed of cuff deflation, and reactive effects of the measurement process.

Consider, now, the additional complexity of construct and measurement validation of more heterogeneous and less-precisely defined constructs with which we are commonly concerned in clinical assessment, such as "depression," "oppositional behavior," "pain," or "borderline personality disorder." Complicated, isn't it?

To summarize a few of the implications (see Sechrest, 2005, for others): (a) Validation of a measure is useful only to the extent that the construct that it measures has been found to be useful; (b) the validation of a measure and the validation of the measured construct are interrelated; (c) multiple operations (i.e., *critical multiplism*) are necessary to validate a construct; and (d) multiple methods of assessment are necessary to measure a construct and to validate a measure of a construct.

The Use of Shortcuts in Clinical Judgment

Because of the large amount, complex nature, and often-conflicting information obtained during clinical assessment, the difficulty in acquiring valid and useful data in some assessment contexts, inadequate training in clinical assessment, insufficient time to gather needed information, or an insufficient emphasis on the importance of clinical assessment, clinicians often use shortcuts, or *heuristics*, to make clinical judgments and decisions. There are several types of clinical judgment shortcuts, all of which increase the risk of biased judgments by the clinician and can adversely affect the services received by a client. Many clinical judgment heuristics were outlined by Garb (1998), Haynes and O'Brien (2000), and Nezu and Nezu (1989) (see also http://en.wikipedia.org/wiki/List_of_cognitive_biases for a list of 73, as of this writing) types of cognitive biases and errors, many of which can affect the accuracy and utility of clinical judgments. Several of the more common clinical judgment shortcuts, biases, and errors are as follows:

1. *Availability*, in which clinical judgments are unduly influenced by the clinician's recent training experiences, workshops, or experiences with other clients.
2. *Anchoring*, in which clinical judgments are unduly influenced by initial information received in the assessment process (i.e., the

initial impressions of the clinician), with less weight given to later information regardless of its relevance or validity.

3. *Representativeness*, in which clinical judgments are unduly influenced by a small and select number of features of a client that are consistent with the clinician's schema about behavior problems (e.g., basing diagnostic decisions on one facet of a behavior disorder).

4. *Base rate misjudgments*, in which clinical judgments are insufficiently influenced by data on base rates and likelihood ratios, such as misjudging the probability of recidivism without posttreatment follow-up sessions based on posttreatment measures or overestimating the likelihood that a client with signs of depression on a projective test is truly depressed (i.e., *positive predictive validity*).

5. *Confirmatory bias*, in which clinical judgments are more strongly influenced by data consistent with, than with data inconsistent with, the clinician's hypotheses.

6. *Insensitivity to measurement errors*, in which clinical judgments are made while ignoring the limitations of measures used in clinical assessment (e.g., assuming that a measure is a "true" indicator of a behavior problem and ignoring the hit rate or positive predictive power of the measure).

7. *Illusory correlation*, in which a clinician infers a pattern or correlation among behaviors or events when none exists.

8. *Ostrich effect*, in which the clinician ignores or undervalues information that is inconsistent with his or her hypotheses.

The adverse effects of these shortcuts are probably obvious: Clients are more likely to receive inadequate or inappropriate services when the clinician uses shortcuts to derive his or her judgments about diagnosis, case formulation, and treatment selection and outcome.

STRATEGIES FOR REDUCING CLINICAL JUDGMENT SHORTCUTS AND ENHANCING THE VALIDITY AND UTILITY OF CLINICAL JUDGMENTS

The ultimate goal of a scientific approach to clinical assessment, and the ultimate goal of this book, is to reduce clinical judgment errors and to strengthen the validity and utility of clinical judgments. Many resources on clinical judgment (e.g., Garb, 1998; Harding, 2007) provide eminently sound suggestions for enhancing decision-making skills, such as being open to information (particularly disconfirming information) collected throughout the assessment process, awareness of personal biases and habitual decision-making patterns, decreasing reliance on memory, and using decision aids such as decision trees and EBP guidelines whenever possible. Moving beyond these strategies, every chapter in this book provides guidance on principles and strategies to improve clinical judgments. A science-based approach to clinical assessment promotes the idea that the validity and utility of clinical judgments can be strengthened if the clinician understands and applies concepts and principles discussed in subsequent chapters. Concepts and principles advanced in subsequent chapters include:

1. Concepts and methods of estimating internal consistency, temporal stability, interrater reliability, and homogeneity of measures and the relations between reliability and validity (Chapter 2)
2. Concepts, various forms of, applicability of, methods of measuring, and the conditional nature of validity evidence (e.g., incremental, content, convergent, construct, discriminant) (all chapters)
3. Measurement errors associated with assessment methods, instruments, informants, and measures, their impact on assessment strategies and clinical judgments, and how these errors can be reduced through multisource assessment (Chapters 2, 9)
4. Assessment strategies for monitoring a client's change across time, aspects of measures that affect their sensitivity to change, and how to estimate the *clinical significance* of change (Chapters 2, 4, 5)
5. How *cut scores* are established and the conditional applicability of cut scores across populations and assessment contexts (Chapter 4)
6. The concepts of sensitivity, specificity, positive predictive value, and negative predictive value of a measure and their differential applicability, depending on the goals of a clinical assessment occasion (Chapter 4)
7. How *base rates* of disorders can affect validity evidence for measures and the judgments, especially diagnostic judgment and predictive power, derived from measures (Chapters 4, 8)
8. How the effectiveness, cost-benefits, and feasibility of particular clinical assessment strategies, instruments, and data differ across assessment contexts and the decisions that are to be made (e.g., screening, diagnosis, case formulation, treatment outcome evaluation) (Chapters 5, 9)
9. The conceptual basis, utility, and limitations of idiographic assessment strategies (Chapter 5)
10. Different measurement models for investigating the psychometric evidence of measures (e.g., CTT, IRT, GT) (Chapters 2, 3)
11. The importance of adhering to science-based procedures in the initial development and later refinement of an assessment instrument to increase its validity and utility (Chapters 2, 3, 7)
12. Analytic strategies for examining patterns among multiple measures (i.e., covariances) and the clinical relevance of those patterns (e.g., through exploratory and confirmatory factor analysis) (Chapter 6)

13. How to interpret commonly encountered statistical procedures and outcomes in clinical assessment research, such as statistical significance, effect size, and analyses of variance (Chapter 8)
14. Variables that affect the convergence or divergence of data on a client from multiple sources (Chapter 9)

In summary, clinicians often make errors associated with the clinical judgment process, even in the context of good assessment data. A major tenet of this book is that a clinician's judgments are more likely to be valid and clinically useful when the clinician understands and conducts assessments in a manner consistent with the scientific bases of clinical assessment. When the clinician deviates from sound science-based assessment practice, clients are placed at risk.

SUMMARY

The goal of this chapter was to introduce concepts and methods of the scientific foundations of clinical assessment. We noted that clinical assessment is one application of psychological assessment and is designed to answer questions about a client's diagnosis, behavior problems and their causes, treatment goals, treatment effects, and the variables that might facilitate or impede treatment outcome. We emphasized the major tenet of this book: Measurement is central to the clinical assessment process, and the degree to which the clinician understands and adheres to science-based clinical assessment strategies affects the degree to which the ultimate clinical judgments will be valid and helpful to the client.

The scientific foundations of clinical assessment derive from four domains. First, a science-based approach to clinical assessment is guided by what we know about the nature of behavior problems, such as their multiple attributes and the functional relations among a client's multiple behavior problems. Second, a science-based approach to clinical assessment is informed by findings from treatment research. For example, understanding the mechanisms that account for treatment-related changes in clients' behavior affects the focus of clinical assessment strategies: Treatments are more likely to be effective to the degree that their mechanisms of action address the causal relations underlying a client's behavior problem. Third, psychometric methods and evidence contribute strongly to the scientific foundations of clinical assessment. Psychometric evidence such as validity and reliability of clinical assessment measures are important indicators of the quality of assessment data and affect the validity and utility of the clinician's judgments and decisions about a client. Fourth, research on clinical judgment and decision making has identified many sources of random and nonrandom error in the assessment process. The clinical assessment concepts and principles in subsequent chapters are designed to decrease the influence of the clinician's judgment errors and strengthen the degree to which the clinician's judgments are based on the best available evidence and optimally beneficial for the client.

RECOMMENDED SOURCES

Basic Concepts of Measurement and Assessment

Linn, R. L. (Ed.). (1989). *Educational measurement* (3rd ed.). New York: Macmillan.
National Council on Measurement in Education. (1999). *Standards for educational and psychological assessment.* Washington, DC: Author.
http://en.wikipedia.org/wiki/Measurement (last revised 11/01/2010).

Behavior Problems and Their Causes

Andrasek, F. (2006). *Adult psychopathology.* New York: Wiley.
Haynes, S. N. (1992). *Causal models in psychopathology.* New York: Kluwer.
Hersen, M., Turner, S. M., & Beidel, D. C. (2007). *Adult psychopathology and diagnosis* (5th ed.). New York: Wiley.

Treatment Research

Nezu, A. M., & Nezu, C. (Eds.). (2008). *Evidenced-based outcome research: A practical guide to conducting randomized controlled trials for psychosocial interventions.* New York: Oxford University Press.

Psychometrics

Furr, M. R., & Bacharach, V. R. (2008). *Psychometrics: An introduction.* Thousand Oaks, CA: Sage.
Nunnally, J. C., & Bernstein, I. H. (1994). *Psychometric theory* (3rd Ed.). New York: McGraw-Hill.

Clinical Judgment, Decision Making, and Cognitive Errors

Dickson, D. H., & Kelly, I. W. (1985). The "Barnum effect" in personality assessment: A review of the literature. *Psychological Reports, 57,* 367–382.
Gambrill, E. (2005). *Critical thinking in clinical practice: Improving the quality of judgments and decisions* (2nd ed.). Hoboken, NJ: Wiley.
Garb, H. N. (2005). Clinical judgment and decision-making. *Annual Review of Clinical Psychology, 1,* 67–89.
Gilovich, T., Griffin, D., & Kahneman, D. (2002). *Heuristics and biases: The psychology of intuitive judgment.* Cambridge, UK: Cambridge University Press.
Schacter, D. L. (1999). The seven sins of memory: Insights from psychology and cognitive neuroscience. *American Psychologist, 54,* 182–203.
http://en.wikipedia.org/wiki/List_of_cognitive_biases (a long list of cognitive biases and errors, along with numerous citations); last revised 10/25/2010.

CHAPTER

2

Reliability

INTRODUCTION

At one time or another, probably every psychology graduate student and, for that matter, every clinician has asked, "How reliable is the test?" or concluded, "The test is reliable." Attributing the characteristic of reliability to the instrument, instead of to the scores obtained with the instrument, is undoubtedly one of the most common measurement errors made in psychology (cf. Thompson, 1994). In this chapter, we focus on a wide range of issues related to the reliability of the *scores* or *measures*[*] derived from psychological assessment instruments and methods such as interviews, observational coding systems, performance tasks, and self-report questionnaires. In addition to presenting several ways to operationalize the concept of reliability and describing the various types of reliability that might apply to a measure, we examine a number of the implications of score reliability for clinical assessment in both applied and research contexts. Our intention is to provide a firm grounding in the concept of reliability, not just the statistical indices commonly used to assess reliability. Even the most robust statistical equations can be meaningless or misleading if used in an ill-informed or inappropriate manner. Moreover, as indicated in Chapter 1, elaborate

---

[*] Science dictionaries typically define *measure* as an amount, quantity, extent, or proportion of something. *Measurement* is then the process involved in obtaining a measure. In psychology, however, the term *measure* is frequently used to refer to the tool used to collect data, and the term *score* is frequently used to refer to the data themselves. Throughout the text, we use the terms *measure* and *score* interchangeably to refer to the data that results from the process of measurement.

clinical assessment procedures are of little value if the data obtained on the client are not reliable.

Many definitions of reliability have been offered over the years. The *Standards for Educational and Psychological Testing* (American Educational Research Association, American Psychological Association, & National Council on Measurement in Education, 1999) defines reliability in the following manner:

> A test, broadly defined, is a set of tasks designed to elicit or a scale to describe examinee behavior in a specified domain, or a system for collecting samples of an individual's work in a particular area. Coupled with the device is a scoring procedure that enables the examiner to quantify, evaluate, and interpret the behavior or work samples. *Reliability* refers to the consistency of such measurements when the testing procedure is repeated on a population of individuals or groups. (p. 25)

Note the misuse of the term *measurement* in this definition; see the definitions in Text Box 1.3 and in the Glossary.

In essence, then, in the terminology used throughout this text, reliability deals with the repeatability of measures or scores. Streiner (2003c) nicely captured this by defining reliability as the degree to which measures taken by similar or parallel instruments, by different observers, or at different points in time yield the same or similar results.

OPERATIONALIZING RELIABILITY

The most straightforward way to establish the reliability of a score on instrument X is to develop two instruments, X and Y, that measure exactly the same construct. These are typically called *alternate forms* of a test. Correlation of scores on X and Y provides an indication of the reliability of the score on instrument X. A correlation of 1.0 indicates perfect reliability inasmuch as the rankings of individuals assessed with Y were identical to the rankings of the same individuals when assessed with X. In other words, across the two instruments, the individuals' rankings based on their scores were perfectly replicated. Of course, there is always some error associated with any measurement, so no instrument can yield scores that are perfectly reliable. We discuss this in more detail in this chapter. If the scores received by each individual on the two instruments were identical, then the two instruments could be described as equivalent or parallel forms. The development of equivalent or parallel forms can be useful. For example, to provide testing stimuli unaffected by practice effects when repeated administrations of a memory test are required, Sullivan (2005) developed several equivalent forms of paragraph-length stories based on key features of the Logical Memory subtest of the Wechsler Memory Scale.

Returning to our discussion of alternate forms of an assessment instrument, using them to evaluate the reliability of scores implies that some time, however small, passed between the completion of the first instrument and the completion of the second instrument. In its purest sense, alternate forms reliability assumes that one form is completed immediately after the other, thus minimizing the duration of time between the administrations of the two forms. In test-retest reliability (or temporal stability), this time duration is lengthened so that the focus is on the correlation or degree of agreement between scores obtained at different assessment occasions. Most typically, rather than using alternate forms of an instrument, the same instrument is administered at two or more distinct time points, and the test-retest reliability of scores on a single instrument is then determined. Of course, if this type of reliability is calculated, there is an assumption that the behaviors assessed are truly stable within the testing interval. Test-retest score reliability is influenced by the interplay between the dynamic nature of the construct assessed (i.e., is it transitory, state-like, or trait-like?) and the time interval chosen to assess reliability. We discuss these matters further in the chapter.

Score reliability can also be determined for instruments that require coding (or rating) by judges (or observers). In this case, all judges observe the same behavior for each individual and then code the behavior using the same instrument; the degree to which judges agree in their ratings reflects interrater reliability. The behavior can be observed live, via recordings, or via a completed test protocol (such as a completed test of intelligence). Thus, interrater reliability (also called interobserver or interscorer reliability or agreement) can be determined for data from observational coding systems, semistructured interviews, behavior checklists, or performance tests (such as measures of academic skill or cognitive functioning). Because two observers are not assumed to be equivalent instruments, it has been argued that interobserver agreement indices are more a measure of convergent validity than of reliability (Suen & Ary, 1989).

The most common way that score reliability is assessed is by examining the internal consistency of an instrument (Hogan, Benjamin, & Brezinski, 2000). This form of reliability evaluates the degree of consistency of the items or elements within an assessment instrument. Rather than developing alternate forms and evaluating the reliability of data obtained from the individual forms, internal consistency reliability artificially generates alternate forms by splitting the instrument in half. In other words, items are randomly assigned to two "new" forms that are, in effect, equivalent halves of the total instrument. We describe further in this chapter the strategies available for generating such internal consistency reliability estimates. The primary reason for the popularity of internal consistency reliability coefficients is the relative ease with which score reliability can be obtained; there are relatively few instruments that have alternate forms, and test-retest reliabilities are, by definition, time-intensive approaches for calculating score reliability (Osburn, 2000). As we noted in Chapter 1, clinicians often err in assuming that a measure with a high level of internal consistency (e.g., alpha > .80) means that the measure validly represents the targeted construct.

RELIABILITY: SOME INITIAL CONCEPTS

As mentioned at the beginning of the chapter, it is the reliability of the scores derived from an instrument, not the measuring instrument itself, that is described by a reliability coefficient. The reason for this is simple: Reliability coefficients are (for the most part) correlations, and all correlation coefficients are influenced by the nature of the sample from which the data were obtained (Anastasi & Urbina, 1997). Accordingly, across samples that differ on relevant characteristics (such as age, gender, and ethnicity), there are likely to be variations in the size of the reliability coefficients derived from the obtained scores. Furthermore, compared to homogeneous samples, heterogeneous samples are likely to have higher reliability coefficients (Thompson, 1994). This is because the range of scores on an instrument will be greater in heterogeneous samples than in homogeneous samples. Relatively speaking, homogeneous samples suffer from a restriction of range problem; therefore, any correlation based on data from such a sample will be lower than if no restriction of range occurred. To illustrate this point, consider an extreme example. Let us assume that a measure of depressive symptoms was administered to a large, nationally representative community sample of adults. By definition, the sample would be heterogeneous in terms of age, gender, ethnicity, and level of psychological distress. Compared to the reliability estimate obtained with this sample, the reliability obtained from a sample of Hispanic American women over the age of 65 who are hospital inpatients diagnosed with depression would likely be considerably smaller.

Reliability Estimates and Sample Characteristics

The conditional nature of reliability estimates, and the impact this can have on the interpretation of assessment data, is dealt with in greater detail in Chapter 7. At this point, though, we would like to emphasize one important implication of the fact that reliability estimates are influenced by sample characteristics. To conform to the requirements of the *Standards for Educational and Psychological Testing* (American Educational Research Association et al., 1999), reliability information must be reported as part of the instrument development process. However, any reliability estimates reported from the normative or standardization samples used in this process may not be accurate estimates for data collected from other samples. For clinical assessment purposes, this means that the assessment data may not provide an accurate reflection of the behavior of the client who is assessed. Clinicians sometimes err in presuming that a high published reliability coefficient for a measure means that the measure provides a reliable estimate of the phenomenon for a particular client. However, the relevance of the published reliability coefficient for a particular clinical assessment occasion depends on how well the client matches the sample used to generate the coefficient.

The sample dependence of reliability coefficients also means that researchers should report score reliability values for all instruments used with their research samples. Unfortunately, all too often researchers presume that reliability coefficients are generalizable across samples, and this type of psychometric information is not reported. Surveys of published articles in psychology, educational, and social science journals have found that approximately three quarters of the articles failed to provide sample-based reliability estimates (Meier & Davis, 1990; Whittington, 1998). Without knowing the reliability of the data collected in a study, it is impossible to determine the likely accuracy of the obtained results or the power of the study to detect statistically significant effects. This also has a direct effect on the clinical value of these results as research findings serve as the basis for making empirically based interpretation of clinical data. For example, the interpretation of a high score on an Openness to Experience scale is based on the body of research evidence indicating that high scores on the scale are associated with certain beliefs and behavioral tendencies. If some of this research is based on data with low reliability, the empirical findings may not be wholly accurate and therefore the validity and accuracy of any clinical interpretation will be undermined.

Measurement Error and True Scores

When interpreting the reliability of scores on an instrument, it is crucial that the role of measurement error be acknowledged and actively considered. We discuss this further in the chapter. For now, it is sufficient to recognize that factors such as imprecise content in the instrument, irregularities in instrument scoring, the vagaries of the situations in which instruments are completed, and fluctuations in the attention and concentration of those assessed, among other factors, can all contribute to measurement error. The flip side of acknowledging the role of error is that there is an assumption that an instrument is measuring, at least in part, something that is stable, repeatable, or reproducible. This, then, represents whatever it is the instrument is actually measuring (it is hoped the construct it is intended to measure). At the level of the individual assessed, this is typically referred to as the person's true score on the instrument. By definition, true scores are implicit or latent and therefore can never be assessed directly. Sophisticated statistical analyses such as confirmatory factor analysis and structural equation modeling can be used to estimate true scores.

Test Theories

As we introduced in Chapter 1, the concept of a true score is a central component of what is known as *classical test theory* (CTT). CTT, so called simply because it is the measurement theory that has been around the longest (stemming from the early 20th century), disaggregates a person's score on an instrument in the following way:

$$O = T + E,$$

where O is the observed score, T is the true score, and E is the total error associated with the measurement.

Throughout most of this chapter and, indeed, much of this book, we use the CTT framework to present psychometric details and the implications of reliability and validity estimates. However, we occasionally touch on the other measurement frameworks introduced in Chapter 1, including generalizability theory (GT) and item response theory (IRT). We noted that GT differs from CTT in that it partitions measurement error into separate, discrete components and employs an analysis of variance approach to estimate the main effects of each component (Cronbach, Gleser, Nanda, & Rajaratnum, 1972; see clinical application of GT in Lakes & Hoyt, 2009). Depending on the nature of the analysis, components of measurement error can be treated as part of the "true score" or as part of the measurement error. For constructs that are relatively unstable (such as measures of the frequency of a child's aggressive behavior over time or a distressed couple's level of marital satisfaction), this is a substantial improvement over the way in which CTT deals with test-retest reliability. Low test-retest reliability in CTT terms could be examined differently in GT by constructing components related to behavior in different contexts that are separate from observer error.

IRT differs from CTT in the way in which individual items on a scale are treated. CTT assumes that all items are comparable inasmuch as they all contribute to a total score, and it is this total score that is the focus of CTT. IRT focuses on the pattern of a person's responses across items and does not assume that all items are similar. In fact, the opposite assumption about items is made, namely, that some items are more relevant to evaluating a person's true score (in IRT this is called a latent trait or ability). This is because, depending on the level of one's ability, some items are better than others at accurately evaluating a person's ability. Many references are available that provide accessible, relatively nontechnical accounts of IRT statistics and procedures, including those by Embretson (1996) and T. J. B. Kline (2005). The reason for our emphasis on CTT in this book is two-fold: It is the dominant measurement theory that has been taught to most graduate students, and the psychometric details most commonly reported in the professional and research literatures stem from CTT (although the use of IRT statistics with clinical instruments is growing rapidly).

Reliability and Validity

Before we begin examining the various types of CTT-related reliability in detail, there are two final points we wish to raise about reliability. First, contrary to the assumptions made by many clinicians, a consistently high level of score reliability from an instrument does not guarantee that the scores are valid indicators of the construct the instrument was designed to measure. In other words, reliability does not provide an assurance of validity. For example, a self-report measure composed of items dealing with how calm, relaxed, tense, and nervous the respondent usually feels may well generate high score reliability estimates across samples or over time. However, if the instrument was intended to assess intelligence, the scores from this instrument are unlikely to be valid. Second, the reliability of an instrument's scores has an impact on the maximum value of the validity coefficient that could be obtained with the scores. The reliability coefficient provides a direct estimate of the variance in the observed scores that is attributable to true score variance. It is the square root of the reliability coefficient, termed the *index of reliability*, that provides the best estimate of the upper limit of validity for the instrument when used with the sample on which the reliability coefficient was based (Anastasi & Urbina, 1997; Williams & Zimmerman, 1966). So, for example, a reliability coefficient of .80 means that the index of reliability is .89 and, therefore, the maximum validity coefficient possible with the sample is .89. We go into much greater detail on validity in the next chapter.

TYPES OF RELIABILITY

Internal Consistency

As discussed in this chapter, there are a number of ways to evaluate the reliability of scores, and the relevance of each in a clinical assessment context depends on the judgments that will be affected by the score. The most common approach to estimating reliability is the evaluation of internal consistency (for details on the construction and evaluation of alternate forms, see Anastasi & Urbina, 1997). Internal consistency indices, such as coefficient alpha, essentially evaluate the degree of consistency in scores across all items in an instrument. This means that having homogeneous items (i.e., items that are all similar in nature and, thus, highly intercorrelated) in an instrument is the best strategy for obtaining high internal consistency values for scores on the instrument. The important question of whether it is best to optimize item homogeneity for the purposes of having scores that are valid is addressed in detail in the next chapter. Internal consistency values can also be high for less-substantive reasons; using redundant items (i.e., simple rewording of items) and using a large number of items (even if only some of them are truly prototypic of the construct being measured) can generate high values (and using data from a large number of examinees can almost guarantee statistically significant values).

As a result of the many aspects of an instrument that can affect internal consistency coefficients of its measures, it is insufficient for a clinician simply to glance at the name of the instrument and the reliability values in the test manual when deciding to administer the instrument to a patient. Closer review of both item content and supporting empirical evidence is necessary to ensure that the instrument is measuring what it is supposed to measure and is appropriate for use with the patient (i.e., considering reading level, age, ethnicity, etc.).

All indices of internal consistency rely on the calculation of some form of split-half reliability. This approach means that a reliability estimate can be generated from a single administration of an instrument to a single sample. Of course, the question arises of how to create two split halves of an instrument—how does one decide which items go in each half? The best answer to this question is to calculate an internal consistency value that is the average of all possible split halves. This is what is done with *coefficient alpha* (often referred to as Cronbach's alpha or, simply, alpha), an approach to evaluating internal consistency for scores on items that have a continuous response format (e.g., a 1 to 7 response option format). The formula for coefficient alpha (Cronbach, 1951), reflecting all of these correlations, is as follows:

$$\alpha = nr_M/[1 + r_M(n - 1)]$$

where n is the number of items, and r_M is the mean intercorrelation among all the items.

This is not a particularly user-friendly approach to calculating alpha, although it does show that both (a) a large number of items that are only weakly intercorrelated and (b) a small number of highly intercorrelated items (i.e., redundant items) can yield a high alpha value. The more useful formula is

$$\alpha = [n/(n - 1)][1 - \{(\Sigma SD^2_i)/SD^2_T\}]$$

where n is the number of items, SD^2_i is the variance for each item, and SD^2_T is the variance for the total score.

A special version of this formula is used for items that are dichotomous (e.g., present vs. absent, yes/no) in nature. This is known as the Kuder-Richardson 20 formula (KR-20; Kuder & Richardson, 1937), so named because it was the 20th formula presented in their publication:

$$KR\text{-}20 = [n/(n-1)][1 - \{(\Sigma p_i q_i)/SD^2_T\}]$$

where p is the proportion of "correct" answers (correct inasmuch as the score contributes positively to the total score on the instrument, such as a "yes" response or a "1" response), and q is the proportion of "incorrect" answers.

All commonly used statistical software packages will allow for the direct calculation from group data of both coefficient alpha and KR-20. These two internal consistency indices are appropriate for many, but not all, psychological instruments. For example, coefficient alpha will yield spuriously high reliability values for scores from many timed performance tests (such as the Coding subtest on the WAIS-IV [Wechsler Adult Intelligence Scale–Fourth Edition]). Because the content of such tests is typically cognitively easy, the resulting scores depend far more on speed than on correct responding, and this leads to inflated internal consistency values (Anastasi & Urbina, 1997). Similarly, inflated estimates of reliability are often found for tests in which items are presented in order of increasing difficulty (such as Vocabulary on the WISC-III [Wechsler Intelligence Scale for Children–Third Edition]). The expected pattern of results for such tests is that correct answers will be obtained until the difficulty of the items exceeds the examinee's ability, at which point all (or almost all) answers will be incorrect. Calculating coefficient alpha values on such results inevitably leads to values that are only slightly below 1.0 (Streiner, 2003c). Both coefficient alpha and KR-20 are split-half measures, so they are not appropriate for instruments that have components that differ dramatically in length, complexity, or item type (this is often the case in achievement tests). For these situations, a host of other internal consistency indices are available (see Feldt & Charter, 2003, and Osburn, 2000, for further guidance).

As we emphasized at the outset of the chapter, it is the reliability of scores, not instruments, that is calculated, and these reliability estimates are likely to vary across samples. In recent years, meta-analytic procedures have been developed that allow researchers to determine the usual level of score reliability across samples, the variability in score reliability across samples, and the major sources of variability in score reliability estimates (Rodriquez & Maeda, 2006; Vacha-Haase, 1998). These procedures, known as *reliability generalization,* can provide invaluable information for both researchers and clinicians. For example, Yin and Fan (2000) reported that the mean coefficient alpha value for scores on the Beck Depression Inventory was .837. Moreover, despite finding that the standard deviation of the score reliability values was relatively small (.007 across 142 samples), they found significantly lower score reliability estimates in samples of adults who were abusing substances compared to other adult samples. This kind of information can be invaluable in applied settings, where decisions must be made about which instruments to use with clients. As emphasized throughout this book, such decisions should be made on the basis of sound scientific evidence, including evidence of score reliability and validity. Although it is beyond the scope of the present general discussion on reliability, it is worth noting that if there are no reliability generalization studies on an instrument or instruments, there are easily calculated formulas that allow for the determination of whether two coefficient alphas differ significantly from each other (see Feldt & Kim, 2006).

Despite its frequent use, coefficient alpha does have limitations. We alluded here to the fact that measurement error could be broken down into specific components and systematically studied. This is precisely what Schmidt, Le, and Ilies (2003) did to determine the extent to which a specific form of measurement error, namely transient error, affected the accuracy of coefficient alpha. They defined transient error as variations over time in responses to instruments due to random variations in respondents' psychological states. The score variance produced by transient error is not relevant to the construct measured and, because internal consistency indices are calculated on the basis of a single-occasion completion of an instrument, the effect of transient error is not taken into account by coefficient alpha. By collecting longitudinal data with a series of instruments, these researchers were able to calculate the impact of transient error on several cognitive, personality, and affective trait measures. Because it cannot correct for transient measurement error, coefficient alpha overestimated the reliability of scores on cognitive and personality measures by 2.2% to 11.3%; for affective trait measures, the overestimation was more substantial and was in the range of 14.5% to 17.8%. In fact, the reliability of the Positive Affect scale of the Positive and Negative Affect Schedule was overestimated by almost one third. As this means that scores on the Positive Affect scale are far less stable than they appear to be, considerable caution should be exercised in making clinical interpretations about the consistency and generalizability of an examinee's attentiveness, enthusiasm, excitement, and related concepts based on this scale. As other research has found that coefficient alpha underestimates the true reliability of scores on heterogeneous or multi-faceted instruments (Osburn, 2000), considerable caution should be exercised in interpreting score reliability estimated by coefficient alpha.

Note how these aspects and limitations of internal consistency support our contention in Chapter 1 that to make the best assessment decisions the clinician must be familiar with psychometric research in clinical assessment: The clinician can easily misinterpret the meaning of a reliability coefficient when considering which assessment instruments to use with a client and can be more confident than is warranted in the meaning of an obtained score if he or she is unfamiliar with basic psychometric concepts.

Standard Error of Measurement

Information about internal consistency can be used in clinical assessment settings to establish *confidence intervals* (sometimes known as a confidence band) around the score obtained by a client on an instrument. Although this does not get around the problems associated with measurement error, it does serve as an explicit reminder that a client's observed score for a construct is not the same thing as his or her true score on that construct. Confidence intervals are based on the *standard error of measurement* (*SEM*), which is the standard deviation of a hypothetically infinite number of observed scores around the person's true score (Hogan, 2007) and is calculated as follows:

$$SEM = SD_T[\text{sqrt } (1 - r_{xx})]$$

where SD_T is the standard deviation of the total score for the sample on which the reliability was determined, and r_{xx} is the reliability (alpha) of the instrument.

A confidence interval of ±1 *SEM* around the observed score means that one can be 68% confident that the confidence band includes the client's true score on that construct. As an example, let us assume that a client scores 14 on a measure of depression, and in the normative sample of relevance to the client, let us also assume that the reliability of the measure was .80 and the standard deviation for the sample was 5.0. Entering these values into the equation yields an *SEM* of approximately 2.3. Thus, we could be 68% sure that the client's true score on the depression measure is somewhere between 11.7 and 16.3.

Of course, other confidence bands can be set, such as 90% (±1.65 *SEM*) or 95% (±1.96 *SEM*). Confidence intervals can be extremely helpful in interpreting a person's scores on indices of an intelligence test. Brooks, Strauss, Sherman, Iverson, and Slick (2009) provided a good illustration of this. The reliability of Visual Delayed Index (VDI; *SEM* = 6.18) scores on the WMS-III (Wechsler Memory Scale–Third Edition) is lower than the reliability of Verbal Comprehension Index (VCI; *SEM* = 2.88) scores on the WAIS-IV, and this has implications for making decisions on the basis of these scores. For someone who received a score of 100 on the VCI, 95 times out of 100 the range of 94–106 includes the true score. In contrast, because of having a larger *SEM*, if the same person received a score of 100 on the VDI, 95 times out of 100 the range of 88–112 contains the person's true score. The implications of these differences in reliabilities (and therefore *SEM*s) are substantial. Note the potential for clinical judgment errors if the clinician is unfamiliar with the concept of *SEM* or with the *SEM* value for a score he or she is using for diagnosis, case formulation, or treatment outcome evaluation.

Because of the value of the *SEM* in interpreting a person's score, the *Standards for Educational and Psychological Testing* (American Educational Research Association et al., 1999) require that the SEM must be reported for a psychological test. In CTT, the SEM is assumed to be the same at all levels of scores on an instrument. In contrast, in the IRT approach an SEM can be calculated, but it varies depending on score levels. This means that there may be greater, or less, measurement precision depending on the obtained score under consideration. Regardless of whether in CTT or IRT terms, the bottom line is the same: Clinicians must be cautious in interpreting measures and must attend to reliability considerations in the selection and interpretation of instruments.

Test-Retest Reliability (Temporal Stability)

The calculation of the test-retest reliability is straightforward; it is an indication of linear relations across measurement occasions. In other words, it is simply a correlation of scores, on the same instrument, obtained at two different points in time. If all those providing responses to the instruments provided exactly the same responses each time or their responses changed to exactly the same degree (e.g., all participants scored 3 points higher on the second than the first administration), the resulting correlation would have a value of 1.0. Not surprisingly, these scenarios almost never occur for two main reasons. First, events that occurred during the interval between the two data collection periods may influence individuals' responses, and they may influence individuals' differently. If the interval is long (such as months or years), true developmental changes may have occurred that are then reflected in respondents' data. Even if the interval is relatively brief (such as hours, days, or weeks), changes in scores may well reflect true changes in respondents' experiences. For example, the effects of interventions specifically designed to alter respondents' experiences (such as treatments for acute pain, anxiety, or depression) might well result in dramatically different scores for some respondents at the second test period. Of course, one might well ask why temporal stability would be assessed when change was expected between the two testing periods. We will return to this point. The second reason that test-retest correlations never have a value of 1.0 is the effects of error, especially transient error. Transient error can exert a substantial effect on test-retest reliability estimates. Chmielewski and Watson (2009), for example, reported that almost a quarter of the variance in scores over time on scales of personality and trait affectivity was due to transient error.* For reasons such as this, forms of coefficient alpha and a split-half coefficient that incorporate transient error effects have been developed for test-retest data (Green, 2003), although they are not yet widely used.

Given the ease of calculating the reliability of test-retest data, the real challenge in measuring and interpreting these reliability estimates comes in determining the appropriate duration for the interval between data collection periods. Bearing in mind the nature of the construct assessed, the time frame covered by the instrument (e.g., past week, past year) and the characteristics of the sample being assessed, only a small set of durations is likely to provide meaningful information about reliability. Trait-like variables (e.g., measures of extraversion, neuroticism, intelligence), for example, should exhibit temporal stability over a relatively long period of time; thus, the reliability of their scores should probably be assessed with an interval of at least several months. In other words, the duration of the intertest interval should be determined primarily by the degree of temporal stability expected to be exhibited by the construct assessed. As the time between data collection points diminishes, concerns about instrument recall effects may increase. If the intervening interval is a matter of hours, days, or weeks, it is possible that responses obtained at the second time point may be influenced by recall of the items on a test or even of one's previous responses to the items. Finally, respondent characteristics such as age and cognitive status should also influence the choice of intertest intervals. When developmental changes (such as with young children) or cognitive deterioration (such as with individuals with dementia) are occurring relatively rapidly, longer intervals between data collection points are likely to reflect real changes in the construct being evaluated, thus negatively affecting both the size and the meaning of derived reliability estimates.

Difference Scores

There may, of course, be situations for which one is interested in determining the extent to which changes in respondents' true scores have occurred. This would be the case when, for example, a treatment or some form of training has been provided to respondents after the first

---

* Having just mentioned the concept of variance in scores, this is an appropriate time for a reminder that when considering reliability values, it is the reliability value itself that indicates the proportion of shared variance (e.g., T. J. B. Kline, 2005). As is well known, when considering a correlation between two different variables, it is the squared value of the correlation that indicates the proportion of shared variance (e.g., a correlation of .80, when squared, equals .64, thus indicating that the two variables share 64% of their variance). When considering reliability estimates, though, the correlation is already a squared value (it measures the variance in observed scores due to variance in true scores). Thus, a test-retest correlation of .80 means that 80% of the variance in the scores obtained at the two time points is shared variance.

administration of an instrument. By administrating the instrument a second time, it is possible to obtain a difference score for each respondent (i.e., posttest score minus pretest score). It is tempting to use this difference score as an index of how much change has occurred. However, things are not quite so simple because the reliability of this difference score is likely to be rather low. Indeed, the more highly correlated the scores on the two administrations are, the lower the reliability of the difference score (those interested will find the formula for the reliability of difference scores in any tests and measurement text, such as the work of T. J. B. Kline, 2005, p. 180). This means that measures that may appear to indicate substantial treatment or training effects may, in reality, reflect substantial measurement error. For this reason, Streiner and Norman (2008) recommended that difference scores should only be used when the reliability of the difference scores exceeds .50.

Fortunately, as described in Text Box 2.1 on assessing clinically significant change, there are other options for determining whether meaningful change has occurred for a person following treatment or training.

Interrater Reliability (Interrater Agreement)

A number of commonly used assessment methods require some form of decision making by the assessor in coding the responses of the individual assessed. For example, semistructured interviews involve decisions about which questions should be asked and how responses should be coded; observational coding systems require decisions about how to classify specific statements, gestures, or facial expressions; and the scoring of responses on performance tasks (such as tests of intelligence, memory, ability, etc.) necessitate judgments about the accuracy and sophistication of responses. But, regardless of the extent to which there is standardization of instructions to those evaluated and those conducting the evaluation, the stimuli used for the assessment method, the response or scoring options available to the assessor, or the decision rules provided to guide the scoring judgments of the assessor, there is the possibility of variability occurring in the scores of the same phenomenon given by different assessors. Thus, there is a need for estimates of the congruence of the scores, ratings, or judgments made by assessors. Although such estimates are typically described by psychometricians and test developers as indices of interrater reliability, it has been argued that they are really indices of interrater agreement. This is because these estimates focus not on the consistency of responses provided by those assessed (see the definition of reliability provided at the outset of this chapter) but on the consistency of the ratings provided by those who are evaluating the responses of those assessed (Heyman et al., 2001). Thus, by using GT, interobserver agreement can be conceptualized and evaluated as an indication of the

TEXT BOX 2.1   ASSESSING CLINICALLY SIGNIFICANT CHANGE DUE TO TREATMENT

A perennial question for clinicians is how best to use assessment data to determine the extent to which clients make meaningful gains in treatment. Of course, asking clients directly if they feel that treatment has been worthwhile and if they have made important changes are important options to consider. However, such questions may not be relevant for all clients (such as those for whom services were mandated or those with significant cognitive impairments), and a host of biases may color clients' responses to such questions. Many clinicians limit their evaluation of treatment outcome with their clients to this nonspecific, bias-prone, and unscientific strategy.

Traditional methods to assess statistical significance require group data and therefore cannot assist in the interpretation for changes observed for individual clients. Fortunately, there is a host of interrelated options for using data from standardized instruments to determine whether a client has experienced clinically significant change. Even more fortunately, assuming that instruments are used for which high levels of internal consistency are typically found (i.e., coefficient alpha $\geq .85$), these options all yield similar results (Atkins, Bedics, McGlinchey, & Beauchaine, 2005). Accordingly, we focus on the most straightforward and easily calculated method developed by Jacobson, Follette, and Revenstorf (1984) and Jacobson and Truax (1991).

Jacobson and Truax's (1991) approach to *clinical significance* consists of two criteria. The first criterion requires that a client's posttreatment score falls within the functional range. They proposed several ways of operationalizing this criterion, including the use of a cutoff at two standard deviations from the pretreatment mean of clients receiving treatment. Second, the client's change on an outcome scale completed prior to and following treatment must be statistically greater than what might occur simply due to measurement imprecision (using the standard error of measurement). This second part is known as the *Reliable Change Index* (RCI; Jacobson et al., 1984). The formula for the RCI is as follows:

$$RCI = (X_{post} - X_{pre})/\text{sqrt}\{2[SD_{pre} * \text{sqrt}(1 - r_{xx})]^2\}$$

where X_{post} is the posttreatment score, X_{pre} is the pretreatment score, SD_{pre} is the standard deviation of the client sample scores

(continued on next page)

at pretreatment, and r_{xx} is the reliability (coefficient alpha) of the instrument (if sample values are not available for the last two values they can be estimated from research studies relevant to an individual client's treatment).

The RCI value must at least ±1.96 to be considered significant. If a client's score passes both criteria, the client is deemed to be recovered, whereas if the RCI criterion is met but the move into the functional range is not, the client is deemed to be improved. If neither criterion is met, the client is classified as unchanged, and if the RCI is passed in the negative direction, the client's functioning is said to have deteriorated. Note how this more science-based strategy can strengthen clinician confidence in the effects of an intervention.

degree to which measures obtained from one observer can be assumed to be generalizable across observers (Suen & Ary, 1989).

The focus in interrater reliability/agreement is on the ratings or scores assigned to specific aspects of the behavior of the person evaluated. Data are provided by different judges who are classifying the person's behavior (such as indicating the presence or absence of a behavior during prescribed time periods with an observation coding system) or by different raters who are scoring a sample of the person's behavior (such as ratings of social skills during analog social interactions, responses to interview questions, or performance on memory tasks). In other words, the focus is on a specific sample of behavior obtained during an evaluation period. This is different from the situation in which ratings of an individual are obtained by multiple informants who know the individual (e.g., parent, spouse, teacher). Data from multiple informants provide invaluable information about convergent validity but not interrater reliability/agreement (for more on this, see Chapter 9).

There is a range of options for assessing interrater reliability, all of which assume that the raters involved made their ratings independently of one another. The most common include percentage agreement, interrater correlation, intraclass correlation coefficient, and Cohen's kappa coefficient. Information about these options is presented in Text Box 2.2.

A significant challenge in using all of these options is determining the level of data that is to be assessed for interrater reliability. In some instances, it may be important to have an estimate of reliability at the level of each response produced by the person evaluated (i.e., how similarly did all raters rate a specific response? e.g., did raters consistently give a rating of 0, 1, or 2 for an answer on an intelligence test?); in others, it may be more relevant to estimate the interrater reliability at the level of a summary score (i.e., how similar were the total scores given by

---

TEXT BOX 2.2   ASSESSING INTERRATER RELIABILITY/AGREEMENT

PERCENTAGE AGREEMENT
- Involves the calculation of the percentage of ratings or scores on which the raters agree
- Does not take into account chance agreements, which can greatly inflate the size of the reliability estimate
- Is recommended for use only when other options are not appropriate, such as when very low base rate behaviors or events are scored (Bartko & Carpenter, 1976)

INTERRATER CORRELATIONS
- Used when the ratings are continuous in nature or are ranked
- Simply correlates a rater's ratings with the ratings of another rater

Intraclass Correlations (ICCs)
- Used when continuous or ranked data from more than two raters are considered, even when multiple raters do not all rate the same behaviors (Shrout & Fleiss, 1979)
- Use mean square values generated by an analysis of variance to provide an indication of the average level of agreement across raters
- Can also be used to reflect rater differences in both the mean level and rank ordering of scores

Kappa
- Used when ratings are made on nominal or dichotomous categories (Cohen, 1960)
- Adjusts for the level of chance agreement between raters, which, depending on the base rate of the behaviors rated, can be considerably greater than 50% (see Wood, 2007, who provided a useful tutorial on understanding and calculating kappa)

---

raters to the responses rated? e.g., how comparable were the total scores given by raters on a subtest of an intelligence test?). A basic premise of CTT is that summary scores will be more reliable than scores on an individual item because random variations in measurement error are likely to be attenuated when summary scores are used.

Such attenuation effects must be kept in mind when interpreting the interrater reliability estimates for differing levels of aggregation in the data under consideration. This is another example of the value of a functional approach to assessment—the relevance of different reliability indices depends on what decisions are to be based on them. From a clinical perspective, focusing on the reliability of summary scores may be most relevant when considering instruments used for diagnostic purposes or for treatment outcome evaluation purposes. A focus on individual responses or items may be more useful in developing more specific clinical case formulations.

HOW RELIABLE SHOULD SCORES ON AN INSTRUMENT BE?

One of the most vexing measurement questions is determining what constitutes an acceptable level of score reliability. Given the emphasis we have placed on the fact that reliability is a property of scores, not of an instrument, it is easy to see why the question is so challenging. Score reliability will depend on the purpose for which an instrument is used and who is evaluated. The development of reliability generalization analyses, described previously, has done much to provide "ballpark" estimates for likely score reliability and to disentangle the elements that affect score reliabilities across assessment purposes and samples. Nevertheless, the question remains and is important for clinicians when they select assessment instruments: What is a scientifically acceptable level of reliability? Some have suggested that there can be no sound basis for recommending a minimal level of reliability (e.g., Streiner & Norman, 2008). Others have stressed that the answer depends on the purpose for which the instrument will be used; indeed, Hogan (2007) likened the question to asking how long a ladder should be. In this regard, it is useful to recall that, in CTT terms, the higher the reliability value, the higher the likelihood that information on true scores comprises a substantial part of the observed scores from an instrument. Conversely, higher reliability values are likely to indicate a lower effect of measurement errors in the observed scores. Therefore, within limits (discussed on page 51) higher reliability values are desirable as they introduce less measurement error into statistical analyses or applied decisions when using the observed scores from an instrument. Concretely, it is also worth remembering that low reliability mandates low validity for a measure, which in turn means that you cannot be confident in the meaning of a score on the measure.

Concern about measurement error is also the reason that most psychometrics texts suggest that the acceptable level of reliability is lower for research purposes than for applied purposes in which decisions based on test data may significantly affect the lives of those assessed (e.g., Hogan, 2007). In a research context, increased measurement error may increase the likelihood of making Type II errors in examining, for example, between-group differences on a clinical instrument (such as whether two groups of patients with different forms of head injury differ on a memory test). The failure to reject the null hypothesis (that there are no significant differences between the groups) when it is false (when there truly are significant differences) is problematic from a scientific perspective but is likely to have little impact on any specific research participant. In a clinical context, however, an increased level of measurement error means that the scores on an instrument are less likely to accurately reflect a client's true score on the construct measured. For example, if scores on a memory test have relatively poor reliability, then the scores of someone who recently experienced a traumatic brain injury may greatly under- or overestimate the true nature of any memory impairment. This in turn could result in denial of clinical services (i.e., no indication of memory impairment) or provided unnecessarily (i.e., scores indicate poor memory functioning).

This still begs the question of what an acceptable level of reliability is, a question that is important to clinicians and researchers alike as they are both faced with making decisions about whether an instrument is likely to be appropriate, scientifically speaking, for the assessment task at hand. For this reason, Hunsley and Mash (2008a) developed a framework of "good enough" criteria for evaluating various aspects of the scores obtained from psychological instruments. Rather than defining ideal standards for psychometric properties, including reliability, they used both (a) reasoned arguments from respected psychometricians and assessment scholars and (b) summaries of various assessment literatures to guide their selection of criteria for rating the psychometric properties associated with scores on an instrument. Their recommendations for adequate, good, and excellent levels of reliability are presented in Text Box 2.3.

A brief comment on Hunsley and Mash's (2008a) recommendations for test-retest reliability is warranted. As discussed previously, test-retest reliability values must be interpreted in light of the relation between the intertest interval and the hypothesized temporal stability of the construct evaluated. Hunsley and Mash's (2008a) test-retest reliability recommendations focused on increasing longer intertest intervals and therefore may not be entirely applicable to measures of phenomena hypothesized to exhibit only short-term temporal stability.

The use of a tripartite system (adequate, good, excellent) to interpret reliability estimates reflects the reality that the likely reliability of scores on an instrument is only one factor that should be considered when selecting an instrument. Other factors, such as the cost, length, validity of measures derived from it, complexity, and utility of an instrument, are also important in instrument selection decisions

TEXT BOX 2.3   GUIDELINES FOR LEVELS OF RELIABILITY

INTERNAL CONSISTENCY

Adequate = Coefficient alpha values of .70 to .79
Good = Coefficient alpha values of .80 to .89
Excellent = Coefficient alpha values ≥ .90

TEST-RETEST RELIABILITY

Adequate = Test-retest correlations of at least .70 over a period of several days to several weeks
Good = Test-retest correlations of at least .70 over a period of several months
Excellent = Test-retest correlations of at least .70 over a period of a year or longer

INTERRATER RELIABILITY/AGREEMENT

Adequate = Kappa values of .60 to .74; Pearson correlation or intraclass correlation values of .70 to .79
Good = Kappa values of .75 to .84; Pearson correlation or intraclass correlation values of .80 to .89
Excellent = Kappa values ≥ .85; Pearson correlation or intraclass correlation values ≥ .90

Adapted from Hunsley and Mash (2008a)

(more on this in Chapter 7).* For example, when considering internal consistency values, a decision might need to be made about whether to use a short (say, 12 items) self-report test of relationship functioning that has been found to yield coefficient alpha values around .75 or a self-report test of relationship functioning that typically yields coefficient

---

* The relation between test length and reliability in CTT is well known, largely because of the widespread presentation of the Spearman-Brown prophecy formula (also known as their "correction formula") in texts on test construction (e.g., Hogan, 2007, p. 135). The formula is

$$r_c = (nr_o)/[1 + (n - 1)r_o]$$

where r_o is the "corrected" reliability value, n is the factor by which the length of the test is changed (lengthened or shortened), and r_o is the original reliability value. For more on the use of corrections for attenuation due to measurement error, see the work of Charles (2005). The relation between test length and reliability is different in IRT situations. For example, adaptive tests, in which only test items appropriate for the respondent's trait level are used, can be short yet have small *SEM* values.

alpha values around .85 but is substantially longer (say, 80 items). All else being equal, the longer test may appear to be preferable, but things are rarely equal as issues such as (a) the cost of purchasing and scoring the test, (b) the appropriateness of the items vis-à-vis the sociodemographic characteristics of those evaluated (e.g., age, ethnicity, educational level), and (c) respondent fatigue (if the test is only one of a dozen others administered in a battery) must all be considered.

Before leaving the topic of what constitutes an adequate level of reliability, there is one final point worth making. It is possible for a reliability estimate, especially coefficient alpha, to be too high. One way to achieve a high alpha value is to have high interitem correlations. This can be achieved by having an instrument composed of almost identical items, which is the issue of redundancy that we mentioned. Whereas focused operationalization is likely to be a strength for most instruments, overly narrow operationalization or limited sampling of potential items may be problematic. In essence, enhancing reliability with nearly identical items (e.g., "How satisfied are you with your life today?" "How satisfied were you with your life yesterday?" "How satisfied do you think you will be with your life tomorrow?") comes at the expense of a possible reduction in validity due to the inappropriately restricted manner in which the construct assessed by the instrument was operationalized. By itself, a large number of redundant items would not reduce validity unless some elements of the construct were missing—we say more about this type of issue in the next chapter. Thus, a coefficient alpha of .98 may not always be a good indication of psychometric strength. Furthermore, as we discuss in Chapters 5, 7, and 9, there are several strategies for increasing the validity and utility of clinical judgments when the clinician is faced with measures with less-than-optimal reliability indices, including the use of more than one measure of the same construct.

IS RELIABILITY EVER IRRELEVANT?

Simply put, reliability information is never irrelevant, and information on reliability estimates is always germane to the scientific evaluation of scores from an assessment instrument. Of course, as described at the beginning of the chapter, not all types of reliability are relevant to every instrument. For example, internal consistency estimates may not be relevant to measures that consist of items that, theoretically, should not demonstrate much interitem correlation. Streiner (2003a) referred to instruments such as these as indexes, with stressful life events inventories and quality-of-life scales as two prime examples of instruments in which the endorsement or degree of endorsement of one item may be unrelated to responses to other items. The reliability of these indexes can be considered via test-retest reliability methods that use a retest interval brief enough to reduce the likelihood that recent events affect the responses to the index. In short, some form of reliability is relevant for every instrument. For example, interitem or interday coefficient alphas can be calculated for behavioral, affective, or cognition checklists or self-monitoring diaries designed to be completed repeatedly within or across days; other strategies to assess intraindividual response consistency on these instruments are also available (see Moskowitz, Russell, Sadikaj, & Sutton, 2009).

As we have stressed throughout the chapter, the clinician should consider the nature of the construct measured and its temporal stability when (a) choosing the type of reliability that best evaluates measures of that construct and (b) interpreting the meaning of the resulting reliability values. An instrument designed to evaluate a construct that is, by nature, broad and multidimensional will be comprised of items that are heterogeneous in coverage. Scores on instruments designed to assess such broad constructs are likely to evidence less internal consistency than will scores on instruments designed to assess more narrowly defined, unidimensional constructs. Interpreting the relative size of the score reliability estimates for measures from these two sets of instruments requires an appreciation of the nature and scope of the constructs measured. Similarly, low reliability values for scores on self-monitoring forms or observational coding systems may not necessarily be an indication of a poorly performing instrument. Rather, they may indicate that some target behaviors occur relatively infrequently, that they vary across short time periods, or that they are situationally determined rather than occurring across situations.

SUMMARY AND RECOMMENDATIONS

Reliability is a critical aspect of any score derived from psychological instruments. Internal consistency, test-retest reliability, and interrater reliability are the most commonly encountered reliability estimates. Knowing which forms of reliability are relevant to a specific instrument requires an appreciation of the nature of the instrument, the nature of the measured phenomenon, and the nature of reliability. Measurement error is present in any form of evaluation; for this reason, the clinician should carefully consider measurement error when interpreting the scores obtained from an instrument. Statistical procedures (using the standard error of measurement) are available to assist in the interpretation of scores; likewise, contemporary guidelines regarding "good enough" levels of reliability are available to aid in the selection of assessment instruments. The bottom line, then, is that reliability evidence, and an informed appreciation of the meaning of this evidence, is essential if the clinician is to make scientifically informed choices when selecting and using assessment tools.

RECOMMENDED SOURCES

American Educational Research Association, American Psychological Association, & National Council on Measurement in Education. (1999). *Standards for educational and psychological testing.* Washington, DC: American Educational Research Association.

Kline, T. J. B. (2005). *Psychological testing: A practical approach to design and evaluation.* Thousand Oaks, CA: Sage.

Osburn, H. G. (2000). Coefficient alpha and related internal consistency reliability coefficients. *Psychological Methods, 5,* 343–355.

Rodriquez, M. C., & Maeda, Y. (2006). Meta-analysis of coefficient alpha. *Psychological Methods, 11,* 306–322.

Streiner, D. L. (2003a). Being inconsistent about consistency: When coefficient alpha does and doesn't matter. *Journal of Personality Assessment, 80,* 217–222.

Streiner, D. L. (2003c). Starting at the beginning: An introduction to coefficient alpha and internal consistency. *Journal of Personality Assessment, 80,* 99–103.

Streiner, D. L., & Norman, G. R. (2008). *Health measurement scales: A practical guide to their development and use* (4th ed.). New York: Oxford University Press.

International Test Commission. Classical test theory. http://www.intestcom.org/Publications/ORTA/Classical+test+theory.php

3

Validity

INTRODUCTION

In Chapter 2, we discussed the conceptual foundations and means of estimating the reliability of scores on assessment instruments. Each form of reliability calculation provides an estimate of the degree to which scores on an instrument are repeatable, reproducible, stable, or internally consistent. As we pointed out in Chapter 2, none of these terms speaks to the question of what the scores actually mean, a distinction often missed in selecting and interpreting the results from clinical assessment instruments. Most basically, the concept of validity refers to the question of what an instrument measures: Validity refers to the degree to which variation in scores on an instrument reflects variation in the psychological entity or process of interest. Therefore, it is best to think of reliability as a necessary precursor to validity (we also noted exceptions to the usual relation between reliability and validity, such as when we expect behavior to change over time).

Once we have evidence that scores on a measure are reproducible, we can then consider what those reproducible scores mean. Imagine the opposite: If scores were not reliable, we could not even consider whether they were valid. We would have nonrepeatable scores, and we would not know which score truly represented the measured construct.

Now, imagine that you are in a situation in which you have evidence for the reliability of a measure. How do you go about testing whether the scores are valid? Suppose that you are the first person to develop a measure of depression. (At least, you hope it is a measure of depression.) How will you determine whether variation in responses to your assessment instrument reflect variation in depression? You might think,

"Let's compare a group of depressed people with a group of nondepressed people." If the depressed people score higher on our measure, we have evidence that the measure is valid (an example of *discriminative validity*; see Glossary). Although your conclusion is correct up to a point, consider the difficulties with this plan. First, in the absence of an existing measure of depression, how do you know which people are depressed and which are not? It is probably true that, since there is no measure, individual clinicians have made judgments that certain individuals are depressed. If that is true, then the criterion by which you are validating your measure is clinician judgments. That criterion may be good, but the problem is you do not know. Because there is no perfect, gold standard assessment for depression (if there were, you would probably not be developing your measure in the first place unless your intent was to develop a brief form of a measure), you should assume that there is some degree of error in the clinician judgments. You cannot know how much error, so you cannot be sure how useful those judgments are as a criterion for your new measure. Because you are not sure about the validity of your criterion, you cannot be sure how successfully you have tested the validity of your depression measure. Thus, if your validation test worked (clinically identified depressed people scored significantly higher than nondepressed people), you would probably have more confidence than you did before that you have measured depression, but you would be far from sure that you have a valid measure of depression.

In this example, we have so far skipped an important step. To measure depression, you must begin with a definition of what depression is. How will you develop such a definition? There are two important considerations that affect your definition of depression. The first is the content domain of concerns, maladaptive behaviors, or symptoms expressed by individuals who are understood to be depressed. To decide what goes into that content domain, you might want to consider clinically identified cases of depressed individuals, study their records and behaviors, and try to specify what constitutes the central characteristics of those cases. In doing so, you might conclude that depressed persons tend to be higher than others in negative affect (they are more distressed), lower than others in positive affect (they derive less pleasure from things), they have appetite disturbances, and they have sleep disturbances. Based on this analysis, you might write depression questionnaire items to represent each of these four symptoms. This process is directed at enhancing the *content validity* of the new assessment instrument (see Glossary).

The second contributor to a definition of depression is how you understand what depression is, the role it plays in a person's life, how depression relates to other psychological processes, and how depression is different from other forms of distress. In other words, for you to understand what depression is, you need to have a model of its relationship to other aspects of life functioning, other forms of psychopathology, and other psychological processes. These aspects of the measure and the targeted construct address the *convergent* and *discriminant validity* of a measure. Together, all of these psychometric and conceptual issues pertain to the *construct validity* of the new measure, an important concept discussed further in this chapter.

There are two reasons why having such a model is necessary. The first is that you want to make sure your items measure what you believe constitutes depression and not other, similar things, like anxiety or sadness. The second reason is perhaps more basic: You will need to support your claim that it is valuable to define and measure the construct of depression.

As you consider these issues, perhaps it will become apparent that the core experience you mean by "depression" is not, itself, directly observable. Rather, you can observe markers of depression. By our definition, high negative affect and low positive affect are both contributors to the experience of depression. You are developing a measure of depression rather than just relying on measures of negative affect, positive affect, appetite, and sleep because you believe that there is clinical value in defining the cooccurrence of these things as an entity in and of itself; it is useful to identify a diagnosis of depression. In this way, your decision to measure depression thus represents a statement of theory. It is critical to appreciate that measure development and validation cannot be separated from the theory underlying the measure.

The complexity of this instrument development process further illustrates the challenges that a clinician faces in selecting the best measure to use with a client. Different assessment researchers may have defined depression differently and therefore included or excluded different markers. Consequently, different assessment instruments that purport to measure the same construct may in fact emphasize different facets of the construct or include markers of different constructs. This reminds us of one frequent clinical judgment error (Text Box 1.2): presuming that an instrument provides a valid measure of the construct just because the construct name appears in its title.

So, you believe it is useful to define this disorder of depression, and defining the disorder involves developing a theory of depression. (Of course, we are using depression as an example, but the same set of concerns applies to attempts to measure other constructs.) Depression is not directly observable; rather, it is an inferred entity. You infer its existence because, you believe, doing so will prove useful for understanding psychological distress and for developing interventions to help suffering people. Because depression is an inferred entity, you can have no direct, concrete, definitive measure of it. We refer to such entities as *constructs* or psychological constructs. We call them constructs because we construct them to help us develop theory and understanding (and presumably, in this case, interventions). How, then, do you validate your construct of depression?

Over the course of this chapter, we discuss validation procedures in detail. For now, though, we can focus on the basic validation process. First, it would be important to acquire empirical evidence that the content of your depression scale conforms to your definition of depression. For example, you would want experts to confirm that your measure (a) includes content assessing each of the four domains we decided on and (b) does not inadvertently include content in other, nondepression domains. As we noted, this step is part of the content validation process. The clinician should be aware that many frequently used clinical assessment instruments have been developed without following science-based content validation procedures (e.g., many self-report questionnaires are generated solely on the basis of the authors' concepts of the targeted construct). This step is important, but there are important aspects of the validity of your measure it does not address.

So far, you actually have no evidence supporting your claim that it is valuable to define and measure the construct of depression. What kind of evidence would support such a claim? Consider these types of validity evidence that would pertain to this question: You could acquire evidence that (a) your scale measures variability in your chosen criterion of clinician judgment of depression; (b) your scale is unassociated with variability on measures of other constructs thought to be different from depression, such as phobias, dependent personality disorder, and avoidant personality disorder (if your scale is associated with variability on measures of these disorders as well, you cannot be confident that your measure really permits assessment of variation in depression specifically); (c) when individuals undergo a behavioral intervention designed to treat depression by improving positive mood (e.g., Dimidjian et al., 2006), their scores on your measure improve; and (d) when individuals undergo a treatment for a different, unrelated disorder, their scores improve to a lesser extent. Positive results for each of these tests would increase your confidence that it is useful to define a construct of depression that is distinct from other psychopathology-related constructs, and that you have constructed an instrument that provides a valid measure of that construct.

At the same time, there are other sources of uncertainty in your validation process. If you were to conduct the four tests just described, you would also be accepting, at least provisionally, the claims that (a) clinician judgments of depression have reasonable validity; (b) there is good reason to develop the constructs of phobias, dependent personality disorder, and avoidant personality disorder; (c) there are reasonably valid measures of each of those disorders; (d) there is empirical support for the theoretical claim that depression is minimally related to those disorders; (e) the behavioral intervention for depression has been adequately validated; and (f) the intervention for the different disorder has been validated for that disorder and does not influence depression levels substantially. As you can see, you must accept these claims for your validation studies to make sense. For all of these and other reasons, it is best to say that you have growing confidence in the validity of your measure, but not that you have established the validity of your measure.

The multiple assumptions and validation processes associated with the development of a clinical assessment instrument illustrates a point made in Chapter 1: There are multiple indices for the validity of a measure, which may diverge from one another. Accordingly, the clinician should attend to those indices that are most relevant to how he or she intends to use the instrument (e.g., for diagnosis vs. treatment outcome evaluation).

To sum, there is indeterminacy to the validation process. Even if your validation results were all positive (i.e., consistent with your predictions), you would still not be in a position to be sure your theoretical and measurement claims, in total, are valid. Just as one example, maybe depression is not distinct from dependent personality disorder, and it only seemed to be because of deficiencies in your measure of depression (or in the measure of dependent personality disorder). That is, a finding consistent with your theory could occur as a result of a combination of a measurement mistake and theoretical inaccuracy. Now, think about the possibility that some of your validation results were not as expected (such as a predicted relationship turns out not to be present). You would have to consider many possibilities: Maybe your theory of the existence of depression and its relation to other constructs is valid, but your measure lacks validity. Maybe your measure is valid, but one of your theoretical statements regarding the relationship of depression to other constructs is incorrect. Maybe your measure and theory are correct, but the measure you used for one of the other constructs lacks validity. As you can see, after each study, your evaluation of the validity of your theory and measure changes, and after each study, you must make judgments concerning the likely explanations for the findings that you obtained. In a real sense, the process of measure validation is never finished; each study provides information about the validity of your measure *and* the theory of which it is a part.

A BRIEF HISTORY OF VALIDITY IN PSYCHOLOGY

Having this background in mind and understanding the importance of validation for the decisions a clinician must make during the assessment process is a good way to understand the history of measure validation efforts in clinical psychology. Examining one early, prominent attempt to measure psychopathology—the Woodworth Personal Data Sheet

(WPDS)—provides a good opportunity to demonstrate the importance of the theoretical issues we just presented. Inspired by the needs of the U.S. Army in World War I, the WPDS was constructed in 1919 to help screen prospective recruits vulnerable to the stress of war by evaluating emotional stability (Garrett & Schneck, 1928). Woodworth wrote 116 dichotomous items; the items were developed on both rational grounds (case histories of identified patients provided item content) and empirical grounds (items endorsed by 50% or more of a normal, comparison group were deleted; Garrett & Schneck, 1928).

As you can see, Woodworth took real, important steps to develop a scale that would have validity. His use of content from clinical cases seems wise, as does the precaution of dropping items that, although they appeared in clinical records, also characterized the functioning of many healthy, normal adults. Despite these good efforts, the scale did not perform well. Total WPDS score did not differentiate between college freshmen and "avowed psychoneurotics" (i.e., clinical patients) (Garrett & Schneck, 1928). This failure was striking, particularly because in the 1920s college students were a much more elite group than they are today; the finding that the clinical patients did not endorse the items with greater frequency than the students (i.e., it had insufficient discriminative validity) seriously undermined the argument that the scale was valid. In another blow, the scale also failed to correlate with teacher ratings of students' emotional stability (i.e., it had insufficient convergent validity; Flemming & Flemming, 1929).

Following failures of validation efforts, researchers of course seek an explanation for the failure. In the case of the WPDS, researchers focused on the item content and concluded that the total WPDS score appeared to combine multiple, different forms of dysfunction (Garrett & Schneck, 1928; Laird, 1925). Consider this diverse array of sample items: "Have you ever lost your memory for a time?" "Can you sit still without fidgeting?" "Does it make you uneasy to have to cross a wide street or an open square?" and "Does some particular useless thought keep coming into your mind to bother you?" At the time, no fully developed models of psychopathology existed that differentiated among different forms of dysfunction that exist today; it thus made sense to combine item responses into a single score. But, based on today's more advanced understanding of psychopathology, each of these items seems to represent a different form of psychological dysfunction. Combining them into a total score necessarily produces a score with heterogeneous items and an unclear meaning; for any one respondent, one cannot know the degree to which the score reflects memory problems, hyperactivity, phobias, or obsessional tendencies.

Thus, from today's perspective, we might conclude that there was a failure in the theoretical specification of psychopathology underlying the WPDS; the construct to be measured was actually a combination of many different constructs, such that the total score did not reflect variation on any single dimension of dysfunction. Our conclusion is that variation in WPDS scores did not represent variation in an identifiable, definable construct. As a result, researchers were not actually testing the hypothesis that emotional stability was related to combat performance, college student group membership, or teacher ratings of emotional stability. Today, it seems to us that efforts to validate the WPDS were doomed because the core knowledge base concerning psychopathology was not well enough developed to lead to more precise, more differentiated, and hence more accurate descriptions of dysfunction. This leads us to an important concept, discussed in greater detail in Chapter 7, that validity of a measure can change over time as our understanding of the nature of the measured construct changes. For the clinician, it means that the validity of some older assessment instruments may have diminished over time even though they are still frequently used.

At the time, some researchers noted the diversity of mental complaints that were summed to yield an overall score. For example, Garrett and Schneck (1928) concluded the following:

> It is this fact, among others, which is causing the present-day trend away from the concept of mental disease as an entity. Instead of saying that a patient has this or that disease, the modern psychiatrist prefers to say that the patient exhibits such and such symptoms. (p. 465)

Garrett and Schneck (1928) then investigated the performance of individual items rather than the test as a whole; they did so by seeking to validate individual items against narrower, specific diagnoses. This early study was remarkable in that it reflected an appreciation of the need for specificity in defining psychological constructs for both predictors and criteria. Garrett and Schneck's (1928) approach anticipated two important subsequent advances in psychometrics. First, their use of an empirical approach to determining the efficacy of item responses in classifying persons produced different results from prior rational classifications (Laird, 1925), thus indicating the importance of empirical validation of measures in clinical assessment. Second, they anticipated the recent emphasis on construct homogeneity, which is the idea that each measured construct should represent a single dimension (rather than having a single score reflect the average of multiple dimensions; see Chapter 2 and McGrath, 2005; Smith et al., 2009; Strauss & Smith, 2009). In Chapter 6, we address this issue further by discussing concepts and analytic strategies for examining the multiple factors that may underlie some measures in clinical assessment.

Validation of Measures in Terms of Their Ability to Predict Criteria: The Early and Middle 20th Century

The failure of the WPDS to demonstrate discriminative validity was an important event in the history of validity theory and remains an important concept in current-day clinical assessment: Psychological tests constructed by experts do not automatically have validity. At the same time, philosophers of science were espousing considerable wariness of theories describing unobservable entities (Blumberg & Feigl, 1931). To respond to these concerns, clinical psychological researchers turned to an empirical and narrow understanding of validity. A test was considered valid if, and only if, it predicted a specific, practical criterion (Kane, 2001). We now refer to this form of validation as *criterion-related validity*. In fact, prominent validation theorists held that the only meaning a test had was its ability to predict a criterion. The idea that scores on a test mean anything beyond their ability to predict an outcome was rejected. As Anastasi (1950) put it: "It is only as a measure of a specifically defined criterion that a test can be objectively validated at all. ... To claim that a test measures anything over and above its criterion is pure speculation" (p. 67).

Although narrow in scope, this approach to measure validation led to many useful advances in knowledge. Concerning the process of constructing tests, it led to a new approach called *criterion keying*, in which items are selected entirely on the basis of whether they predicted the criterion. No thought was given to the content of the item; such considerations were deemed immaterial. Instead, items were included on a scale only if they predicted the outcome of interest; in fact, the direction they were keyed (which response was considered positive and which negative) was determined on strictly empirical grounds. If the target group (say, depressed individuals) tended to endorse the item in one direction, then the item was keyed that way on the test.

The emergence of criterion keying represented an important advance: Validity, in the form of successful prediction of a criterion, was built into the test. Criterion keying worked well in many ways. Two widely used measures of personality and psychopathology, the MMPI (Minnesota Multiphasic Personality Inventory; Butcher, 1995) and the California Psychological Inventory (CPI; Megargee, 2009), were developed using criterion keying. Both measures have generated important new knowledge concerning personality, psychopathology, and adjustment. For example, the MMPI-2 successfully distinguishes between psychiatric inpatients and outpatients (Butcher, 1990; Greene, 2006; Nichols & Crowhurst, 2006) and provides improved prediction in normal populations, head-injured populations, and individuals in correctional facilities (Butcher, 1995). The CPI predicts a wide range of criteria successfully as well (Gough 1996).

Of course, the criterion-related validity method also had limitations, and these became more apparent over the course of time. One of those limitations is already referenced in this chapter: Tests of a measure's criterion-related validity depend, for their validity, on the validity of the criterion. Reliance on criterion-related validity "involves the *acceptance* of a set of operations as an adequate definition of whatever is to be measured [or predicted]" (Bechtoldt, 1951, p. 1245). Often, it was assumed that the criterion was valid in the absence of empirical support for that assumption. From today's perspective, many criteria used in the past may have lacked validity; frequently, they represented judgments that were made with an insufficiently developed knowledge base (such as crude diagnostic classifications). These limitations necessarily limited researchers' capacity to validate measures.

The second limitation of criterion-related validity methods is one that was only identified as philosophers of science moved away from the reluctance to focus on unobservable processes. Over time, it became clear that many of the most important scientific advances were in the realm of theory (think of Einstein's special theory of relativity). Thus, it increasingly came to seem that theoretical advances would provide the basis for the most meaningful empirical studies conducted by clinical psychological scientists. But, when a test is developed specifically to predict an identified criterion and when the test is validated only with respect to how well it achieves that predictive task, the test validation process adds little to basic theory. Because such tests are only validated with respect to their prediction of the specific target criterion and because the content domain represented in the tests is not a focus of consideration, these tests do not readily lead to tests of theories describing relations among psychological processes and our understanding of those processes.

To test such psychological theories, one often needs measures that represent psychological processes that cannot be represented by a single criterion; that is, one needs measures of inferred psychological constructs. One might want to measure inferred constructs as diverse as basic personality processes that contribute to psychopathology (for example, extreme levels of excitement seeking may contribute to maladaptive risk taking), level of intelligence, visual perceptual processing, and so on. If one can measure constructs of this kind, one can develop theories that help explain healthy functioning, unhealthy functioning, factors that trigger and maintain one or the other, and the causal relations associated with different forms of dysfunction. Lee Cronbach and Paul Meehl, writing in 1955, compellingly articulated this need. The development of such theories is important; in their absence, clinical scientists lack a basis for proposing and testing new possible relations among clinically important variables. Many of the core, comprehensive theories that shape clinical scientific thought today, such as comprehensive theories of personality functioning (Costa & McCrae, 1992), could not have been developed if researchers continued to operate using a narrow, criterion-related validity perspective.

As real as the limitations of criterion-related validity are, it is wise to remember that when the focus on this approach to validity began, the level of knowledge concerning psychopathology and many other psychological phenomena was not far enough advanced to permit the development of measures based on well-developed theory. The predictive failure of the WPDS speaks to that reality. At that time, the reliance on criterion-related validity methods was helpful and led, in the end, to considerable growth in knowledge, which in turn has made it possible to develop new theories. Ironically, the success of the criterion-related validity method led to its ultimate replacement with a new approach that emphasized theory testing and the measurement of unobservable, inferred constructs. The new approach is known as *construct validity* theory and was ushered in by several authors in the middle of the 20th century (Campbell & Fiske, 1959; Cronbach & Meehl, 1955; Loevinger, 1957).

Construct Validity and Theory Testing

The construct validity perspective is the one implied by the example of developing and validating a measure of depression with which we led off this chapter. We next present the construct validity concept in more detail before turning to recent advances in validation theory and ongoing issues in the field. We also highlight the relevance of the construct validation process for clinicians who are selecting and applying clinical assessment instruments and interpreting the measures derived from them.

As we noted, the concept of construct validation emerged in the middle of the 20th century. In 1948, MacCorquodale and Meehl published a paper arguing that psychological researchers needed to make use of hypothetical constructs: hypotheses about the existence of processes, psychological functions, or entities that are not directly observable. This crucial paper promoted the legitimacy of inferring the existence of psychological constructs that cannot be directly observed but that contribute to observed behavior. In 1954, the Committee on Psychological Tests of the American Psychological Association published technical recommendations that included the introduction of the concept of construct validity by Meehl and Challman. Then in 1955, Cronbach and Meehl published their seminal paper introducing construct validity into the broader literature.

As recognized by Cronbach and Meehl (1955), it is necessary to infer the existence of unobservable psychological constructs to develop and validate theories of psychological functioning. Construct validity has been defined in different ways (see Glossary) but generally refers to the degree to which individual differences on a measure reflect individual differences on the underlying, unobservable construct of interest. This definition points to a central problem for psychological researchers and clinicians who use the definitions: If one cannot observe psychological constructs, how can one then validate measures of them?

Cronbach and Meehl (1955) said that to validate measures of unobservable constructs in a convincing way, it is necessary to show that a measure of a construct relates to measures of other constructs in ways that are predictable by theory. For hypothetical constructs, the only way to judge whether a measure represents a construct validly is to test whether scores on the measure conform to a theory that includes the target construct. We gave an example of such a process in the beginning of this chapter: To provide persuasive evidence that your measure of depression is valid, you needed both to confirm the validity of the content of the measure and to show that scores on the measure related to scores on other measures in the ways that you predicted from your theory.

One of the problems that was evident in our hypothetical example of constructing the first measure of depression was that we did not have great confidence in the validity of the criterion of clinician judgments of depression. Cronbach and Meehl (1955) addressed this problem directly by talking about the process of *bootstrapping* scientific knowledge.* They gave the example of temperature measurement. They noted that scientists began with the general sense that some things feel hotter than others. Through a series of experimental efforts, over many years, they learned that mercury expands with increased temperature, that there can be good interobserver agreement on the amount of mercury expansion, that one can use the degree of mercury expansion to define temperature differences even of small magnitude, and that those differences are associated with important events (points at which things freeze or melt, for example). Ultimately, they developed a theoretical structure to explain the relationship between temperature and mercury expansion. The end products of this line of investigation were a much more developed and precise understanding of temperature and the development of instruments to measure small differences in temperature. The development of the thermometer was an integral part of advances in understanding the nature and impact of temperature on the physical world.

In the case of temperature, researchers started with a vague, unsatisfying criterion of subjective ratings of the phenomenon, and their investigations, through an iterative process, led to more precise measurement and a better understanding of temperature. The implication for psychological science is that efforts to validate theories and the measures used to test them can, by an analogous bootstrapping process, lead to advances in knowledge, advances in theory, and measures that are more reliable and valid than were the original criteria. And indeed, researchers often do develop measures, like measures of depression, that outperform the original criteria used in their development. In Text Box 3.1, we provide an example in clinical assessment: the development of measures of intelligence.

---

* Bootstrapping as a strategy for refining constructs and their measurement refers to an ongoing process of building a knowledge base by developing hypotheses, testing them, using those results to both improve the hypotheses and improve the ability to measure the target constructs (see Glossary).

TEXT BOX 3.1   BOOTSTRAPPING TOWARD MEASURING INTELLIGENCE

Alfred Binet's effort to develop a measure of children's intelligence represented a welcome advance from previous efforts because he used a real-world criterion: Scores on his scale had to be associated with teachers' judgments. Although his use of a criterion was noteworthy, the criterion was not strong; teacher judgments, like all human judgments, are subject to various forms of perceptual and memory biases, along with other sources of error. Nevertheless, validation against this criterion led to the development of the Stanford-Binet scale, which provided measures of individual differences in intelligence. Even relatively small differences in intellectual functioning could be recorded as differences in Stanford-Binet scores.

The scale included a wide variety of tasks. Over time, researchers studied the scale, its correlates, and possible empirical differences between different types of tasks. As this work advanced, researchers began to recognize a difference between verbal and nonverbal intelligence (the latter includes things like spatial reasoning). David Wechsler then developed a new intelligence test that provided different quantitative indices for the two kinds of intelligence. Research using the Wechsler-Bellevue scale confirmed the value of the distinction: The two scales had different correlates, and interestingly, deficits in performance on them appeared to be associated with damage to different brain regions. In recent decades, further research, conducted by those studying intelligence and those studying cognitive processing, has led to the identification of two more domains of intellectual functioning: working memory and processing speed. Today, measures of intelligence assess all four domains, and the different domains play different roles in explaining other psychological phenomena.

Thus, we now have quantitative indices of human variation on four important dimensions of intellectual functioning. We can describe individuals' strengths and weaknesses on these dimensions, and we can use the results to inform academic and other interventions. Note how the scores from the four dimensions often have greater clinical utility than an overall IQ score that aggregates scores from these four dimensions.

Today, we view a profile on the most recent version of the Wechsler scale as a much more valid and detailed assessment than one could get from teacher judgments (although teacher judgments are often important in planning school-based interventions). The bootstrapping process has taken us from a relatively vague original criterion to the detailed, empirically validated, and clinically useful assessments now available. Those interested can turn to the work of Lichtenberger and Kaufman (2009) and Sattler (2001) to learn more about the history of intelligence tests.

CURRENT PERSPECTIVES ON THEORY AND MEASURE VALIDATION: CONSTRUCT VALIDITY UPDATED

At this point in the chapter, you have a good sense of the basic process of construct validation and a sense of how perspectives on the validation process have evolved over the last century. In this next section, we describe five advances that have been made in how researchers understand construct validity. As you will see, these advances represent either slight modifications of construct validity theory or straightforward extensions of the theory. All have implications for judgments made during clinical assessment.

Advances From the Philosophy and History of Science in Understanding the Process of Theory Testing

Early in the 20th century, a widespread view among philosophers of science was that theories could be fully proved or fully disproved based on empirical evidence. This perspective was called *justificationism* (Lakatos, 1968), and from this point of view, the validity of a theory, and the validity of measures, could be directly and unequivocally established by a series of critical experiments.

In the latter half of the 20th century, historians of science and philosophers of science have converged on a different perspective, known as *nonjustificationism* (Bartley, 1987; Weimer, 1979). From this perspective, no theory is ever unequivocally proved or disproved. Rather, the development of measures and theories is an ongoing process. At any one time, certain theories are judged to perform better in terms of important clinical predictions than others, and evidence favors the validity of certain measures over others. As you can see, from this perspective, science is characterized by a lack of certainty. We noted this lack of certainty at the start of this chapter in our example of measuring depression.

Here is why uncertainty is unavoidable, especially in clinical science: When one tests any theoretical claim, such as that psychopathy is characterized by high levels of impulsiveness and angry hostility but low levels of anxiety and self-consciousness (Lynam & Widiger, 2007), one is presupposing the validity of multiple measures and multiple theories to conduct the test. In this example, one must accept that (a) there are reliable individual differences in each of four personality dimensions that are not solely a function of context; (b) one has measured each of those four dimensions in reliable and valid ways—variation on each of four measures represents variation in the relevant underlying, unobserved constructs; (c) each of the four unobserved constructs has been validly defined; (d) one has not excluded other, important contributors to psychopathy that would alter the apparent impact of the four traits of interest; (e) one's measures of the four personality dimensions do not represent other, theoretically unrelated processes to any substantial degree; (f) the concept of psychopathy is useful in explaining human behavior and dysfunction, such that inclusion of the concept provides an increment in explanatory power beyond what is available without it; (g) one has identified a sample with sufficient variability on each dimension to test the theoretical claim; and so on.

Obviously, a failed test of the core theoretical claim could be due to many different things; the theory may be inaccurate, any one of the measures may lack sufficient reliability or validity to conduct the test, the theory that each of the four dimensions exist as useful descriptions of human functioning could be incorrect, and so on. Philosophers sometimes refer to the many theories that one presumes to test the theory of interest as "auxiliary theories," and they note that problems with either the target theory or any of a number of auxiliary theories could explain a negative result. As a practical matter, researchers typically do consider a number of different possibilities when faced with a nonsupportive finding. If one believes there is other strong support for one's theory, one might question the validity of an auxiliary theory or a measurement. In the absence of external support for the core theory under investigation, one might be more inclined to question it.

Inquiry into a given theory is often characterized by ongoing debates between those who support and those who oppose the theory. What makes these debates part of science, rather than simple opinion debate, is that scientists subject every aspect of their research to critical scrutiny; as a field, we embrace that scrutiny as the best way to advance knowledge. Research methods and assumptions are described in the publications that report findings. There is an ongoing process of criticism of theory, measurement, methods, and assumptions. Over time, the debate comes to favor one side over the other. Weimer (1979) observed that this process of conducting science is characterized by "comprehensively critical rationalism" (p. 40): Every aspect of the research enterprise is open to critical evaluation and hence revision. Of course, as we noted in Chapter 1, this ambience of scrutiny of one's hypotheses is part of a scientific approach to clinical assessment. The clinician must continually collect data that that can support or refute his or her hypotheses about the client's problems and goals, their interrelations, and potential intervention strategies based on these hypotheses.

Roles of Content Validity and Criterion-Related Validity in the Construct Validation Process

As you may have gathered, construct validation is a kind of umbrella term that refers to the process of building evidence that variation on a measure reflects variation on the construct of interest. We referred in this chapter to two other kinds of validity: *content validity* and *criterion-related validity*. *Content validity* refers to whether your measure accurately reflects the content domain of the target construct; it has been defined as "the degree to which elements of an assessment instrument are relevant to and representative of the targeted construct for a particular assessment purpose" (Haynes, Richard, & Kubany, 1995). From today's perspective, evidence for the content validity of an instrument is one part of the overall empirical record concerning the instrument's construct validity. In clinical assessment, an instrument with low content validity may fail to capture change in important aspects of a phenomenon (e.g., insufficient representativeness) or may reflect change in irrelevant phenomenon (e.g., insufficient relevance of elements). The problems with instruments with low content validity should now be apparent: When measures are derived from an assessment instrument with low content validity, clinical judgments can be adversely affected by variance in irrelevant behavior and insufficiently informed by variance in relevant behavior.

Criterion-related validity, which again refers to the degree to which a measure predicts a criterion of interest, is also now considered one piece of evidence for the construct validity of a measure. Criterion-related validity can be described as predictive, when a test score predicts a future outcome of interest, or concurrent, when a test score is associated with an outcome measured at the same time. An example of criterion-related validity would be when one is interested in predicting presence or absence of a criminal history (whether predictively or concurrently). To make the prediction, one might choose a measure of psychopathy. Presumably, individuals high in psychopathy are more likely than others to have a criminal history. The degree to which that relationship is present in a sample can be understood as evidence of criterion-related postdictive validity for the psychopathy measure (postdictive because the criminal history is present before the assessment of psychopathy). From a construct validity perspective, the finding that the psychopathy measure successfully predicts criminal history is viewed as one piece of evidence for the construct validity of the measure. Of course, prior to the introduction of construct validity, the ability of the scale to predict criminal history would be the only relevant evidence of its validity, and it would be known as a predictor of criminality, not a measure of the inferred construct of psychopathy. Note again the challenges posed by the criterion: The postdictive validity of the psychopathy measure would vary depending on how criminal history was measured.

Informative Programs of Construct Validation: Toward a Resolution of a Difficulty

There are problems with the use of construct validity as a system for understanding the process of validating theories and the measures used to test them. The idea depends on the assumption that one can specify a set of relations between one's target construct and other constructs;

one needs to do so to conduct empirical validation tests. The problem for clinical psychological science, as for many branches of science, is that researchers often do not have precisely specified theories on which to draw or theories about a construct can be specified differently across researchers. When that is true, the meaning of construct validity, and what counts as validation evidence, is not clear.

Cronbach (1988) contrasted what he called strong and weak programs of construct validation. Strong programs depend on spelled out theory, so that one conducts tests of whether a measure of a construct conforms to the set of theoretically specified predictions. Because well-developed, elaborated theories are rare, it seems that strong construct validation programs represent something of an ideal rather than a description of standard practice. Cronbach observed that when developed theories are not available, thus ruling out strong validation programs of research, investigators often rely on weak construct validation research. Without developed theory-guiding predictions, it is less clear what counts as validity evidence. It sometimes seems that researchers count almost any correlation as validation evidence: If one's measure correlates with some variables and not others, one generates an explanation for the observed pattern, which is then described as evidence for construct validity. But, such approaches often have a kind of ad hoc, opportunistic quality (Kane, 2001); empirical results from such approaches may not be highly informative.

For the clinician, this means "buyer beware," in that a clinical researcher's interpretation of findings from validity tests of an instrument may not be warranted by a less-biased interpretation of the data. All authors of this book have served as journal editors and reviewed many assessment research manuscripts in which the authors exhibited a strong positive investigator bias in discussions of the results of validation studies. In these cases, the authors operate more as advocates than as clinical scientists.

Although it may seem that we are stuck between the unattainable ideal of strong construct validation and unacceptable, weak construct validation, the dichotomy between strong and weak does not actually capture the nature of the validation process. Remember the concept of bootstrapping: Early in any new line of research, one proceeds without a fully elaborated theory. As results come in, measures are improved, and theoretical claims are developed, one moves to stronger validation processes. Smith (2005) argued that, rather than think in terms of strong and weak construct validation, we should apply the standard of how informative is a validation test given the state of knowledge we have about the construct.

The bootstrapping, iterative process leads to ongoing refinement of measures and of theories and hence to progressively improved empirical tests of each. Thus, researchers can properly ask whether their empirical tests are likely to be informative (Smith, 2005). As one considers conducting an empirical test, one might ask whether the results of the test will shed light on the validity of one's measure or one's theory. Does a test of a hypothesis represent a direct comparison between two, competing theoretical explanations? If it does, the results are likely to be informative; they are likely to advance knowledge. Does a test of a hypothesis involve a claim that, if supported, undermines criticism of a theory? Does a hypothesis test involve a direct challenge to the validity of a measure? Does it involve direct criticism of a theory? Tests of these kinds are likely to be informative; they can advance knowledge and facilitate the development of elaborated theories and better measures of the targeted constructs.

Construct Homogeneity

The recent focus on construct homogeneity addresses one threat to successful, informative construct validation efforts. Imagine developing a measure of a construct domain that has multiple dimensions. One example, described in Text Box 3.2, is the familiar concept of neuroticism (emotional instability and the tendency to experience distress frequently). One current theory of neuroticism (Costa & McCrae, 1992) is that it includes six separate traits. If you then use a single score for neuroticism, your construct validation efforts have a great deal of uncertainty built into them. This problem is especially important for clinical assessment because often there is a need to attend to only certain facets of neuroticism. A frequent error in clinical assessment is to rely on a highly aggregated, composite score to draw inferences about one facet of that score. This would be illustrated by using a "neuroticism" measure to evaluate the outcome of an intervention designed to reduce a client's impulsiveness (see Text Box 3.2).

Suppose you use a single score to represent a multidimensional construct domain, and you correlate individual differences on that score with measures of other constructs. If you do so, you will have built two sources of uncertainty into your test. The first is that, with a single score, you cannot know how much each different trait contributed to that correlation. Let us say that you correlate neuroticism with physical health concerns; although it may be true that each of the six traits has the same correlation with health concerns, it is unlikely. You have no way of knowing which of the six traits do correlate with health concerns and which do not; instead, you essentially have an average of different relationships. As a result, you lack information you need to develop a useful case formulation, design the best intervention strategy, or evaluate the effects of an intervention.

The second problem has even more severe implications for clinical research: The same composite score will tend to reflect different

TEXT BOX 3.2   NEUROTICISM AND CONSTRUCT HOMOGENEITY

In their measure of the five basic factors of personality, Costa and McCrae (1992) identified six personality traits within the domain of neuroticism: anxiety, depression, self-consciousness, vulnerability, angry hostility, and impulsiveness. These six scales correlate with each other more highly than they do with scales measuring other personality traits, hence their placement together in the neuroticism domain. But, the six scales are not alternate forms measures of the same construct; as their different names imply, they are thought to measure different traits from one another. The traits thus differ in the nature of their clinical implications.

There is good empirical evidence that the scales do measure different constructs. To understand this evidence, we can first compare the reliability of the scales to their intercorrelations. Internal consistency (Cronbach's alpha) estimates of reliability, as given in the test manual, range from .68 to .81 for these scales. Correlations among the six scales range from a low of .31 to a high of .60. We consider one pair of scales as an example: self-consciousness (alpha = .68) and angry hostility (alpha = .75). Recall from Chapter 2 that these values can be understood as estimates as the proportion of variance on these scales that is reliable or repeatable (i.e., true score variance). Now, consider the correlation between the two scales reported in the manual; it is $r = .37$. As you may know at this point, the square of that correlation is called the *coefficient of determination*, an index of how much variance is shared between the two scales. So, $(.37)^2 = .14$. If 68% of the variance in self-consciousness is reliable but only 14% is shared with angry hostility, then 54% of the variance in self-consciousness is estimated to be reliable, true score variance unrelated to angry hostility ($68 - 14 = 54$). In the same way, we estimate that 61% of the variance in angry hostility is true score variance unrelated to self-consciousness. So, for each of these constructs, there is a great deal of reliable variance not shared with the other construct.

The unrelated variability in the two scales turns out to be important for understanding the form of dysfunction known as psychopathy. Lynam and Widiger (2007) found that psychopaths are characterized by unusually low levels of self-consciousness but unusually high levels of angry hostility: The difference between the two traits matters. As you can see, simply summing the scores on these two separate traits does not produce a number with clear psychological meaning and doing so is less useful to the clinician

(continued on next page)

> when drawing clinical judgments about a client. An overall neu-
> roticism score (i.e., the sum of these two traits plus four others)
> does not refer to a definable psychological entity. If one correlated
> such a score with another measure, one would not be in a position
> to know what the correlation means. If a clinician wanted to mea-
> sure change, perhaps following treatment or following important
> life events, an overall neuroticism score would not tell him or her
> what had changed.

combinations of the six traits for different individuals in your sample. Two people could easily have the same neuroticism score even though one is high in self-consciousness and low in angry hostility, and the other is low in self-consciousness and high in angry hostility. The same score would reflect different personality patterns for different people. For example, a psychopath and a nonpsychopath could have identical neuroticism scores. Because that is true, you cannot know the meaning of a correlation between overall neuroticism and other variables: Scores on a measure of a multidimensional construct do not mean the same thing for everyone in your sample. Clearly, the use of more specific measures will provide more information to clinicians.

For these reasons, many construct validity theorists emphasize the need to use single scores to represent homogeneous dimensions of psychological functioning (McGrath, 2005; Smith et al., 2009). When you do so, you are in a much better position to meaningfully interpret the results of validation tests, and the clinician is in a much better position to make valid and useful clinical judgments. When scores representing heterogeneous constructs are used in research and clinical assessment, interpretations lack clear meaning. In this chapter, we do not discuss the empirical means to investigate whether one has defined a homogeneous construct and developed a homogeneous scale, although we do address one way to answer this question in the chapter on factor analysis (Chapter 6). For now, though, we want to emphasize that a claim that a construct, or its measure, is homogeneous is a theoretical claim that itself needs to be validated. One conducts systematic validation research to investigate whether a measure includes multiple dimensions that relate differently to other psychological phenomena or not. When one identifies multiple dimensions in a measure, and when one shows that those dimensions relate differently to other measures (that is, they play different roles in understanding psychological functioning), one should then represent each dimension with its own score. There are many straightforward empirical and statistical methods for studying each separate construct within a larger domain (e.g., multivariate statistical analyses enable study of the impact of each of several constructs as well as the impact of combinations of constructs).

Construct Representation

The term *construct representation* is used most often in reference to laboratory tasks. Many clinical psychology researchers test hypotheses relating certain forms of cognitive functioning to psychological dysfunction; often, a laboratory task is used to measure cognitive functioning. An example would be the hypothesis that patients with schizophrenia have more difficulty than controls in inhibiting their response to high verbal associates (Rattan & Chapman, 1973). To evaluate that hypothesis, researchers need a task of responsiveness to verbal associates, that is, a task such that individual differences in response to the task reflect individual differences in responsiveness to verbal associates. Rattan and Chapman developed two multiple-choice vocabulary subtests, one with associates to the stimulus word as incorrect alternatives and the other without associates. Patients diagnosed with schizophrenia, compared to persons without a diagnosis of schizophrenia, showed greater deficit on the "with associates" vocabulary test than on the other vocabulary test. The resulting inference that schizophrenia is associated with distraction by verbal associates depends on the degree to which variation on the verbal associate test is truly associated with variation in response to verbal associates.

Construct representation is similar to the concept of external validity in that it refers to whether variation in responses to a task represent variation in the underlying construct of interest; the idea is that the construct is represented validly by the task. Just as it is necessary to develop evidence for the construct validity of measures of individual differences, so it is necessary to establish evidence supporting claims of construct representation.

There is a growing appreciation of the need to engage in construct representation research (Strauss & Smith, 2009). Too often, experimental laboratory tasks are simply developed and used by a researcher for a specific study, even though there is little or no independent evidence for their validity. Providing independent evidence of validity, that is, providing evidence of construct representation, is a complex task. For example, schizophrenia researchers have begun to develop methodological models to investigate construct representation and to avoid the many confounds that can be present when one compares clinical groups to nonclinical controls (Strauss, 2001). Many tasks involve the simultaneous operation of multiple cognitive processes; for example, a working memory task may require one to retain several pieces of information, but retention may also depend on attentional processes and accurate visuospatial perception. This reality makes it difficult for researchers to be sure which processes are relevant for a given disorder. For experimental psychopathology research to advance, it is necessary to confirm that tasks that are used do reflect the psychological processes they are thought to reflect.

Many clinical assessment instruments require clients to participate in some form of cognitive activity (memory tests are one example). When using such instruments in clinical assessment, it is important that you evaluate the evidence that individual differences in response to the instrument do in fact covary with individual differences in the clinical construct of interest (such as memory deficits).

APPLICATION TO CLINICAL PRACTICE

Although much of what we have presented in this chapter concerns basic aspects of theory development and validation, this material has direct implications for clinical practice; we have frequently alluded to clinical implications over the course of the chapter. One important implication concerns how clinicians choose measures to aid in clinical decision making. In Text Box 3.3, we review things for clinicians to consider in light of the information in this chapter.

SUMMARY AND RECOMMENDATIONS

In this chapter, we highlighted a number of things that are important for you to understand as you prepare to conduct clinical assessments, evaluate the validity of assessment instruments you might use, and develop and evaluate new assessment instruments. These keys points are presented in Text Box 3.3. Clinical psychology has seen enormous advances in the past century; those advances make the development of sophisticated theory and valid measures ever more possible. This time is an exciting one to conduct theory and measure validation research.

Key Points From This Chapter

1. The validity of a measure, including laboratory tasks, can never be assumed; it must be investigated empirically, and there are many possible validation strategies.
2. Because so many psychological constructs are not directly observable, tests of the validity of measures are also tests of the validity of theories on the relationships among constructs and the measurement of constructs.
3. The validation process is ongoing, and validity evidence is dynamic; you have never definitively established the validity of a measure, and validity can change as theories evolve.
4. It is important to define constructs in specific ways so that you can develop procedures to measure your target construct and select the best measures for a construct in clinical assessment without inadvertently measuring other constructs at the same time.

TEXT BOX 3.3 CHOOSING ASSESSMENT INSTRUMENTS IN CLINICAL PRACTICE

One of the most important contributions clinicians can make to the welfare of their clients is to assess accurately the nature of clients' difficulties. Our discussion of the validation process suggests that the clinician adopt the following strategies:

- Define the nature of the client's possible difficulties as precisely as possible. For an assessment procedure to prove valid and useful for your particular purpose, it must assess the domain of interest to you and the client with minimal overlap into the assessment of other, less-relevant domains.
- Investigate the validity evidence of the prospective measure carefully. How strong is the validation evidence? Is there validation evidence for populations relevant to your clinical task? Is there evidence that the measure assesses the construct of interest to you with minimal overlap into the assessment of different constructs? Is there evidence for the validity of the measure in the context or setting of interest to you? Does variability on the measure predict clinical outcomes of interest to you? Does the measure differentiate among related disorders in the ways you would like? What are the gaps and uncertainties in the validation evidence? Do those gaps compromise the validity of the measure in your context, for your purpose?
- Decide whether you are interested in assessing change using the prospective measure. If so, determine whether there is evidence that the measure can be used for that purpose. Harkening back to the preceding chapters, consider all issues relating to the reliable measurement of change. Is there evidence that scores on the measure change as a function of time or intervention?

---

5. Researchers should try to define informative validation tests; that is, tests that bear directly on the validity of a theory and the measures used to test it. In selecting measures to use in clinical assessment, clinicians should examine the degree to which validation studies are appropriately focused on important aspects of the targeted construct.
6. Validation tests will most likely be useful when focused on homogeneous measures of constructs because one can then avoid averaging scores reflecting different psychological processes.

7. Clinicians should evaluate the validity evidence of prospective measures, particularly with respect to the degree to which this evidence is relevant to the populations and settings of interest to them.
8. Our understanding of the validation process has changed with time and with scientific advances; researchers should continue to evaluate critically the validity perspectives we have described.

RECOMMENDED SOURCES

Campbell, D. T., & Fiske, D. W. (1959). Convergent and discriminant validation by the multi-trait multi-method matrix. *Psychological Bulletin, 56,* 81–105.

Cronbach, L. J., & Meehl, P. E. (1955). Construct validity in psychological tests. *Psychological Bulletin, 52,* 281–302.

McGrath, R. E. (2005). Conceptual complexity and construct validity. *Journal of Personality Assessment, 85,* 112–124.

Messick, S. (1995). Validity of psychological assessment: Validation of inferences from persons' responses and performances as scientific inquiry into score meaning. *American Psychologist, 50,* 741–749.

Smith, G. T. (2005). On construct validity: Issues of method and measurement. *Psychological Assessment, 17,* 396–408.

Strauss, M. E., & Smith, G. T. (2009). Construct validity: Advances in theory and methodology. *Annual Review of Clinical Psychology, 5,* 89–113.

Applying Psychometric Evidence to Clinical Decisions

INTRODUCTION

The focus in this chapter is on statistics and psychometric evidence that are involved in the process of using assessment data to make clinical decisions. As we emphasized in the first three chapters, a wide range of clinical decisions, from determining whether a client's symptoms are consistent with the criteria associated with a diagnostic category and whether some form of intervention is indicated for the client, to determining whether an intervention should be terminated and whether a client has made meaningful gains in functioning, are all based on assessment data. Within psychometric theory, considerations about the implications and applied value of assessment data have been termed *consequential validity* (Messick, 1995). Both the ways in which test data and other assessment data are interpreted (e.g., the data indicate that a client's distress is of a clinically significant magnitude) and judgments based on those data (e.g., the level of impairment in memory functioning indicates the need for special rehabilitation services) provide information pertinent to considerations of consequential validity.

We begin the chapter by discussing what are called diagnostic efficiency statistics; these statistics apply psychometric evidence to the process of making diagnostic and prognostic decisions. We then discuss *incremental validity*, which addresses the question of whether predictions made with a set of assessment data can be meaningfully improved by adding information from another set of assessment data. Finally, we examine *sensitivity to change*, which is a key consideration in the development, evaluation, and use of instruments designed to inform the clinician about the impact of interventions.

In previous chapters, we discussed the role of error in measurement and emphasized the importance of using the standard error of measurement in estimations of an individual's true score (i.e., ability, knowledge, severity of symptoms). We also discussed the (ongoing) process of validating an instrument and how the nature of validity evidence should influence your choice of instruments for a specific purpose with a specific client or sample of participants. As we move into the current chapter, it is important to remember that no instrument provides data that are perfectly reliable or perfectly valid—there is always some error and uncertainty involved in measurement. Moreover, as you will see in this chapter, scores on psychological instruments may possess generally good reliability and validity but may be of limited value in making clinically relevant predictions or decisions.

On the basis of extensive empirical literature, we know that health professionals and the public alike have difficulty grasping and using many of the concepts we present in this chapter (Gigerenzer, Gaissmaier, Kurz-Milcke, Schwartz, & Woloshin, 2008; Reyna, Nelson, Han, & Dieckmann, 2009). For this reason, we present these concepts in a manner that builds on knowledge graduate students in various health disciplines already possess (probably from undergraduate psychology courses). We encourage you to pay close attention to the examples we use to illustrate concepts such as sensitivity, likelihood ratios (LRs), positive predictive power (PPP), and incremental validity. The statistics on which these and related concepts are based are relatively simple and require only rudimentary mathematical skills (addition, multiplication, and division). Nevertheless, it is clear that correctly making simple calculations is far from straightforward for many people.

DIAGNOSING AND PREDICTING CLIENT BEHAVIOR

As an introduction to our presentation of statistical concepts used for making diagnostic or prognostic decisions, we begin with a common clinical question: If a client successfully completes treatment, what is the likelihood that the client will experience a relapse in the near future? It is well known that relapse occurs all too frequently for individuals successfully treated for depression, regardless of the type of efficacious treatment provided. For this reason, Jarrett et al. (2001) examined the impact on subsequent relapse of adding a continuation phase to standard cognitive therapy. Following successful treatment with cognitive therapy, half of their research participants received 10 additional sessions of treatment in the 8 months following the "termination" of cognitive therapy; the other half received no additional treatment. Participants in both groups were assessed on a regular basis. The authors found that, over a 16-month follow-up, the rate of relapse among those receiving continuation cognitive therapy was one third that of the rate among those who received no additional treatment. In clinical settings, providing continuation-phase treatment for all depressed clients who successfully completed cognitive therapy would be a difficult undertaking for both practical and financial reasons. Moreover, based on the Jarrett et al. (2001) data, not all clients are likely to relapse; therefore, not all need continuation treatment. An important question stemming from this research is whether it might be possible to identify those at greatest risk for relapse to offer these individuals continuation treatment.

This is the question that Jarrett, Vittengl, and Clark (2008) addressed in their reanalysis of the Jarrett et al. (2001) data. These researchers used participants' scores on a range of outcome measures, taken at the last regular treatment session, to predict the likelihood of subsequent relapse. For our purposes, we focus only on the Beck Depression Inventory (BDI) data presented by Jarrett et al. (2008). BDI scores can range from 0 to 63; using regression techniques, they found that BDI scores at termination were significantly related to the probability of subsequent relapse. For example, participants whose BDI scores were 0 or 1 had a .36 or lower probability of relapsing; in contrast, those with BDI scores of 7 or greater had a .68 or higher probability of relapsing.

This kind of information seems immediately clinically relevant; for example, a low BDI score at termination may lead the clinician simply to encourage a client to contact him or her if symptoms of depression reappear, whereas a moderately elevated BDI score at termination may lead the clinician to schedule two or three monthly follow-up appointments to monitor the client's recovery more closely and provide "booster" sessions when needed. However, there are several questions that need to be addressed before the full clinical value of this type of information is evident. Given the imprecision of any measurement and any regression equation, how accurate is the regression equation likely to be when applied to a new, independent sample of clients? This can only be answered by independent research studies in which the equation is applied. What is the critical BDI score that should be used to determine who is (and who is not) offered follow-up appointments or continuation-phase treatment? How many errors are we likely to make in determining who would benefit from continuation-phase treatment, and relatedly, how many errors are we likely to make in determining who does not need continuation-phase treatment? These are the type of questions to which we now turn; we address the related question of cost-benefit considerations in the next chapter.

Decisional "Hits" and "Misses"

Table 4.1 provides a simple way of thinking about the use of assessment data to make clinical decisions and illustrates some errors that clinicians can make in their decisions. When we use assessment data, we are really making predictions about an "event," such as the ability of test scores to indicate the presence of a specific diagnosis, a preferred treatment for a client, or whether a treatment will significantly change the client's rate of aggressive behaviors, decrease his or her blood pressure, or reduce the likelihood that the client will relapse following successful treatment. Continuing with our previous example, the event we are predicting is whether our client is likely to experience a depressive relapse less than a year and a half after successful treatment (in this instance, the nonevent would be no relapse). Based on making a simple, binary prediction, four outcomes are possible. Our prediction that the person would experience a relapse might be borne out. In other words, a relapse did occur (i.e., a "true event")—this is called a *true positive*. On the other hand, if we predicted that the person would not relapse and no relapse occurred (i.e., a "true nonevent"), this is termed a *true negative*. Obviously, both true positives and true negatives are good things (at least from a statistical or clinical decision-making perspective), as our predictions turned out to be accurate. Thus, both true positives and true negatives are decision-making "hits." Unfortunately, errors are an inevitable part of any decision making—these are called "misses." Misses comprise both situations in which we predicted relapse and no relapse occurred (a *false positive*) and situations in which a relapse occurred, but we had predicted that no relapse was likely (a *false negative*). Readers familiar with industrial/organizational theory and research will recognize these concepts as part of test decision theory, which has been used for many decades for making decisions on hiring and admission to academic programs (see, for example, Anastasi & Urbina, 1997, and Hogan, 2007, for more details). An important tenet of this book is that a scientific approach to clinical assessment will increase the chance that the clinician's decisions will be hits; for example that the clinician will more accurately identify clients who are likely to maintain treatment benefits across time and identify those who are likely to relapse without additional interventions.

TABLE 4.1   Accuracy and Errors in Clinical Prediction

Prediction	True Event	True Nonevent
Event	True positives (A)	False positives (B)
Nonevent	False negatives (C)	True negatives (D)

Hits: A and D
Misses: B and C
Sensitivity: A/(A + C)
Specificity: D/(D + B)

Cut Scores, Sensitivity, and Specificity

There is a host of useful concepts and statistics stemming from the information in Table 4.1. But, before examining these in detail, we first need to consider how one determines what prediction to make. In other words, what is the basis for making a prediction of an event or a non-event? The answer to this stems from a decision made about the assessment data used for prediction purposes: These decisions often involve the determination of a cut score. *Cut scores* divide a test score (or other assessment data) into two (or more) categories, with the implication that there is something different about scores that fall within the different categories (Dwyer, 1996). The implication of a binary categorization might involve decisions such as pass/fail on a test of cognitive performance, depressed/nondepressed on a self-report measure, or treatment required/no treatment required during an intake assessment. The use of multiple categories is also common in clinical work and includes examples such as level of symptom severity (none, minimal, moderate, severe) or cognitive functioning (below average, average, above average). It is essential to recognize that the determination of a cut score (or multiple cut scores) is not a wholly objective process inasmuch as it requires judgment about the nature and value of the categories created and the decisions that might be taken about these categories. For these reasons, psychometricians tend to be reticent about promoting the use of cut scores and view them almost as unavoidable in using data for applied purposes (Dwyer, 1996). As we discuss further in this chapter and in Chapter 7, the validity of cut scores is "conditional"; they can depend on the characteristics of the client to whom they are being applied.

Because no measures are perfect (which is true for both the measurement of the predictor variable and the criterion variable) and no regression equations predict outcomes perfectly, the selection of any cut score is inevitably a task of balancing competing considerations. The goal is to maximize the number of correct decisions and minimize the extent to which erroneous decisions are likely to be made based on the cut score. Returning to the language used with respect to Table 4.1, this usually requires the clinician to carefully consider the rate of hits and misses and the implications for the client associated with the various forms of hits and misses.

There are no firm guidelines in the assessment literature for establishing cut scores. Some researchers develop cut scores based on the distribution of scores associated with the measure or a set of assessment data used for the predictor variable. For example, in establishing a clinical cut score for the Clinical Outcomes in Routine Evaluation—Outcome Measure (a treatment-monitoring and outcome measure), Connell et al. (2007) used the logic and procedures of the reliability change index described in Chapter 2. This meant that they evaluated their assessment data to find the score that optimally distinguished scores in their clinical sample from scores in their general population sample. Another option that uses distribution information is to examine how well extreme scores, based on normative samples, differentiate groups of interest. Loewenstein et al. (2006), in establishing cut scores for the assessment of mild cognitive impairment, decided to focus on the presence of very low scores to distinguish between older adults who were cognitively normal and those who were cognitively impaired. Accordingly, they examined the values of setting cut scores at 1.5 or 2.0 standard deviations below normative mean values on the instrument.

The most common strategy for determining cut scores is to explicitly use the type of information contained in Table 4.1 to calculate some statistics that focus on the decisional hits associated with a specific cut score. Let us assume that we want to use scores from a self-report psychological assessment instrument to classify individuals as meeting, or not meeting, diagnostic criteria for bulimia nervosa. To do this, we would need a group of research participants who, based on a validated external criterion such as a structured diagnostic interview (e.g., Structured Clinical Interview for Axis I Disorders [SCID]), meet criteria for bulimia and a second group of research participants who do not meet these criteria. (For the moment, we ignore questions of the relative sizes of the two groups or the extent to which the nondisordered group meets some or any of the criteria for bulimia.) We would then ask all participants to complete the self-report measure. By setting a cut score on the self-report measure, we use the diagnostic interview data to fill in information for the four cells of Table 4.1 (e.g., the proportion of those who scored above the cut score who, based on the SCID, met criteria for bulimia).

Two statistical terms are central for optimizing cut scores: *sensitivity* and *specificity*. The sensitivity of the cut score describes the extent to which those who met diagnostic criteria based on an external criterion (usually considered to be a "gold standard") were so identified by the measure. Sensitivity is calculated by dividing the number of true positives (those identified as a "case" by the measure who were also identified by the external criterion) by the total number of people who met diagnostic criteria based on the external criterion [or, in Table 4.1 terms, $A/(A + C)$]. Essentially, sensitivity answers the question, "How good is this measure in identifying persons who have a particular disorder [or, have been divorced, experience panic episodes, have experienced a traumatic life event, etc.]?

In contrast, the specificity of a measure is the extent to which those who did *not* meet diagnostic criteria were so identified by the measure. Specificity is calculated by dividing the number of true negatives by the total number of participants who did not meet diagnostic criteria [in Table 4.1 terms, $D/(D + B)$]. Table 4.2 provides some hypothetical details for our bulimia example.

Based on the information provided in Table 4.2, it appears that the cut score we set on the self-report measure does a relatively good job of identifying those who meet criteria for bulimia (sensitivity of .75; meaning that the measure correctly identified 75% of those who were

TABLE 4.2　Using Self-Report Data
(Cut Score) to Predict a Diagnosis of Bulimia

Result of Decision Based on Cut Score	Diagnosis Based on Structured Interview	
	Bulimia	**No Bulimia**
Bulimia	75 (A)	33 (B)
No bulimia	25 (C)	67 (D)

Hits = A + D = 75 + 67 = 142
Misses = B + C = 33 + 25 = 58
Sensitivity = A/(A + C) = 75/(75 + 25) = .75
Specificity = D/(D + B) = 67/(67 + 33) = .67

diagnosed with bulimia) and those who do not (specificity of .67). Moreover, using the cut score we set resulted in comparable levels of sensitivity and specificity. It would be possible to calculate the sensitivity and specificity using each possible score on the self-report measure as the cut score. Moving the cut score affects sensitivity and specificity differently; as sensitivity increases, specificity decreases, and vice versa. Why is this? Assuming that high scores on the measure reflect greater symptom severity, and that the predictor variable and criterion variable are not perfectly correlated, setting a very low cut score would be good for maximizing the number of true positives and minimizing the number of false negatives, thus increasing sensitivity. However, a very low cutoff score also means the number of false positives will increase, which in turn will reduce specificity. It is a trade-off: One cannot have both maximal sensitivity and maximal specificity.

Sensitivity and specificity are important considerations for selecting assessment instruments and interpreting measures from them. When reviewing the information about a cut score on a measure, one must pay close attention to (a) the composition of the sample used to set the cut score and how similar it is to the clients with whom you will be using the measure, and (b) the value judgments about sensitivity and specificity that informed the selection of the cut score (i.e., Was high sensitivity or high specificity of greater value to the researchers, and does this match the value of these statistics in the current assessment context?).

Let us return now to our discussion of the process for determining cut scores. Sensitivity and specificity data can be used to select a cut score for a specific purpose. Most commonly, sensitivity and specificity are treated as equally important; in other words, in selecting the cut score, one tries to obtain maximal correct classifications with simultaneous minimal misclassifications. A simple way to determine this is to use the Youden index (Y; Youden, 1950):

$$Y = \text{Sensitivity} + \text{Specificity} - 100$$

The highest *Y* value will indicate the "best" cut score to use, assuming sensitivity and specificity are equally valued. Examples of this approach can be found in many different assessment domains, including instruments to measure abusive behaviors (Zink, Klesges, Levin, & Putnam, 2007), depressive symptoms (Forkmann et al., 2009), and marital discord (Whisman, Snyder, & Beach, 2009).

Other options are possible, depending on the purpose for which the cut score will be used. For example, Cacciola, Pecoraro, and Alterman (2008) examined the ability of the Addiction Severity Index to detect substance use among individuals diagnosed with Axis I disorders. As they were interested in using the instrument for screening purposes, they were more interested in maximizing sensitivity than they were in maximizing specificity. Because they knew that those classified as likely having substance abuse problems would receive further evaluation, they were most concerned to ensure that they did not miss many individuals who truly had a substance abuse problem—false-positive results were less of a concern for them. Accordingly, they chose a cut score that maximized sensitivity while maintaining specificity of at least .50.

Once a cut score has been established for a measure, it is critical that it is used appropriately. This means that the user must have an appreciation of the likely accuracy associated with the cut score. Further, when applying the cut score the clinician must carefully weigh the costs (psychological and financial) of false positives and false negatives. As we noted, the appropriate use of a cut score also requires an appreciation for the fact that specificity and sensitivity are conditional (see Chapter 7): They are affected by sample characteristics. For example, cut scores on a depression-screening instrument may be appropriate for younger but not older adults. Moreover, if a cut score is intended for classification purposes within a general population, the sample used to establish the cut score must be representative of the general population. Such a sampling strategy is used for the various Wechsler intelligence scales. Most psychological assessment instruments, however, are developed based on data obtained from specific samples, especially clinical samples. For present purposes, the key implication associated with this sampling strategy is that a cut score developed for use with clients having one type of clinical problem may not be optimal or appropriate for use with clients presenting with other clinical problems. Before a clinician uses a cut score to make important decisions about a client, a careful reading of the relevant research literature is necessary, and as discussed in Chapter 9, it may be helpful to collect additional data before making these decisions.

A study by Forkmann et al. (2009), examining the sensitivity and specificity of the BDI, nicely illustrated this point. The BDI (and now the revised version, the BDI-II) is the most commonly used measure of depressive symptoms. It was originally developed to assess symptom severity among individuals already diagnosed with depression. Thus, the cut scores associated with the instrument may not be applicable to other groups of individuals. Forkmann and colleagues (2009) were interested in evaluating the use of the BDI as a screening tool for detecting depression among patients admitted to a cardiology unit. Because the BDI contains several somatic items that may not accurately tap the construct of depression in physically ill individuals (i.e., these items may lack *discriminant validity in this study* because they can also reflect symptoms associated with cardiac problems), they examined cut scores on both the total BDI and the BDI after these somatic items were removed. All participants were diagnosed with a structured clinical interview before completing the BDI. The researchers found that neither version of the BDI exhibited good sensitivity, with the 95% confidence interval for sensitivity falling below .50 (i.e., below chance levels). As a result, they advised against the use of the BDI as a screening tool to detect depression in cardiac patients.

Findings such as these serve to underscore the fact that psychometric evidence (reliability, validity, sensitivity, etc.) is dependent on client/sample characteristics. In Chapter 7, we discuss the conditional nature of all psychometric evidence in much greater detail. The implications for clinical practice are clear: The clinician should carefully consider the degree to which psychometric evidence for a measure is relevant for the clients and the assessment context in which it will be used.

For now, it is sufficient for us to note that there is a statistical procedure that can be used to compare how well cut scores perform for different clinical groups. The procedure involves computing *receiver operating characteristic curves* and calculating data for area under the curve to evaluate the efficacy of various cut scores (more details are provided in Table 7.1; see also McFall & Treat, 1999). These same procedures also can be used for comparing the efficacy of different measures for evaluating a specific clinical group (for an excellent presentation of this in the context of assessing youth bipolar disorder, see Youngstrom et al., 2004).

There is one more way that sensitivity and specificity information can be used to present information about the accuracy of classification based on assessment data. The LR uses both sensitivity and specificity to provide an index of how much the odds of a correct classification are increased by the use of the assessment data. Specifically,

$$LR^+ = \text{Sensitivity}/(1 - \text{Specificity}) = \text{True Positive Rate}/\text{True Negative Rate}$$

and

$$LR^- = \text{Specificity}/(1 - \text{Sensitivity}) = \text{True Negative Rate}/\text{True Positive Rate}$$

The LR^+ index indicates the odds that a person with a positive test result (i.e., a score above a selected cut score) actually has the characteristic, condition, or diagnosis of interest. In contrast, an LR⁻ index indicates the odds that a negative test result (i.e., a score below a selected cut score) does not have the characteristic, condition, or diagnosis of interest.* A value of 1, for either index, indicates that classification based on the cut score does not aid in the accurate identification of the diagnosis (or the lack of the diagnosis). Returning to the example of the self-report measure of bulimia presented in Table 4.2, the LR⁺ value is 2.27; this means that the classification of having bulimia based on the self-report measure is two and a quarter times greater for someone who actually has a diagnosis of bulimia than for someone who does not. The corresponding LR⁻ value is 1.32, which means that the classification of no bulimia based on the self-report data is only slightly greater for someone who truly does not have a diagnosis of bulimia than for someone who does have the diagnosis. LR values are beginning to be reported in the psychological assessment literature. A good example of this is provided by Curtis, Greve, and Bianchini's (2009) presentation of using Wechsler Adult Intelligence Scale III scores to predict malingering among individuals with traumatic brain injury.

Predictive Power

Streiner (2003b) referred to sensitivity, specificity, and LRs as "column-based" indexes inasmuch as they use data from the columns of Table 4.1 to determine the denominators used in calculating these statistics. There is another set of statistics that focus on the use of "row-based" indexes—these are termed *positive predictive power* (PPP) and *negative predictive power* (NPP).† Before defining these indexes, it is important to appreciate the shift in perspective that comes with focusing on row-based data. All of the calculations possible from Table 4.1 assume that we have information about the true classification of individuals that is distinct from the measure that we are evaluating. Thus, for example, in Table 4.2 we assumed that data from a structured diagnostic interview were available to determine a "true" diagnosis of bulimia separate from the data obtained with the self-report instrument. With column-based indexes, the availability of a "true" index allows us to examine the extent to which individuals who truly did or did not meet diagnostic criteria were accurately classified by our use of the self-report data from these individuals. Put another way, the use of column-based indexes starts with information from some criterion (e.g., a diagnostic evaluation) and evaluates how good another measure is at accurately classifying individuals vis-à-vis this criterion. Row-based indexes, on the other hand, start

---

* LR⁻ can be defined as the likelihood ratio of a negative with respect to the person assessed as either having the diagnosis or not having the diagnosis. We follow Streiner's (2003b) approach by defining it with respect to the person not having the diagnosis of interest.
† Positive predictive power is also referred to as positive predictive value; negative predictive power is also referred to as negative predictive value.

TABLE 4.3 Using Self-Report Data (Cut Score) to Predict a Diagnosis of Bulimia

Result of Decision Based on Cut Score	Diagnosis Based on Structured Interview	
	Bulimia	No Bulimia
Bulimia	75 (A)	33 (B)
No bulimia	25 (C)	67 (D)

Hits = A + D = 75 + 67 = 142

Misses = B + C = 33 + 25 = 58

Positive Predictive Power = A/(A + B) = 75/(75 + 33) = .69

Negative Predictive Power = D/(D + C) = 67/(67 + 25) = .73

with the classification of individuals based on this criterion measure and then seeing how many in the sample meet the criterion of interest.

To aid in understanding predictive power, let us return to the bulimia example. Table 4.3 provides information on calculating positive and negative predictive power. Do not worry about the definition of these indexes for the moment—it will be easier to understand them once we work through an example. As you can see in the table, the hits and misses data remain unchanged from the previous table. In fact, all that changes in our calculations is the denominators in the two equations.

The PPP for our example is .69. This means that 69% of those predicted to have a diagnosis of bulimia based on our self-report measure actually met diagnostic criteria. Now consider the NPP, which is .73. Among those classified by our self-report measure as not having bulimia, 73% turned out not to meet diagnostic criteria.

Information on predictive efficacy is particularly valuable when we use data from an instrument to make clinical decisions. Now, it is time for the definitions. PPP is the probability that an individual has a characteristic, condition, or diagnosis when the classification criterion indicates that the person has it. Similarly, NPP is the probability that an individual does not have a characteristic, condition, or diagnosis when the classification criterion indicates that the person does not have it. Although these are extremely clinically valuable statistics, PPP and NPP are not commonly reported in the psychological literature. Doust (2009) provided some good examples of how sensitivity, specificity, LRs, PPP, and NPP can be used in diagnostic decisions typically encountered by family physicians.

The Impact of Base Rates on PPP and NPP

In the example we have been using, there were 200 participants: 100 met diagnostic criteria for bulimia, and 100 did not meet the diagnostic criteria. Thus, in our example, the base rate for bulimia was .50. In this context, it is obvious that our self-report measure does better than chance in identifying those with bulimia (.69 vs. .50) and those without bulimia (.73 vs. .50). It has been known for many decades that base rates (or prevalence) of a characteristic have no impact on column-based indexes (i.e., sensitivity and specificity) but exert considerable influence on row-based indexes (i.e., PPP and NPP). This is because accurate classification of the presence of a characteristic, based on a measure of the characteristic of interest, becomes more difficult as the base rate occurrence of the characteristic diminishes. Or, put another way, the closer the base rate is to .50, the more likely it is that an assessment tool can meaningfully add to the accurate prediction of the presence of a characteristic of interest (i.e., the incremental predictive efficacy of the measure is more likely to increase).

In the industrial/organizational literature, this relation was formalized many years ago by Taylor and Russell (1939) in statistical tables that depicted the expected proportion of correct selection decisions (such as hiring decisions) based on both base rate data regarding successful selection outcomes and the validity coefficients of the tool used for the hiring decision. Meehl and Rosen (1955), in their influential article on cut scores, further highlighted the role that base rates play in the use of psychological instruments to make correct clinical decisions. They proposed the following rule about the likely value of a measure in making decisions: Essentially the decisions made based on the measure are better than chance (i.e., simple knowledge of base rates) when

> (Base Rate of the Characteristic/Base Rate of Not Having the Characteristic) > (False Positives Based on the Instrument/ True Positives Based on the Instrument)

Referring to Tables 4.1 and 4.3 (in which false positives are Category B and true positives are Category A), this yields the following:

$$(.5/.5) > (33/75), \text{ or } 1 > .44$$

As this statement is true, we can claim that the use of the self-report measure adds meaningfully to the prediction of a diagnosis of bulimia nervosa. Similar calculations can be done when the characteristic of interest is not meeting criteria for the diagnosis.

Let us return to the broader issue of base rates and classification errors commonly made by clinicians. Most of the predictions made by clinicians on the basis of assessment data have to do with relatively low base rate characteristics such as particular psychiatric diagnoses (other common examples include malingering, suicide risk, and violence risk). For example, approximately 1% of the general adult population are likely to meet diagnostic criteria for bulimia nervosa. This means that the accurate detection of this diagnosis, by any assessment instrument, is an extremely difficult task. On the other hand, data from an assessment instrument may be valuable in screening out individuals unlikely to meet diagnostic criteria. Streiner (2003b) proposed two rules regarding the impact of base rates: (a) When the base rate (or prevalence) is low, an assessment instrument is best used to rule out a condition, and (b) when the base rate (or prevalence) is high, an assessment instrument is best used to rule a condition in.

Because information about sensitivity and specificity are unaffected by base rates, it is possible to use this information in Bayes's theorem to calculate PPP and NPP for varying base rate levels. Forgoing the Bayesian terminology for the equation, we can calculate PPP and NPP in the following manners (Streiner, 2003b):

$$PPP = (\text{Base Rate} \times \text{Sensitivity})/\{(\text{Base Rate} \times \text{Sensitivity}) + [(1 - \text{Base Rate}) \times (1 - \text{Specificity})]\}$$

and

$$NPP = [(1 - \text{Base Rate}) \times \text{Specificity}]/\{[(1 - \text{Base Rate}) \times \text{Specificity}] + [\text{Base Rate} \times (1 - \text{Sensitivity})]\}$$

Returning again to our bulimia example, using data from Table 4.2 and assuming a base rate of .01, we have the following:

$$PPP = (.01 \times .75)/\{(.01 \times .75) + [(1 - .01) \times (1 - .67)]\}$$

$$= (.0075)/\{(.0075) + [(.99) \times (.33)]\}$$

$$= (.0075)/(.3342)$$

$$= .02$$

This means that, of all individuals in a *sample of the general population* classified as likely to have bulimia based on the self-report measure, only 2% will actually meet criteria. Concomitantly, 98% of those identified as having bulimia will have a false-positive indication. Now, before becoming too discouraged, bear in mind that the population base rate was 1%. Thus, using the test data yields better results than would be expected by chance. It is worth noting, though, that the base rates of disorders for persons seeking services (i.e., those who are the main focus of clinical assessments) are usually substantially higher than what is found in the general population, which means that relatively fewer false positives will be identified.

Turning now to NPP, and remembering that we are predicting who does not meet diagnostic criteria:

$$NPP = [(1 - .01) \times .67]/\{[(1 - .99) \times .67] + [.01 \times (1 - .75)]\}$$

$$= (.6633)/[(.6633) + (.0025)]$$

$$= .996$$

In other words, based on the self-report data, over 99% of those predicted not to meet diagnostic criteria in a *general population sample* will actually not meet criteria. This sounds like an amazingly accurate set of predictions but remember that the population base rate for not having the condition is .99.

What all of this means is that accurately predicting rare characteristics is an incredibly difficult task, one that is, necessarily, fraught with errors. In the next chapter, we deal more explicitly with the nature of these errors and how one can consider options for balancing the costs and effects of false positives and false negatives. Another take-home message from this is that it is critical for clinicians to appreciate the impact that base rates have on their predictions. Numerous authorities recommend that clinicians have a sense of the local base rates for conditions (i.e., the practice context in which one works) and recognize that these base rates may differ dramatically from those on which research on an instrument is reported in the literature (e.g., Finn & Kamphuis, 1995; Garb, Lilienfeld, & Fowler, 2008). It is common for researchers, when developing and evaluating instruments, to have base rates near .5 (i.e., an equal number of participants with and without the condition). Using the Bayesian equations for PPP and NPP, and including local base rate information, will provide useful guidance with respect to the likely predictive power of instruments when used in applied settings. Insensitivity to the role of base rates in the psychometric evidence pertinent to a measure can increase the chance that the clinician will make incorrect judgments about a client during clinical assessments. And of course, incorrect judgments can cause harm to clients.

To assist researchers and clinicians in the identification and use of research studies examining diagnostic efficiency statistics, international standards have been set for the reporting of such studies. Termed the Standards for the Reporting of Diagnostic Accuracy Studies (STARD; Bossuyt et al., 2003), many journals in medicine, epidemiology, chemistry, and biology recommend or require the use of these standards. Among psychological assessment journals, the *Journal of Personality Assessment* is the only one that recommends authors follow STARD in reporting their work. We anticipate that as clinicians become more familiar with these statistics, the use of STARD in psychological research will increase. Key aspects of STARD are presented in Text Box 4.1. Also, for those interested in how diagnostic efficiency statistics can be presented in a simple, user-friendly manner, we recommend reading Frederick and Bowden's (2009) article on their test validation summary approach.

TEXT BOX 4.1 STANDARDS FOR THE REPORTING OF DIAGNOSTIC ACCURACY STUDIES (STARD)

Following initial meetings in 1999, several groups worked to improve the reporting of diagnostic studies. After several meetings, numerous literature searches, and the field testing of draft standards, the STARD statement was published in several journals in 2003 (e.g., Bossuyt et al., 2003). As of 2010, the STARD Web site (http://www.stard-statement. org/) reported that more than 200 journals include the STARD statement as part of their instructions to authors for submission of manuscripts for possible publication. The STARD statement includes (a) a flowchart prototype for reporting on participant recruitment and the sequencing of diagnostic tests and (b) a detailed checklist of items that must appear in any study using STARD. Like other research reporting standards that have emerged in recent years, the goal is to ensure the complete and accurate reporting of research. The type of information required in an article that adheres to the STARD statement may seem fairly obvious to most readers. However, articles that do not include this information (and there are many such articles) make it difficult to interpret the results and to know if the measures are appropriate for use in a particular assessment context. Here are some examples of the checklist items:

TITLE, ABSTRACT, AND KEYWORDS

- Clearly identify the study as relevant to diagnostic accuracy (e.g., include terms such as sensitivity and specificity)

METHODS

- Describe study sample and inclusion/exclusion criteria
- Describe recruitment procedures
- Describe the instruments being evaluated and the reference against which the instruments were compared
- Describe any coders/judges/raters used for generating assessment data and the training they received

RESULTS

- Report severity of symptoms/disorder among participants with the condition and other conditions among participants not having the target condition
- Report relevant estimates of diagnostic accuracy, including confidence intervals when appropriate
- Report any adverse effects associated with the assessment procedures

DISCUSSION

- Discuss clinical applications of the study findings

Before leaving the topic of how base rates affect predictive power, there are two final points we wish to make, both of which deal with strategies for improving the accuracy of clinical decisions made with assessment data and avoiding the misuse of cut scores when making important decisions about a client. One way in which predictive power can be enhanced is by altering the cut score used to make classification decisions. As we emphasize throughout the book, the scientific quality of any assessment data is dependent on the purpose for which they are used and the sample from which they are derived. Thus, it may be appropriate to have different cut scores depending on the nature of the sample (Kamphuis & Noorhof, 2009). Continuing with our bulimia example, different cut scores might be used if we were to use a general population sample, a general clinical sample, or a sample of individuals suspected of having an eating disorder. Likewise, different cut scores might be used if we were screening for the possible presence of a disorder or if we were attempting to formulate a diagnosis. The second way to enhance predictive power is to change the base rate of the condition that is being predicted. A common strategy for doing this is to employ a sequential assessment strategy. This may include, for example, starting with an inexpensive, easily completed measure that has high sensitivity. Even if many false positives are identified, the concern here is to minimize the number of false negatives. The sample that results from this initial assessment is likely to have a base rate for the condition that is much closer to .50 than was the case for the original sample. At this point, a second instrument is used, typically one that is more expensive or time consuming but has high specificity to eliminate from consideration as many false positives as possible. This type of strategy is common for detecting low-prevalence medical conditions (such as breast cancer) and has also been recommended for evaluating psychiatric conditions such as personality disorders (Widiger, 2008).

INCREMENTAL VALIDITY

Incremental validity addresses the question of whether data from one or more assessment instruments increase validity or utility of a clinical judgment beyond what can be accomplished with other sources of data (Hunsley & Meyer, 2003; Sechrest, 1963). An improvement in prediction can be demonstrated in multiple ways, including increased power, sensitivity, specificity, PPP, and NPP of decision-making judgments beyond what is generated based on other data, such as simple base rate or diagnostic data (Haynes & O'Brien, 2000; Hsu, 2002; Sechrest, 1963; Streiner, 2003b; Wiggins, 1973). Some have suggested that incremental validity can also be demonstrated by reducing the costs associated with the predictions or by showing that the predictive validity of a brief form of a measure is equal to that of a longer form (e.g., Elliott, O'Donohue,

& Nickerson, 1993; Sechrest, 1963; Smith, McCarthy, & Anderson, 1998); we address this issue in the next chapter on utility. Further chapters address related questions, such as whether it is worthwhile, in terms of both time and money, to obtain data on the same variable using multiple methods and collect parallel information from multiple informants (i.e., the cost-benefits of multisource assessment).

There are two main ways in which incremental validity is examined in the assessment literature (cf. Hunsley & Meyer, 2003). First, incremental validity analyses are useful in evaluating new instruments or revisions to existing instruments. Although, unfortunately, rarely investigated by researchers, an important consideration associated with any new measure is its incremental validity over alternative measures available to assess the same construct (Haynes and Lench reported in 2003 that, over a 5-year period, only 10% of manuscripts submitted for possible publication in the journal *Psychological Assessment* considered incremental validity). For example, in discussing the development of the MMPI-2 (Minnesota Multiphasic Personality Inventory Version 2) and the adolescent form of the MMPI (MMPI-A), Butcher, Graham, and Ben-Porath (1995) advocated that any new subscale or index should be evaluated to determine whether it has incremental value over existing MMPI measures. A large number of studies have since been published that address precisely this point.

The second (and most commonly employed) way in which the concept of incremental validity is used is in a research-focused testing context: Statistical analyses are conducted in which information from a new source of data (such as a test scale or an observational coding system) is examined in terms of its contribution to improving on the prediction of a clinically relevant criterion (e.g., diagnosis, premature termination, treatment outcome). The focus in this type of research is on the value of adding new test data into a statistical equation, generally based on regression analyses, to predict a criterion. Prediction is assessed by the extent to which the sources of data can account for variance in the criterion of interest. A fine example of this is Watkins and Glutting's (2000) study of using WISC (Wechsler Intelligence Scale for Children) data to predict academic achievement. Specifically, they examined the incremental validity of profile characteristics (i.e., scatter and shape) over subtest scores in predicting both reading and mathematics achievement. Using data from a large, nationally representative sample of students, subtest mean scores were found to be a statistically significant predictor of achievement scores; adding profile scatter information did not significantly increase the prediction of achievement scores, but the addition of profile shape data did.

Two main analytic strategies are used to evaluate incremental validity. The most common strategy involves the use of multiple regression analyses to determine whether newly entered data account for variance in the prediction beyond what was possible with data already entered into the prediction equation. Such analyses can be conducted with either cross-sectional or longitudinal data.* The Watkins and Glutting (2000) study is an example of this multiple regression approach to evaluating incremental validity. The second strategy, the manipulated assessment design (Hayes, Nelson, & Jarrett, 1987), involves the random assignment of participants to two or more conditions in which the collection of assessment data or the availability of the assessment data to clinicians is varied systematically. This type of design allows the researcher to focus on the differential accuracy or validity of clinical decisions based on the type and amount of assessment data available to the clinicians. The critical comparison for the purpose of incremental validity would be to determine whether the validity or accuracy of the obtained predictions improved (or deteriorated) as more data became available to the clinicians. Several examples using this design are presented in the following chapter on clinical utility and in Chapter 9.

The results of incremental validity research have the potential to provide invaluable guidance to clinicians with respect to the nature and scope of their assessment activities. Indeed, in the realm of personnel psychology, there is sufficient focused, programmatic research on incremental validity to allow for the derivation of key assessment implications with respect to the use of employment interview evaluations (Huffcutt, Roth, & McDaniel, 1996), job performance evaluations (Conway, Lombardo, & Sanders, 2001), and personnel selection strategies (Schmidt & Hunter, 1998). Unfortunately, the progress made in addressing issues of incremental validity in this area has not been paralleled by the same degree of progress in clinical assessment. Although there are many excellent examples in the literature of how some types of assessment data demonstrate, or do not demonstrate, incremental validity for specific assessment purposes, there is yet insufficient replicated evidence to guide most of the decisions central to the delivery of psychological services to youth or to adults (Garb, 2003; Johnston & Murray, 2003). This is primarily due to the extremely limited use of research designs and analyses relevant to the question of incremental validity of instruments or data sources. In this context, as emphasized throughout this book, the best a clinician can do is to base his or her judgments on data from psychometrically strong methods and measures that do not share error variance.

One exception to this state of affairs is the research on the diagnosis of attention-deficit/hyperactivity disorder (ADHD) in children. In their review of this literature, Pelham, Fabiano, and Massetti (2005) were able to draw two conclusions with direct clinical relevance to the diagnosis of the disorder. First, as structured diagnostic interviews do not possess incremental validity over rating scales, they concluded that diagnosing ADHD is most efficiently accomplished by relying on data

---

* Secondary analyses of published data can also be subjected to this type of analysis (see Hunsley & Meyer, 2003, for details).

from parent and teacher ADHD rating scales. Second, in ruling out an ADHD diagnosis, it is not necessary to use both parent and teacher data: If, on a measure known to possess good NPP, either informant does not endorse rating items indicative of ADHD symptoms, the youth is unlikely to have a diagnosis of ADHD. These conclusions illustrate the potential clinical value of incremental validity research. This line of research also demonstrates the importance of selecting an assessment instrument that has been shown to provide the most valid data for the purpose at hand and to examine literature to determine what other assessment options might increase validity of the resulting clinical decisions. Given the time and expense associated with some assessment strategies, such as the use of projective assessment methods or long self-report personality inventories, the clinician should be sensitive to the degree that measures from these instruments significantly contribute to the validity and utility of clinical judgments based on more easily attainable data (cf. Garb, Wood, Lilienfeld, & Nezworski, 2002).

SENSITIVITY TO CHANGE

The professional services provided by many psychologists, social workers, counselors, and educators focus on helping clients change, be it evaluating client change over time or trying to influence the type and extent of the change experienced by clients. Most educational, rehabilitation, and clinical services are, by nature, intervention services. Whether the goal is to improve a client's well-being, assist the client in the return to a previous higher level of functioning, or slow the rate of a client's deterioration associated with a chronic, debilitating condition, the intent of the clinician is to intervene to bring about a change in the client's psychological trajectory. Accurate and meaningful measurements are crucial for determining whether real changes are occurring and understanding the variables that might be hindering or facilitating that change. In Chapter 2, we addressed issues related to the reliability of scores that influence our ability to assess client change accurately, and in Chapter 1 we noted some aspects of assessment instruments that can affect their sensitivity to change. At this point, we focus on the question of whether scores on an instrument have been demonstrated to be sensitive to the type and extent of change likely to occur in situations in which the instrument will be used.

To address this question, both the content of the instrument and the evidence for the validity of its scores must be examined. With respect to the content (e.g., items on a self-report or clinician-completed symptom checklist, observational behavior codes), the clinician must determine the degree to which the items are relevant to the nature of the change anticipated for the client. This involves two considerations: (a) Does the content tap specific cognitive, affective, behavioral, physical, or physiological variables that are likely to be associated with successful change efforts? (b) Is the content likely to be sensitive to the form of intervention that will be provided to the client? The first element is germane to claims that the coverage of the measure is congruent with the goal of assessing change. If, for example, the instrument focuses only on automatic negative thoughts or relationship functioning, it is likely to provide only partial coverage of the types of change of interest in treating a depressed client. In such cases, the clinician would be prudent to include additional measures to assess the full spectrum of possible changes. Moreover, if an instrument fails to evaluate change in a manner consistent with the treatment and its goals, it is unlikely to provide an accurate indication of client change. For example, self-report items focused on the frequency of negative affective experiences are unlikely to be highly relevant for a treatment approach that emphasizes the acceptance, rather than reduction, of negative emotional states.

The extent of change potentially assessed by an instrument must also be considered as it should be consistent with what is likely based on the nature of the intervention efforts. For example, standard measures of intelligence and memory may not adequately reflect the type of changes evident in rehabilitation efforts to improve cognitive functioning following a traumatic brain injury. Similarly, administering a measure of personality before and after an 8-week stress management program is unlikely to result in much evidence of client improvement. Finally, as we noted in Chapter 1, the clinician must attend to whether either ceiling or floor effects are likely to reduce the likelihood that scores on an instrument accurately reflect client changes. In short, the content of the instruments must correspond to the nature of the condition, the nature of the anticipated changes, and the nature of the intervention efforts. In many cases, it may also be important to measure changes in potential unwanted side effects of a treatment (e.g., changes in peer or teacher responses to a student treated for ADHD, changes in spouse response to treatment of a client's alcohol use).

Note how these issues further strengthen the mandate to adopt a functional approach to assessment. Clinicians often err by using assessment instruments based on their popularity, availability, or familiarity. However, valid and useful clinical judgments are more likely when a clinician selects assessment strategies that best match the characteristics of the client, the context of assessment, and the questions that the assessment data are meant to answer.

Several types of validity evidence are relevant to evaluating the sensitivity to change of scores on an instrument. The most valuable evidence involves obtaining repeated assessment data (at a minimum, before and after the intervention) and then comparing these data with changes assessed by instruments that are the gold standard for assessing change in the intervention context of interest. If a gold standard does not exist, the use of a reasonable proxy, such as a change in diagnostic status following treatment, is often used. The degree to which change scores (preferably residualized change scores*) on the measure of interest correlate with the change scores of other variables of interest can provide additional validity evidence to determine sensitivity to change. To infer that change occurred for reasons other than maturation, regression to the mean, and the simple passage of time, any changes evident in the data should occur to a significantly greater degree among those who received the intervention than among those who did not receive an intervention.

A study on measuring change in the treatment of obsessive-compulsive disorder (OCD) by Abramowitz, Tolin, and Diefenbach (2005) illustrates the use of several forms of validity evidence to examine sensitivity to change. All clients met diagnostic criteria for OCD prior to treatment, and all were assessed prior to and following treatment on the instrument of interest, the self-report Obsessive-Compulsive Inventory–Revised (OCI-R). In addition, pre- and posttreatment data were available on other instruments, including a semistructured clinical interview for OCD, the BDI-II, and a disability scale. Statistically significant improvements were noted on the OCI-R after treatment, and residualized change scores on the OCI-R were moderately correlated with residualized change scores on the semistructured interview and the disability scale (but only weakly with the BDI-II, which is consistent with the intended focus on changing OCD symptoms specifically).

Many clinicians evaluate their services using both data from instruments specific to the conditions and treatments provided to clients and data from an outcome instrument designed to assess change more broadly. These last instruments may include measures of general psychosocial functioning, well-being, and quality of life. Lambert and Hawkins (2004) summarized some of the supporting data, including sensitivity to treatment effects, of several instruments of this type (see also Hunsley & Mash, 2008b). The Outcome Questionnaire, in particular, has compelling evidence for its sensitivity to change for a broad range of counseling and clinical treatments (e.g., Burlingame et al., 2001; Vermeersch, Lambert, & Burlingame, 2000; Vermeersch et al., 2004).

A question that commonly arises with respect to the use of an instrument for evaluating change is how frequently data should be collected. Generally, the more frequent the better, as frequent assessment allows for more accurate tracking of client functioning and therefore better clinical decisions about whether the intervention is working, whether refinement of an intervention strategy might be warranted, whether meaningful deterioration is evident in a chronic progressive illness, and so on. Of course, there are certain limits to implementing this advice, such as the potential burden to the client and clinician of frequent evaluations. When using symptom checklists, the time duration referred to in the instructions should also influence

---

* Residualized change scores are calculated by regression analyses that remove, from a Time 2 score, the variance that is associated with the person's score on the same measure administered at Time 1.

the frequency of administration (e.g., a self-report instrument requiring the report of symptoms experienced over the past month should not be used on a weekly basis). Unfortunately, there is also some evidence that the repeated administration of an instrument can compromise the validity of the measures; weekly administrations of the BDI and the Child Depression Inventory have been found to overestimate, compared to monthly administration periods, reductions in depressive symptoms (Longwell & Truax, 2005; Twenge & Nolen-Hoeksema, 2002). Thus, decisions about the frequency of measures used to evaluate change should be informed by both the potential risks and the benefits of possible administration schedules.

SUMMARY AND RECOMMENDATIONS

A growing body of research provides guidance to clinicians on the ways in which assessment data can contribute to making scientifically based decisions about services to clients. Simple data on decisional hits and misses can yield enormously valuable information on sensitivity, specificity, PPP, and NPP, all of which are directly germane to decisional tasks by clinicians on a daily basis. Evidence for incremental validity, although relatively limited at present, has the potential to focus clinicians' assessment efforts and thereby save time and money for clients and the health care system. Demands for professional accountability and quality assurance can be met, at least in part, using assessment data to document and evaluate the impact of our professional services. Selecting and using instruments that have been demonstrated to be sensitive to client change can go a long way in meeting these professional obligations. In Text Box 4.2, we summarize the take-home messages from this literature that we provided throughout this chapter.

Although there are a number of resources that can be used to aid in the selection of scientifically sound instruments (e.g., Antony, Orsillo, & Roemer, L., 2001; Hunsley & Mash, 2008b), they provide relatively little information on the issues covered in this chapter. As the field advances, this is likely to change. For the time being, however, the informed clinician must rely on searching databases to find research relevant to, for example, the sensitivity of an instrument for a particular assessment purpose in a particular clinical sample; the potential incremental validity of adding a semistructured interview to self-report data; or the selection of a measure to track treatment-related change. Throughout this work, it is essential to remain mindful of the fact that making error-free decisions is impossible. What is possible, though, is to use scientific evidence to maximize the value of the assessment data collected and then to use these data to reduce the number of decision-making errors made in the course of our professional services.

TEXT BOX 4.2   APPLYING PSYCHOMETRIC EVIDENCE TO CLINICAL DECISIONS

- The determination of a cut score requires judgments about the nature and value of the categories created by using the cut score and the decisions that might be taken about these categories.
- When reviewing the information about a cut score on a measure, the clinician must pay close attention to (a) the composition of the sample used to set the cut score and how similar it is to the clients with whom you will be using the measure and (b) the value judgments about sensitivity and specificity that informed the selection of the cut score.
- A cut score developed for use with clients having one type of clinical problem may not be optimal or appropriate for use with clients presenting with other clinical problems.
- Clinicians must appreciate the impact that base rates have on their predictions. Base rates affect both PPP and NPP (but not sensitivity and specificity), and the closer the base rate is to .50, the more likely it is that an assessment tool can meaningfully add to the accurate prediction of the presence of a characteristic of interest.
- Decisions made on the basis of data from an assessment instrument are better than chance (i.e., simple knowledge of base rates) when:

  > (Base Rate of the Characteristic/Base Rate of Not Having the Characteristic) > (False Positives Based on the Instrument/True Positives Based on the Instrument)

- When the base rate (or prevalence) of a condition is low, an assessment instrument is best used to rule out a condition; when the base rate (or prevalence) is high, an assessment instrument is best used to rule a condition in.
- Evidence of incremental validity for an assessment tool can provide guidance on the nature and scope of an assessment. Clinicians, therefore, should review the relevant research literature when planning their assessment activities. At a minimum, clinical judgments should be based on data from multiple psychometrically strong methods and measures that do not share error variance.

(continued on next page)

- When selecting a measure to track client change, the clinician should consider (a) whether the content of the instrument taps specific cognitive, affective, behavioral, physical, or physiological variables that are likely to be associated with successful change efforts and (b) if the content is likely to be sensitive to the form of intervention that will be provided to the client.
- The selection of a measure to track change should also be informed by considerations such as (a) ensuring that the extent of change potentially assessed by an instrument is consistent with what is likely based on the nature of the intervention efforts, (b) whether ceiling or floor effects may reduce the likelihood that scores on an instrument accurately reflect client changes, and (c) whether changes in potential unwanted side effects of a treatment should also be monitored.
- When assessing for possible client changes, the more frequent the assessments are, the better it is as frequent assessment allows for more accurate tracking of client functioning. However, considerations about the burden of the assessments, the time frame covered by the assessment tool, and the potential reactivity of assessment must also be factored into decisions about the frequency with which assessments are conducted.

RECOMMENDED SOURCES

Frederick, R. I., & Bowden, S. C. (2009). The test validation summary. *Assessment, 16*, 215–236.

Gigerenzer, G., Gaissmaier, W., Kurz-Milcke, E., Schwartz, L. M., & Woloshin, S. (2008). Helping doctors and patients make sense of health statistics. *Psychological Science in the Public Interest, 8*, 53–96.

Hunsley, J., & Meyer, G. J. (2003). The incremental validity of psychological testing and assessment: Conceptual, methodological, and statistical issues. *Psychological Assessment, 15*, 446–455.

Streiner, D. L. (2003b). Diagnosing tests: Using and misusing diagnostic and screening tests. *Journal of Personality Assessment, 81*, 209–219.

Clinical Utility and Decision Making

INTRODUCTION

Imagine a situation in which a clinic or agency is considering implementing the use of an assessment instrument for the treatment services they provide to their adult clients. The first questions that clinicians working there are likely to raise about this decision have to do with the intended purpose for which the instrument will be used: What is it supposed to do, and what is the evidence that it actually can do this? The next question might well be how the data from the instrument will improve on information from the assessment instruments already used by the clinicians. If, for example, the data are supposed to aid in treatment delivery, in a setting in which the majority of people currently receive treatment after an initial evaluation, is the goal to increase the number receiving treatment, decrease the number receiving treatment, alter in some way the determination of who receives treatment, help the clinician select the best treatment for each client, or better track the progress and outcome of therapy? A related set of questions comes from issues raised in Chapter 4: With respect to deciding who receives treatment, what are the rates of false positives, true positives, false negatives, and true negatives, both with and without the use of data from the instrument? What are the costs, both psychological and financial, associated with the current system and with the addition of the new instrument? Moreover, if the instrument is going to be used routinely, how much will it cost to purchase it and have all clinicians receive training in using it? How will the time needed to administer and score the instrument affect the total amount of staff time available for providing treatment services? How open are the clinicians to incorporating this instrument into their practices? All of these questions, in one way or another, touch on aspects of *clinical utility*.

At heart, the clinical utility of psychological assessment deals with the degree to which psychological assessment data have meaningful value with respect to the provision of clinical services. Given the history of the development of psychological assessment instruments (some of which has been touched on in previous chapters), one might reasonably expect that the question of the usefulness or value of assessment data has been a cornerstone of efforts to develop, validate, and disseminate scientifically strong psychological measures. Strikingly, however, there is only limited evidence for the clinical utility of many assessment methods and instruments, even when there is impressive evidence for their reliability and validity (McGrath, 2001). This is perhaps best exemplified by the research literature on two of the most commonly used and researched psychological instruments, the MMPI (Minnesota Multiphasic Personality Inventory) and the Rorschach Inkblot Test. Despite decades of clinical use and empirical investigation, there are virtually no replicated studies demonstrating the utility of these instruments for the range of assessment purposes for which they are typically used (Hunsley & Bailey, 2001). As we noted in Chapter 4, clinicians often use assessment instruments because of familiarity or tradition without reference to the degree to which they enhance the quality of clinical judgments.

Why the limited research on utility given the plethora of psychometric research? The sheer popularity of these and other commonly used assessment instruments in clinical settings may well have reduced the perceived need for evidence of the clinical value of the data provided by such instruments. Nevertheless, it is essential that there is strong evidence for the value of psychological assessment data. This ethical imperative is increasingly echoed by insurance carriers and others, who insist on professional accountability to engage in scientifically supported practice. After all, in most health or educational systems, the time and money devoted to the collection, integration, interpretation, and use of assessment data has a direct impact on the resources available to provide services designed to improve the psychosocial functioning of those assessed.

Regardless of the reasons behind the dearth of utility research and evidence, at present the *potential* for clinical utility is all that is available for most assessment methods, strategies, and instruments (and for clinical case formulations based on assessment data). Evidence for reliability, validity, and clinician interest in using an instrument is certainly a good start (and a necessary condition) but should not be confused with clinical utility evidence. This lack of utility evidence has a direct effect on claims that can be made about most current assessment practices. With respect to the ways in which clinical assessments are usually conducted, at present support for the clinical utility of the assessment data is based more on an implied promissory note than on accumulated scientific evidence. However, with increasing awareness of the importance of clinical utility (e.g., Holmbeck & Devine, 2009), we anticipate that there will be considerable investigation of the utility of assessment in the coming years. As an example, there is a growing number of studies examining the potential benefits of collaboratively working with clients to determine the foci of assessment efforts and then providing extensive feedback to them about the assessment results. Such an approach, sometimes described as *collaborative* or *therapeutic assessment,* has usually been found to have a positive impact on the process of treatment following the initial assessment and to have beneficial mental health effects in its own right (Poston & Hanson, 2010).

With this background in mind, our purpose in this chapter is to provide a sense of the ways in which psychological assessment methods and instruments can demonstrate clinical utility. We begin by examining how the concept of utility has been used in the health care and psychological literatures and then, specifically, how the concept has been applied to clinical assessment. Although utility can be understood as a specific form of validity, we discuss how utility implies more than what is usually understood by construct validity (including being more than just incremental validity). We then discuss how clinical utility is emphasized in screening and diagnostic assessment efforts (i.e., diagnostic utility) before moving on to examine the ways in which assessment-related clinical utility can be demonstrated for intervention purposes (i.e., treatment utility). We conclude our discussion of clinical utility by focusing on cost and feasibility considerations. Along the way, we discuss several factors that directly influence the extent to which studies of clinical utility can inform clinical assessment practices.

DEFINING CLINICAL UTILITY

The concept of utility has had a central role in the assessment literature in industrial, organizational, and personnel psychology for several decades. In these literatures, utility stemming from assessment data is evaluated in terms of improvements in decisions (e.g., whether to hire job applicants or promote employees) or services (e.g., increased productivity) *and* the financial implications of these improvements relative to the cost of collecting and using the data themselves (e.g., Anastasi & Urbina, 1997; Murphy & Davidshofer, 2005). Although "good" decisions are preferable to "bad" decisions, the focus here is on determining exactly how much better a good decision is than a bad decision and then considering whether the various costs associated with these decisions (including gathering the information used to make the decisions) are worth the effort to make better decisions. As we describe, both of these elements—improvements in services and financial costs associated with these improvements—are key elements of the clinical utility of psychological assessment instruments.

The application of the utility concept to the realm of clinical practice is not new as it dates to the mid-20th century (e.g., Cronbach & Meehl, 1955; Sechrest, 1963). However, interest in clinical utility seems to have grown in recent years, and an emphasis on garnering evidence regarding actual improvements in both decisions made by clinicians and service outcomes experienced by clients can be found in literature on diagnostic systems (e.g., First et al., 2004; Mullins-Sweatt & Widiger, 2009); psychosocial treatments (American Psychological Association Presidential Task Force on Evidence-Based Practice, 2006); and psychological assessment (e.g., Hunsley & Bailey, 1999; Hunsley & Mash, 2007; McFall, 2005). With respect to the last, clinical utility involves a demonstration that the use of assessment data leads to improvements in clinical services and, accordingly, results in improvements in client functioning. This can include considerations of diagnostic utility (the extent to which the assessment data result in a more accurate, comprehensive, and useful diagnostic formulation) and treatment utility (the extent to which assessment data contribute to an improvement in the outcomes of psychological treatments) (Hunsley & Mash, 2007).

To examine how the term *clinical utility* has been used in the health care literature, Smart (2006) conducted a keyword search for published articles in which the title contained the term. This search, concluded in mid-2005, yielded over 1,000 articles, the first of which was published in 1961. As the search only examined the use of the term in article titles, this is likely a considerable underestimate of the frequency with which the concept is used in the health care literature. Regardless of the precise frequency, one aspect of the use of the term that is clear is the lack of a consistent conceptual framework for defining it; most commonly, this involves confusion regarding the concepts of validity and utility (Kendell & Jablensky, 2003; Mullins-Sweatt & Widiger, 2009). This does not mean that validity is irrelevant to utility; rather, utility considerations are concerned with, at least in part, evidence of validity under clinically representative situations (i.e., real-world settings).

With all of the foregoing points about utility (and validity) in mind, we suggest that there are three central dimensions that must be considered when evaluating the clinical utility of assessment instruments and data.* These dimensions are effectiveness, cost outcomes, and feasibility. Text Box 5.1 provides more details on each of these dimensions. Although evidence for all of these dimensions is valuable, clearly any

---

* See also Smart (2006), who proposed a conceptual framework for clinical utility that involved four dimensions: appropriate (e.g., is there evidence that the service is effective?), accessible (e.g., is the service cost effective?), practicable (e.g., can the service be implemented in the clinical setting?), and acceptable (e.g., are there ethical, legal, social, or psychological concerns that might affect the provision of the clinical service?).

TEXT BOX 5.1   A FRAMEWORK FOR
DEFINING THE CLINICAL UTILITY OF
ASSESSMENT INSTRUMENTS AND DATA

IS IT EFFECTIVE (I.E., USEFUL) IN CLINICAL PRACTICE?

- As a starting point, does it provide reliable and valid data that can inform clinical decisions?
- Does use of the data result in, or facilitate, appropriate clinical decisions?
- Does use of the data improve on the decisions made based on alternative, less-complex assessment strategies (e.g., decisions based on simple base rate or demographic data)?

ARE THE OUTCOMES OF SUFFICIENT VALUE RELATIVE TO THE COSTS IN CLINICAL PRACTICE?

- What are the full costs of the assessment (including clinician time, client time, materials, equipment, space, etc.) in relation to the full benefits of the clinical outcomes?
- Are the costs of the assessment justified by savings in other services? For example, compared to other assessment and treatment options, does the assessment lead to more appropriate services, which in turn reduce the total costs of services to the client or agency?
- Are the costs of the assessment justified by improvements in client functioning that would be less likely to occur in the absence of having the assessment data available? For example, if an additional 5 hours of assessment results in a 10% further reduction in the frequency of panic attacks, is this worth it relative to the costs of providing the additional assessment time to the client and delaying services for those waiting to receive services?

IS IT FEASIBLE IN CLINICAL PRACTICE?

- Do the clinicians have the knowledge and skills necessary for using the instrument or for learning to use the instrument?
- Does the clinical facility have the infrastructure necessary for using the instrument as it is intended to be used (e.g., specialized equipment or rooms necessary for using the instrument; computer facilities for collecting, analyzing, and storing the data; support staff necessary for collecting data or maintaining equipment necessary for using the instrument)?
- Is the use of the instrument acceptable to clinicians, clients, administrators, third-party payers, and so on?

discussion of clinical utility must start with documented evidence of effectiveness or usefulness. Clinicians' beliefs about the clinical value of an instrument are no substitute for evidence that the assessment data enhance effectiveness as there are many examples in the literature of cherished assessment instruments that have little or no evidence of reliability, validity, or clinical effectiveness (Hunsley, Lee, & Wood, 2003). With effectiveness evidence in hand, then and only then do questions of cost outcomes and feasibility become relevant. In the following sections, we discuss each of these dimensions in turn. We begin with a detailed discussion of the ways in which effectiveness can be examined for various assessment purposes.

CLINICAL UTILITY: EFFECTIVENESS

Thus far, we have argued that to demonstrate clinical utility a measure must demonstrate effectiveness. Demonstrations of effectiveness, in turn, rely on data showing that measures from the instrument increase the validity of clinical judgments based on them. The best evidence that the instrument works well depends heavily on the purpose for which the instrument is used. As we noted in previous chapters, assessment instruments can be used for myriad purposes, but the most common purposes in clinical settings are screening, diagnosis, case formulation, treatment selection and planning, treatment monitoring, and treatment outcome evaluation. Therefore, how effectiveness is operationalized will vary from purpose to purpose. Text Box 5.2 provides examples of the ways in which effectiveness can be operationalized for these different assessment purposes; in the subsequent sections, we provide examples of how the effectiveness of clinical instruments can be evaluated for each of these assessment purposes. Our intention in providing these examples is to sharpen your skills in critically evaluating the degree to which assessment strategies enhance the services provided to your clients.

Screening

Screening is undertaken to identify individuals who are likely to have a clinically relevant disorder or condition or those individuals who are at heightened risk of developing a clinically relevant disorder or condition (and to identify those who are not). In many instances, those screened have not necessarily sought to be screened for one or more disorders or conditions. Medical clinics, schools, and workplaces will often use screening instruments to identify problems such as depression and substance abuse. In most cases, the rationale guiding the screening process is that the early identification of clinical problems will facilitate the provision of treatment services to identified individuals; in other assessment contexts, of course, screening is used to determine who is not

TEXT BOX 5.2   OPERATIONALIZING EFFECTIVENESS
FOR DIVERSE ASSESSMENT PURPOSES

SCREENING

- To what degree can a measure identify people likely to meet diagnostic criteria for the disorder of interest or identify persons who could benefit from mental health services? To what degree can it be used across a range of samples (e.g., community, medical, psychiatric) by varying the cut score?
- Relative to other data sources, to what extent are sensitivity, specificity, positive predictive power (PPP), and negative predictive power (NPP) values enhanced?

DIAGNOSIS

- To what degree does the use of the data yield more accurate or more complete diagnoses when added to clinicians' usual diagnostic practices?
- For brief self-report or clinician-report instrument, compared to the gold standard of a structured diagnostic interview evaluation, how well does the instrument perform?

CASE FORMULATION

- To what extent does inclusion of data from the instrument provide valuable clinical information that might not otherwise be available to the clinician?
- To what extent does the use of the instrument aid in generating more accurate, more comprehensive, or more reliable case formulations?

TREATMENT SELECTION AND PLANNING

- To what extent does the assessment information aid in selecting effective treatment options?
- Does the treatment choice based on the use of the assessment data make a difference in client functioning after treatment?

TREATMENT MONITORING/OUTCOME EVALUATION

- To what degree does the measure help the clinician identify clients for whom treatment is not working?
- Does appropriate use of the data provided by the monitoring instrument or strategy result in enhanced client functioning?

likely to be suitable for some service or opportunity (e.g., being hired for a job requiring a high-level security clearance).

As discussed in Chapter 4, the base rate of the condition in the screened sample will affect the PPP and NPP of any screening effort. Thus, it may be necessary to develop different cut scores for the same instrument when used in different screening contexts (e.g., general population screening, screening within a mental health clinic), and clinicians should consider if published cut scores are relevant to a specific client. Moreover, in selecting the best cut scores, the clinician should consider the implications of false positives and false negatives in the current assessment context. The rationale for screening is predicated on several assumptions, such as the accurate identification of likely cases, the ready availability of intervention services for these individuals, and the likelihood that interventions can effectively treat the problems or meet the treatment goals identified through screening.

Let us now consider a research example and its implications for clinical assessment. Screening for suicidal ideation is a critical but extremely challenging assessment goal. Many instruments have been developed and validated over the years, including the Suicidal Ideation Questionnaire, which was the focus of a study by Gutierrez and Osman (2009). As stated by the authors, the goal of their study was to determine if this instrument could be used for large-scale screening of high school students to detect those at elevated risk for attempting suicide. To this end, they designed a study to evaluate the sensitivity, specificity, PPP, and NPP of the instrument. Their sample consisted of 64 adolescents who had been admitted to an inpatient unit because of serious suicidal ideation, 50 adolescents who had been admitted to an inpatient unit following a suicide attempt, and 56 nondisordered adolescents randomly selected from a high school in the same region as the inpatient settings. A cut score that optimally distinguished between the clinical and non-clinical groups was established, and impressive accuracy statistics were obtained with this cut score. However, detecting suicidal risk in this study was a relatively easy task as over two thirds of the sample was hospitalized and was known to have experienced high levels of suicidal ideation. This is a good example of how study results provide support for the validity of the measure but not necessarily much evidence of its utility in typical clinical assessment contexts. Remember, the authors' were interested in the large-scale screening of students. In this context, data relevant to effectiveness considerations should come primarily from a sample of students similar to those likely to be targeted in large-scale screening efforts. Additional studies, using representative samples with much lower base rates of suicidal ideation, would be necessary for determining a cut score appropriate for use in general population screening efforts. Should evidence of effectiveness be forthcoming, then research on additional aspects of utility (e.g., the psychological "costs" of false positives and false negatives, financial costs related to screening, and the feasibility of collecting and appropriately using the screening data) would be warranted. A clinician who used cut scores derived by Gutierrez and Osman (2009) could make many clinical judgment errors because of base rate and participant characteristic differences.

Diagnosis

The topic of clinical diagnosis needs little introduction as it is a cornerstone of many clinical training programs and clinical activities. Research on the diagnostic utility of instruments has grown substantially in recent years, and detailed reports on diagnostic accuracy statistics and incremental validity are becoming more common in the literature. The essential issue in diagnostic utility is the degree to which the use of an instrument leads to more accurate identification and classification of clinical conditions. If it does, then in many areas of assessment research a second issue must be addressed in determining utility: To what extent does the use of the instrument improve on current diagnostic assessment practices?

Almost by definition, research on diagnostic utility is likely to focus on samples of individuals seeking or receiving services. Returning to the base rate theme we emphasized in the previous section; this means that the base rate of a given disorder is likely to be higher in such samples than is the case in samples drawn from the general population. All things being equal, this means that it should be relatively "easier" to correctly identify disorders in clinical samples than in general population samples. Accordingly, true positive rates in clinical samples should be higher relative to those rates from general population screening efforts. However, all things are not equal, especially given (a) the high degree of comorbidity (often 50% or higher) found in most clinical samples (e.g., Brown, Campbell, Lehman, Grisham, & Mancill, 2001) and (b) the heterogeneity in symptom profiles within a given diagnosis (due, at least in part, to the fact that many disorders share the same markers and to the use of diagnostic criteria that permit substantial symptom heterogeneity). Thus, even with higher base rates, the correct identification of diagnostic categories within a clinical sample is still a difficult task. Moreover, there are substantial differences in diagnostic reliability across disorders, suggesting that some disorders may be particularly difficult to diagnose correctly (Hunsley & Mash, 2008b). As a result of these influences, you will commonly encounter studies in which measures from an instrument demonstrate good diagnostic utility for a class of disorders but not necessarily for a specific disorder within that class. We now briefly describe two examples of this.

The Child Behavior Checklist (CBCL) is one of the most frequently used instruments in assessing youth. Aschenbrand, Angelosante, and Kendall (2005) examined the utility of some CBCL subscales in identifying specific youth anxiety disorders. Their sample consisted of 110 youth referred for treatment at an anxiety disorders clinic and 30 nonanxious youth. They found that the parent reports on the Anxious/Depressed subscale of the CBCL were highly correlated with the severity of clinician-rated generalized anxiety disorders symptoms. Likewise, parent reports on the CBCL Withdrawn subscale were highly correlated with the clinician-rated severity of social phobia symptoms. Not surprisingly, they were able to determine a cut score on the CBCL that worked well in ruling in the likely presence of an anxiety disorder. However, it was not possible to determine a cut score that effectively ruled in a specific diagnosis of generalized anxiety disorder or social phobia (i.e., all possible cut scores demonstrated low predictive efficacy).

Challenges in demonstrating utility for specific diagnoses were also encountered by Ames, Hendrickse, Bakshi, Lepage, and Keefe (2009) in their efforts to determine the utility of the Neurobehavioral Cognitive Status Examination with older adult outpatients in a mental health service. In their study, the instrument proved effective in discriminating the presence or absence of any form of cognitive impairment or dementia. It did not, however, demonstrate utility for the identification of specific forms of cognitive disorders—this is important information for the clinician who is recommending specific intervention strategies to help a client with cognitive impairment.

In our view, many of the problems with the diagnostic utility of an assessment instrument stem from problems with the validity of the diagnostic categories themselves. In Chapter 3, we discussed how including conceptually distinct facets within a multidimensional construct can not only enhance the coverage of the construct but also negatively affect its validity. As an example, including facets of emotional distress, cognitive impairment, and reduced physical functioning as facets in the diagnosis of depression may increase coverage of the range of possible depressive symptoms. However, allowing such symptom heterogeneity to contribute to an aggregated measure also reduces the ability of the measure to differentiate depression from other disorders that share these facets.

As discussed in this section, once a measure from an instrument has demonstrated its value in aiding in the diagnosis of a condition, the next question to consider is whether the use of the instrument also improves on current assessment options available for formulating diagnoses. Perhaps the best example of such research is the use of informant-completed measures in the diagnosis of youth attention-deficit/hyperactivity disorder (ADHD). As mentioned in Chapter 4, Pelham et al. (2005) argued that sufficient replicated evidence exists to conclude that rating scales and structured diagnostic interviews possess the same level of validity for diagnosing ADHD. Thus, diagnosing ADHD is most efficiently accomplished by relying on data from parent and teacher ADHD rating scales. This is strong evidence for the clinical effectiveness of the rating scales. As use of the rating scales is also likely to be less costly and more clinically feasible than using structured diagnostic interviews, rating scales appear to have considerable overall clinical utility for this purpose.

Although, as indicated previously, research on incremental validity is relatively limited, there are some examples in the literature that demonstrated an instrument not only equals but also actually improves on other assessment options in a diagnostic context. For example, Wolf et al. (2008) found that the Keane Posttraumatic Stress Disorder Scale, extracted from the MMPI-2, possessed incremental validity over the MMPI-2 clinical scales and the restructured clinical scales in the prediction of a PTSD diagnosis.

One must not assume, however, that use of an instrument shown to have predictive value in identifying clinical conditions necessarily will demonstrate an improvement on available assessment practices. As with any other assertion in a scientific approach to clinical assessment, empirical evidence is necessary to determine if a measure from one instrument is better than a measure from a different instrument for a specific assessment purpose. For example, Bagby, Marshall, and Bacchiochi (2005) found that the Malingering Depression scale on the MMPI-2 could accurately detect feigned depression, but that it did not demonstrate evidence of incremental validity over other MMPI-2 validity scales. Similarly, Marshall and Bagby (2006) reported that, although the Infrequency Posttraumatic Stress Disorder scale on the MMPI-2 performed well in identifying feigned PTSD, its performance was no better than a number of well-established MMPI-2 validity scales.

Case Formulation/Treatment Selection and Planning

Client assessment is frequently undertaken to formulate hypotheses about how the client's problems or conditions developed and the factors responsible for maintaining them. The results of this assessment are then used to make decisions about possible treatment options. Such an assessment requires, at a minimum, information on the client's functioning and diagnostic status, life history, and current life situation. Client characteristics (e.g., ethnicity, sexual orientation, religious beliefs); life circumstances (e.g., relationship conflict, constraints due to demands of employment or parenting); and medical conditions may necessitate the adaptation of the evidence-based interventions to ensure that treatment is feasible and acceptable to clients. A number of resources are available to aid in developing scientifically informed case formulations; many focus on theory-specific or disorder-specific approaches to case formulation (e.g., Persons, 2008), whereas others emphasize the use of specific broadband assessment instruments (e.g., Butcher & Perry, 2008) or transtheoretical case formulation models (e.g., Beutler, Malik, Talebi, Fleming, & Moleiro, 2004).

Despite the centrality of case formulation to treatment planning and treatment provision, the empirical evidence base for the reliability and validity of these procedures is remarkably limited (Beiling & Kuyken, 2003). A plethora of variables, including locus of control, reactance, readiness to change, ego strength, and psychological mindedness, have shown promise in predicting treatment outcome in many studies (see

Hunsley & Mash, 2008b, and Antony & Barlow, 2010, for more details). At this point in time, though, there really is no cumulative program of research that has demonstrated that incorporating variables such as these into case formulations results in better case formulations, better treatment planning decisions, or ultimately, better treatment outcomes (see, however, Beutler & Harwood, 2000; Haynes, Leisen, & Blaine, 1997; and Haynes et al., 2009, for some promising exceptions). This may be because, although a multitude of possible variables could be assessed as part of case formulation efforts, across a range of clients the likely impact of any single variable on treatment outcome is likely to be relatively small. Text Box 5.3 describes the potential benefits of adopting an idiographic assessment approach in developing case formulations, planning treatments, and evaluating treatment effects.

In principle, studying the impact of data used for case formulation purposes is relatively straightforward. Formal models of case formulation (e.g., Haynes & O'Brien, 2000; Sturmey, 2009) typically emphasize establishing causal relations for client behavior problems (i.e., identifying modifiable causal variables), mapping those relations within an inclusive causal model, then selecting and adapting interventions to address those problems based on knowledge of the hypothesized causal relations. The choice of an intervention is based on matching the hypothesized causal mechanisms underlying the client problem (e.g., avoidance maintaining fear and anxiety) with the mechanism underlying an appropriate treatment (e.g., exposure to feared stimuli results in reductions of fear and anxiety responses). If one understands a mechanism of treatment and can match that to individual causal mechanisms, treatment should be improved in comparison to an intervention not matched to variables maintaining a client's behavior problems.

Rather than employing a formal causal model that maps out relations among mechanisms and behaviors, many clinicians employ informal case formulation models that are, essentially, general descriptions of hypothesized causes underlying client problems. The manipulated assessment design (Hayes et al., 1987) described in Chapter 3 can be used to test such informal case formulation models. This design involves the random assignment of participants to two or more conditions in which the collection of assessment data or the availability of the assessment data to clinicians is varied systematically. A study by Lima et al. (2005) illustrates the value of using such a design in the context of informal or varied case formulation approaches. In their study, clients completed the MMPI-2 prior to commencing treatment; half the treating clinicians received feedback on their client's MMPI-2 data, and half did not. The clients involved in the study presented with a range of diagnoses, including anxiety disorders, mood disorders, substance-related disorders, adjustment disorders, eating disorders, and personality disorders. To address questions of clinical utility, the researchers conducted between-group comparisons on variables related to treatment outcome. Overall, providing clinicians with the MMPI-2 results as a potential aid

TEXT BOX 5.3 IDIOGRAPHIC ASSESSMENT: INDIVIDUALIZED ASSESSMENT TO REDUCE ERROR IN CLINICAL ASSESSMENT MEASURES AND JUDGMENTS

Idiographic assessment is the measurement of variables and functional relations that have been individually selected, or derived from assessment stimuli or contexts that have been individually tailored, to maximize their relevance for a particular client (Haynes et al., 2009). Idiographic assessment contrasts with *nomothetic assessment*, in which judgments about a client are based on comparison with other persons using data from the same assessment instrument administered in a standardized manner.

Although there are disadvantages of idiographic assessment, especially in terms of diagnostic utility and generalizability of findings across clients, there are several advantages. In particular, idiographic assessment is consistent with hundreds of studies (summarized in Chapter 1) that have found significant differences across clients in the attributes of their behavior problems.

Figure 5.1, from Haynes et al. (2009), illustrates hypothetical relations among multiple attributes of a behavior problem and multiple elements of a standardized measure of the behavior problem for one client. Line thickness indicates the relative strength of relation. For this client (e.g., a client who is experiencing depression), the measure of the behavior problem (e.g., a standardized multi-item self-report questionnaire on depression) is most strongly affected by Element D (e.g., a disproportionate number of the items address the cognitive aspect of depression). However, based on other information gathered in the assessment, we know that this client's behavior problem is most strongly associated with Attribute C (e.g., this client most strongly experiences the fatigue or anhedonia aspect of depression). Note also that the measure is also affected by Element A (e.g., sleep aspect of depression), which is not an attribute of the behavior problem for this client, and omits Attribute E (e.g., the client's "agitation"), which is an important aspect of the client's experience.

Observe how the mismatch (Haynes et al., 2009) between the standardized measure elements and the attributes of the targeted behavior problem for this client introduces error in the measure: Variance in the measure would be affected by sources irrelevant to this client and would not be affected by sources that are relevant to this client. This incongruence reduces the precision of this measure of this behavior problem for this client; the incongruence would compromise the validity of judgments about treatment outcome or when attempting to identify causal variables for this

(continued on next page)

client's depression, as part of the clinical case formulation. An individualized measure that more strongly focused on Attribute C, included Attribute E, and omitted Attribute A would facilitate a more precise measure of causal relations for this client's depression and of treatment-related changes in this client's depression.

Haynes et al. (2009) described a psychometric paradigm for idiographic measurement (a multilevel random effects factor model) designed to increase the congruence between clinical measures and the unique aspects of the individual that also is compatible with traditional psychometric principles. The authors also described the limitations of idiographic assessment, recommended its use as a supplement to nomothetic assessment, and outlined key principles and procedures for the development of an idiographic instrument for use in clinical assessment.

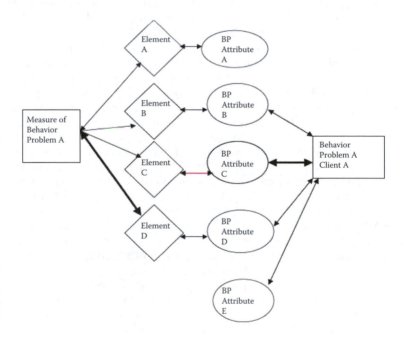

Figure 5.1 Illustrating incongruence between a nomothetic measure of the attributes of a client's behavior problem and the elements that contribute variance in the measure. Line thickness illustrates the relative strength of functional relations. (From Haynes, S. N., Mumma, G. H., & Pinson, C., *Clinical Psychology Review, 29*, 179–191, 2009.)

in case formulation and treatment planning had no discernible impact on variables such as client improvement ratings or premature termination rates.

To date, one case formulation/treatment-planning variable shown to have clinical utility for informal case formulation approaches is diagnosis. Diagnosis has utility in determining the best treatment options for clients by directing clinicians to the evidence base on which treatments are most efficacious for clients with the diagnosis or diagnoses in question. However, it has been argued that this apparent utility might be better described as "pseudotreatment utility" (Nelson-Gray, 2003). The reason for this is simple: The manipulated assessment design or other similar experimental designs have rarely, if ever, been used to determine the treatment utility of diagnostic information. This could be done by, for example, intentionally matching and mismatching treatment to client diagnosis (depressed adult clients could be randomly assigned to receive either interpersonal therapy for depression or exposure treatment for specific phobias). Of course, ethical considerations in mounting such studies are considerable, which probably explains why they are not conducted. Regardless, this leaves us with only indirect evidence of the utility of diagnosis in case formulation and treatment-planning tasks.

Evidence for the enhanced benefit for the client of the main goal of clinical case formulation—matching treatment foci and mechanisms to identified causal variables—is limited to specific populations, mostly from research on children and adults with developmental disabilities, cognitive impairment, and severe behavior problems (such as self-injury, aggression, and severe deficits in self-help). Many studies presented in the *Journal of Applied Behavior Analysis* have compared the outcome of treatment based on the functional analysis (e.g., identifying response consequences that might be maintaining a problem behavior) with the outcome of treatment based on best-practice models without a functional analysis. Many of these have found significant positive benefits for best-practice treatments but significantly enhanced benefits for basing treatments on the results of the functional analysis (e.g., Wilder, Chen, Atwell, Pritchard, & Weinstein, 2006).

Treatment Monitoring/Outcome Evaluation

The evaluation of treatment outcome typically focuses on the attainment of treatment goals and the evaluation of a client's overall psychosocial functioning. To some extent, then, some instruments shown to have utility for monitoring treatment process purposes may also have utility for monitoring treatment outcome. There are, however, additional types of measures commonly used only prior to and following the completion of treatment; instruments used to gather information for case formulation purposes, diagnostic interviews, broadband functioning scales (e.g., MMPI-2), and quality-of-life measures may all be useful in evaluating treatment outcome. As noted, a measure can be insensitive to short-term change (i.e., over days or weeks) but valuable in measuring longer-term change (i.e., over months or years). For present purposes, we focus first on the type of evidence that demonstrates that an assessment strategy (specifically, a treatment-monitoring system) has utility for monitoring or outcome evaluation and next on a major threat to validity that can limit the utility of an instrument.

To have utility for treatment-monitoring or outcome evaluation purposes, a measure must demonstrate sensitivity to treatment effects, whether this sensitivity is apparent over the span of one or two sessions or over the whole course of treatment (of course, the nature of this sensitivity should determine whether the instrument is used to assess short-term or long-term changes). A number of concepts mentioned in previous chapters, such as the time frame covered by the measure and whether the measure focuses on facets or aggregated elements, will influence the degree to which a measure is likely to be sensitive to change. Sensitivity to treatment effects, however, is not sufficient to establish utility as a monitoring or treatment outcome measure; to do this, there must be evidence that the information provided by the instrument makes a meaningful difference in the validity of the clinician's inferences about treatment effects, the way in that treatment unfolds, or the eventual impact of the treatment.

The evaluation of utility for treatment outcome measures is not straightforward. This is because such measures themselves typically serve as indicators of effectiveness (i.e., they are the "criteria" on which judgments about treatment outcome are made). However, one could examine the utility of treatment outcome measures by considering, for example, the degree to which the measures help the therapist to detect failing treatment or improve on treatment success rates obtained when the measure is *not* used.

In the previous chapter, we briefly mentioned the Outcome Questionnaire-45 (OQ-45). This frequently used treatment-monitoring instrument focuses on symptom distress, interpersonal relations, and social role functioning and has considerable supporting validity evidence for measuring client progress in treatment. For our present purposes, we focus on a line of research conducted with the OQ-45 that, using a manipulated assessment design, nicely illustrates how clinical utility of a monitoring instrument can be evaluated. Lambert et al. (2003) presented meta-analytic results from three utility studies in which more than 2,500 adult clients completed the OQ-45 after each therapy session. Clinicians in the control condition in these studies did not receive information about the client scores. On the other hand, clinicians in the experimental condition received feedback about the scores that was limited to an indication of whether clients, based on normative data, were making adequate treatment gains, making less-than-adequate treatment gains, or experiencing so few benefits from treatment that they were at risk for negative treatment outcomes. By the end of treatment, based on OQ-45 data, 21% of clients in the control condition had experienced a deterioration of functioning, whereas only 13% of clients in the experimental condition had deteriorated. Supportive results were also found for improvements in functioning: In the control condition, 21% had improved, whereas in the experimental condition 35% of clients had improved. The demonstration that the use in routine clinical practice of the OQ-45 data by clinicians reduced deterioration rates by a third and increased improvement rates by two thirds provides compelling evidence for the clinical utility of the instrument.

Before closing this section, there is one potential threat to the validity and utility of treatment monitoring and outcome evaluation that we mentioned in Chapter 4 and reiterate here. It has been long known that there is the potential for the act of measuring a behavior to have an impact on the nature or expression of the behavior. Such *reactive effects* (also known as reactivity) result in the modification of the behavior of the person assessed or the behavior of others in the target person's environment. There is evidence that some self-report symptom measures may be affected by reactive effects when used repeatedly, such as when monitoring the effects of treatment. For example, there are a number of studies showing that the repeated administration of the Beck Depression Inventory II, in the absence of any efforts to change depressive symptoms, can yield an appreciable reduction in scores on the instrument (e.g., Longwell & Truax, 2005; see also Sharpe & Gilbert, 1998, and Twenge & Nolen-Hoeksema, 2002, for similar results on other self-report symptom measures, and Christensen & Hazzard, 1983, and von Baeyer, 1994, for reactivity associated with other assessment methods). This underscores the fact that the clinical utility of an instrument must be well supported by the results of comprehensive and thorough validity studies.

Acknowledging the challenges, clinicians do a disservice to clients by not systematically monitoring their treatment process and outcome. Without frequently collecting valid, sensitive-to-change measures of treatment outcome and process with their clients, clinicians are more liable to use biased shortcuts in judging the effects of their intervention efforts. Doing so can result in harm to clients.

CLINICAL UTILITY: COST OUTCOMES

Assuming that there are data supporting the effectiveness of using measures from the assessment instrument for a specific clinical purpose, the next question to be addressed with respect to clinical utility is one of costs. An extensive literature on the costing of health care services is available to provide guidance on how best to operationalize the costs of assessment, the benefits (measured in monetary terms) that result from the assessment, and the effectiveness (measured in terms of psychosocial variables) of the services that result from the assessment. Although it may seem strange at first to consider monetary factors as part of clinical utility, the reality of all clinical assessments is that someone must pay for these services. Whether delivered in a private or public context, there is a financial bottom line associated with the use of assessment instruments. If the costs and outcomes associated with the use of the instrument are not deemed acceptable to those responsible for the costs of the service, the simple fact is that the instrument will not be used regardless of its scientific merits. This does not mean that the costs of the assessment should be minimal or that the costs must be precisely balanced by savings in other services received by a client. It does mean, however, that, as is increasingly the case for other health care services, evidence regarding the costs and the various outcomes resulting from the assessment data are needed to make the strongest case possible for the clinical use of an instrument. In this section, we draw on Yates and Taub's (2003) thorough presentation of these issues, and those interested are encouraged to consult their article for more details.

To be of value, the calculation of the assessment costs must include all accrued costs. The costs of purchasing the assessment instrument, along with the costs of the materials necessary for the use of the instrument (e.g., scoring sheets, disposable electrodes for psychophysiological instruments), are obvious components of a full costing estimate. There are, however, numerous other cost elements that must be included. For example, there are the costs stemming from the time required for the clinician to administer, score, and interpret the assessment data and to provide feedback (verbal and written) to the client or other service providers. Relatedly, there are also the costs associated with the clinician receiving the initial training in the use of the instrument or, in the case of the release of a revised instrument, becoming competent in the use of the new edition. On the material side, there are also costs associated with the use of software programs to score and interpret the assessment data. Furthermore, infrastructure costs, such as costs associated with the space used for the assessment and computer equipment used for storing and scoring the data, must be considered. Examples of these costing estimates are provided in Text Box 5.4.

To determine all resources used in the assessment, the best option is to disaggregate the components involved in the entire assessment process and then consider the resources used in each component. In most instances, this would mean breaking down the assessment into components such as (a) initial client contact and assessment planning (i.e., determining the nature and scope of the assessment); (b) administration of assessment instruments and procedures (i.e., the actual collection of the data); (c) examination and, if appropriate, scoring of assessment data; (d) integration and interpretation of assessment data; (e) provision of feedback on the results of the assessment; and if appropriate, (f) supervision of trainees or other professionals involved in conducting the assessment. Note that the cost associated with delaying treatment to conduct the assessment could also be considered; in other words, are assessment activities beyond a "bare minimum" warranted by improved benefits to the client?

TEXT BOX 5.4   CALCULATING ASSESSMENT COSTS

The basic formula for calculating costs related to assessment services is straightforward—the challenge is ensuring that all costs are included in the calculations. As described by Yates and Taub (2003), there are four steps in calculating total costs:

- Measure the amount of each "resource" used for the assessment (e.g., how many hours of clinician time were required)
- Determine the unit cost for each resource (e.g., the hourly rate for the clinician)
- Multiply the amount of the resource used by the unit cost of the resource
- Add the costs for all resources used to determine the total cost

---

After each component of the assessment has been identified, the next step is to enumerate the resources used in each component. Generally, these resources are likely to be (a) professional time; (b) assessment equipment; (c) assessment material used with each client (e.g., recording media, scoring sheets); (d) office space; (e) overhead (e.g., computer equipment, electricity, telephone connections); and (f) client time. Remember, to provide a complete and accurate cost estimate, it is important to include all resources used. This would mean that, in the case of a psychoeducational assessment conducted in a school context, time for teachers to be involved in the collection of data and in receiving feedback at the end of the assessment should be considered. Of course, one can tailor the breadth of the costing estimate to suit the purpose of the exercise; obtaining the total cost for the service provided by a clinic would not include expenses associated with anyone not employed by the clinic, whereas a comprehensive cost estimate would include all expenses associated with the assessment process (e.g., client's lost income during the time devoted to the assessment, client transportation costs). What is critical is that the cost estimate include an explicit description of the scope and limits of the estimate.

Costing procedures and cost-benefit analyses are only useful when they yield data that allow for comparisons among multiple service options. For example, knowing the costs of using parent and teacher self-report measures in the assessment of possible ADHD is only informative when alternative assessment strategies (e.g., structured diagnostic interviews, neuropsychological evaluations) are available. Simply knowing the costs of a single set of assessment procedures is not particularly enlightening.

In cost-outcome analyses, outcomes can be of two main kinds: outcomes that can be expressed in monetary terms and outcomes that are not reducible to monetary terms, such as improved productivity on the job or increased quality of life. With respect to assessment practices, both types of outcomes are likely, which means that both cost-benefit analyses (i.e., outcomes in monetary terms) and cost-effectiveness analyses (i.e., outcomes in nonmonetary terms) are likely to be relevant. Although common in the larger health services research literature, cost-benefit or cost-effectiveness studies of psychological services are relatively infrequent.

By definition, then, the measurement of benefits in a cost-benefit analysis requires that a monetary value can be attached to an outcome. For example, if the introduction of a new diagnostic assessment process results in a reduction in the time devoted to determining client diagnoses, this decrease in professional time, materials required, space requirements, and so on can be converted in dollar figures. Similarly, if a new assessment process results in an improvement in the assignment of treatments to clients, the monetary value of this could be determined by examining costs associated with, for example, fewer appointment reminder phone calls and fewer missed appointments.

In determining benefits, it is crucial to distinguish between benefits that are associated with the setting in which the assessment was provided (i.e., program or service benefits) and benefits experienced by a client across settings (i.e., including benefits experienced in health care services separate from those received at the setting in which the assessment was conducted).* For example, assessment procedures for a client presenting with sleep disturbance may result in better treatment planning, which in turn results in better treatment outcome. This may mean that the client will require fewer future treatment sessions once the initial course of treatment for the sleep disorder is completed (i.e., program benefits); it could also mean that a reduction occurs in the need for other health care services due to the successful resolution of the sleep disorder. To model these costs accurately, data must be available on alterations in service needs experienced by the average client who received the assessment and the average client who did not receive the assessment.

Effectiveness in the context of cost-effectiveness analyses for health care services is typically defined as enhanced health or functioning. With respect to clinical assessment services, effectiveness can include the gamut of psychosocial health-related variables, ranging from decreases in symptoms (depression, anxiety, etc.) to improvements in role functioning (e.g., parenting, marital, occupational) and quality of life. These variables should be measured in a standardized manner using well-validated measures so that alterations in functioning can be

---

* For information on medical cost offsets found for psychological services, see the work of Hunsley (2003).

compared across clients. Those interested can find numerous costing examples, derived within the context of neuropsychological assessment, in the work of Prigatano and Pliskin (2003).

From this discussion, we can distill several important considerations in clinical assessment strategies: Assessment strategies will differ in the degree to which they are warranted by enhanced benefit to clients. Some commonly used strategies (e.g., the routine use of projective and broadly focused personality assessments) will have insufficient cost-benefit or cost-effectiveness ratios for some clients, in some assessment contexts, and for some assessment purposes. The clinician must consider if the use of an assessment instrument is warranted by enhanced validity and utility of judgments about diagnosis, case formulation, or treatment monitoring.

CLINICAL UTILITY: FEASIBILITY

The final factor to be considered when determining the clinical utility of an assessment instrument is that of feasibility. Even if there is evidence that the instrument is effective in a clinical context and the costs of using the instrument, relative to the outcomes associated with the availability of the assessment data, are deemed to be reasonable in the clinical setting, a host of other elements will influence the feasibility of collecting and using the data. These elements can be roughly grouped into clinician, client, and system elements.

Based on the results of numerous clinician surveys, we know that a wide range of barriers can interfere with the implementation of assessment procedures. Clinician-related barriers include theoretical orientation (e.g., when routine collection of standardized data is inconsistent with the clinician's beliefs about the benefits of standardized assessment); beliefs that instruments are inadequate to cover the issues presented by clients; concerns about the administrative burden associated with use of instruments (i.e., skill development, time devoted to administrative and scoring); concerns about the scientific value of instruments (i.e., doubts about reliability and validity); concerns about the applicability of instruments to specific types of clients; and doubts that an instrument considered for use can yield any information beyond what is typically gathered during assessment or treatment (Garland, Kruse, & Aarons, 2003; Gilbody, House, & Sheldon, 2002; Hatfield & Ogles, 2007; Palmiter, 2004). Professionals well versed in measurement and assessment principles know that many of these objections are valid when applied to many assessment contexts. However, as generic obstacles to the use of scientifically sound instruments, most of these objections have little validity. This underscores the need for solid education in the principles and scientific basis for clinical assessment and the importance of addressing clinicians' assumptions about assessment when introducing new assessment procedures in a clinical setting.

There is one clinician-related element in particular to address more fully. Concerns about instrument length and complexity often lead to calls for shorter forms of psychological instruments. Indeed, a well-performing but briefer form of a longer validated instrument has the potential to increase the cost benefits or cost effectiveness of an assessment. This has resulted in the development of a large number of brief or short forms of assessment instruments. These brief instruments must be seen for what they are: new instruments that must undergo the process of scientific evaluation we outlined in the previous chapters (Yates & Taub, 2003, referred to this as establishing "decremental" reliability and validity). The validity evidence for an original long form of an instrument does not apply automatically to a short form of the same instrument. Rather, a short form must undergo the same critical process of construct validation as the original measure did. Smith, McCarthy, and Anderson (1998) provided a discussion of methodological and other considerations in developing and validating short forms. They emphasized the need for (a) tests of construct validity that are independent of validation tests conducted on the original long forms; (b) adequate representation of the content domain of the long form in the new short form; (c) demonstration of equivalence between the long and short forms using independent administrations of the two versions; and (d) demonstration that the short form provides meaningful savings in time and resources. Clinicians often select elements or parts of long forms of assessment instruments to use with their clients, particularly for treatment outcome monitoring. Although such a strategy can be useful (see discussion of idiographic assessment in Text Box 5.3), the clinician must remember that validity evidence relevant to the long form is no longer applicable.

There is an extensive treatment literature on the evaluation of the acceptability of clinical services to clients, potential clients, and their family members. Stemming from the behavior analytic tradition, the focus on *social validity* emphasizes the evaluation, by the users of psychological services, of treatment methods, goals, and outcome (Foster & Mash, 1999). Although not a replacement for evidence of treatment efficacy, social validity is important in addressing questions about the likely engagement and continuation in services offered to clients. Little research has examined issues of assessment acceptability, presumably because most assessment instruments are not particularly time consuming or onerous for clients. However, extensive batteries of tests (as often used in psychoeducational and neuropsychological assessments), elaborate self-monitoring diaries, or ambulatory psychophysiological recording devices may well place significant demands on some clients. In such instances, investigating the social validity of these assessment procedures may yield data that influence the way in which these assessment instruments are used by clinicians. For example, Rhule, McMahon, and Vando (2009) examined the social validity (i.e., acceptability) of analog observation of parent-child interactions. The authors not only found high levels of acceptability for this assessment method but also found that acceptability differed as a function of characteristics of the parent and child.

Finally, the clinician must consider a number of systemic issues when considering the feasibility of using an assessment instrument. These include the extent to which (a) assessment activities (and the time necessary for them) are valued in a clinical setting; (b) colleagues support the use of the assessment instruments; (c) administrators actively support the adoption and use of scientifically sound assessment practices (including providing the time and financial support to learn to use an instrument); and (d) calls for greater accountability are linked to the benefits derived from use of the assessment data. The growing literature on the dissemination and implementation of evidence-based psychological services provides invaluable guidance in examining how the adoption of assessment practices could be affected by systemic issues (e.g., Gotham, 2004; Jensen-Doss, Hawley, Lopez, & Osterberg, 2009). In many cases, the clinician must serve as an advocate for science-based clinical assessment strategies within a clinical setting composed of other professionals less well versed in the benefits of such an approach to clinical services.

SUMMARY AND RECOMMENDATIONS

In this chapter, we highlighted the nature of clinical utility and the ways in which it could be evaluated (i.e., incorporating effectiveness, cost-outcome, and feasibility considerations). At present, however, there is little or no evidence for the clinical utility of many commonly used assessment instruments. Therefore, our first main recommendation is that, when available, evidence for clinical utility should strongly influence a clinician's decisions about whether an instrument should be used for a specific assessment purpose. Thus, for example, ongoing and frequent evaluations of client progress in therapy are likely to be valuable in enhancing the impact of the treatment and reducing the likelihood of treatment failure. In the absence of such evidence, our second main recommendation is that a clinician should be mindful of the importance of utility considerations in selecting and using instruments. Being aware that there is a considerable conceptual and empirical gap between an instrument that has been found to produce reliable and valid data and one that is clinically useful is a good starting point in making scientifically informed decisions about assessment matters. In addition, be sure to match the instrument to the goal of assessment and to consider base rate data when making diagnostic decisions with obtained data. There are also a number of additional recommendations based on material presented in the chapter and echoed in other chapters in this book: Consider the incremental validity and utility of an instrument before including in an assessment, measure treatment process and outcome frequently, select measures for treatment outcome monitoring that have been shown to be sensitive to treatment change, and carefully consider the psychometric implications of using short forms or subscales of an instrument.

Although not often considered as central elements in the assessment process, we encourage bearing in mind both cost and feasibility issues. It is always tempting to obtain more data in an effort to have a comprehensive evaluation. This, however, can be a costly and time-intensive enterprise that may not be clinically necessary. Further in the book, we say more about the benefits and limitations of gathering assessment data using multiple methods and multiple informants. In sum, keeping in mind the issues raised throughout this chapter should enhance the likelihood that scientifically sound instruments and justifiable procedures are followed when assessing clients.

RECOMMENDED SOURCES

Holmbeck, G. N., & Devine, K. A. (2009). Editorial: An author's checklist for measure development and validation manuscripts. *Journal of Pediatric Psychology, 34,* 691–696.

Nelson-Gray, R. O. (2003). Treatment utility of psychological assessment. *Psychological Assessment, 15,* 521–531.

Prigatano, G. P., & Pliskin, N. H. (Eds.). (2003). *Clinical neuropsychology and cost outcome research: A beginning.* New York: Psychology Press.

Smart, A. (2006). A multi-dimensional model of clinical utility. *International Journal for Quality in Health Care, 18,* 377–382.

Yates, B. T., & Taub, J. (2003). Assessing the costs, benefits, cost-effectiveness, and cost-benefit of psychological assessment: We should, we can, and here's how. *Psychological Assessment, 15,* 478–495.

6

Understanding Patterns Among Measures Through Factor Analysis

INTRODUCTION

As you read scientific reports describing clinical assessment instruments, you are likely to encounter many studies that describe factor analyses of assessment measures. The term *factor analysis* refers to a set of statistical techniques that, although mathematically complex, have the conceptually straightforward property of identifying a small number of underlying dimensions within a large number of data points. This set of techniques is used frequently in clinical assessment research. Clinicians often measure numerous behaviors, events, markers of personality traits, attitudes, or aspects of intellectual functioning. Frequently, researchers are interested in either exploring whether those numerous indicators can be summarized in terms of a smaller number of underlying dimensions or testing hypotheses about underlying dimensions of the measured phenomena.

Before we go further into technical and definitional aspects of factor analysis, we first give an intuitive feel for what this analytic technique does. Suppose we develop a measure of what we believe to be intelligence, and we include three measures of various aspects of verbal performance (word definitions, analogies, proverbs) and three measures of various aspects of visual/spatial performance (puzzles, matrices

TABLE 6.1 Hypothetical Correlation Matrix for Six Dimensions of an Intelligence Test

	V1	V2	V3	VS1	VS2	VS3
V1	—	.70	.65	.10	.20	.15
V2		—	.75	.15	.10	.20
V3			—	.20	.15	.10
VS1				—	.75	.65
VS2					—	.70
VS3						—

V, verbal tests; VS, visual/spatial subtests.

to complete, blocks to arrange in a certain design). Thus, we have six measures: three verbal and three visuospatial. We administer the overall test to a sample and examine the correlations among the six measures. As we look at the correlations among the measures, we notice that the verbal measures all tend to correlate highly with each other, but they do not correlate highly with the visual/spatial measures. In contrast, the visual/spatial measures all tend to correlate highly with each other but again not with the verbal measures. This pattern of associations indicates that, in general, individuals who do well on some verbal tasks will tend to do well on other verbal tasks, and individuals who do poorly on some verbal tasks will tend also to do poorly on other verbal tasks. The same is true for the visual/spatial tasks. Table 6.1 provides an example of what such a correlation matrix might look like.

One way to view this pattern is to say that there appear to be two underlying (or higher-order) dimensions to responses to our intelligence test items; one dimension reflects variation in verbal skill, and another dimension reflects variation in visual/spatial skill. But so far, our impression of two underlying dimensions is based solely on our visual inspection of a correlation matrix. Factor analysis provides a quantitative, mathematical description of the nature of underlying dimensions that characterize data such as these. Thus, as part of our test development process, we can use factor analysis to determine whether our impression that our intelligence measure consists of two underlying dimensions of intellectual functioning is truly accurate. Simply put, factor analysis mathematically identifies and defines the underlying dimensions of a set of items or measures.

You can see how important this technique can be for test development and theory validation and for the clinical judgments based on test scores. In the example, you might have developed your scale based on well-validated theory that distinguished between verbal and visual/spatial functioning. If so, a factor analysis of your measure that confirmed the presence of the two dimensions would speak to the validity of your measure and of the underlying theory. Or, if there was no previous, well-validated theory, your factor analysis might facilitate development of a theory that distinguishes between the two types of intellectual functioning.

We hope that, even at this early stage of the chapter, you can see how important it is for clinical practice to understand well the dimensional structure of assessment instruments. If the results of factor analytic strategies indicated that there are two types of intellectual functioning, the clinician must consider which type is most relevant for the judgments that he or she is making with a client. Suppose that (a) there are separate verbal and visuospatial dimensions to intellectual functioning; (b) you, the clinician, do not know that; and (c) you test someone who is actually well above average in verbal skill and well below average in visuospatial skill. Because you are unaware of the dimensional structure of the instrument, you calculate a total score (unknowingly averaging above-average and below-average skills) and describe the person as of average intelligence. As you can see, your description of your client is inaccurate and likely to be unhelpful.

Practicing clinical scientists must understand the dimensionality of the constructs they assess, and the measures used to assess them, to draw accurate, useful clinical conclusions. For that reason, we devote this chapter to helping you understand one common method for the determination of dimensionality (factor analysis). When you have completed this chapter, you will be prepared to read factor analytic reports in an informed way and with a critical eye so that you can draw the best clinical inferences from the relevant, published research.

As Rummel (1988) put it many years ago, a central goal of science is to discover pattern, order, and regularity in phenomena; factor analysis is one way to discover order and patterns in psychological measures, so it serves as an important instrument of scientific inquiry in psychology. That is why so many clinical assessment instruments are factor analyzed and why it is useful for you to have a clear understanding of this mathematical tool. In this chapter, we describe the role of factor analysis in inductive approaches to measure and theory validation; the observation of underlying factors or dimensions can lead researchers to develop theories concerning the constructs that are measured. We also describe the role of factor analysis in deductive approaches to measure and theory validation; the technique can be used to test specific, theory-driven hypotheses concerning the underlying structure of clinically important responses or behaviors. It is also important to understand the limitations of factor analysis. Always remember that factor analysis is a mathematical/statistical technique and has many limitations. We describe those as we move through the chapter. Our discussion of each of these topics will improve your ability to understand reports of factor analyses and thus to make decisions concerning how to select clinical assessment instruments and use the measures from them in a way that best benefits the client.

RATIONALE FOR FACTOR ANALYSIS AND CLINICAL USES OF THE OUTCOMES OF FACTOR ANALYSIS STUDIES

The recognition that certain behaviors, test responses, physiological indices, or other psychological phenomena covary (or that they do not) can provide important information to a clinician. As discussed in Chapter 1, it is often crucial to know which sets of behaviors tend to occur together, just as it is critical to know which sets of behaviors tend to occur independently of each other. Examples of the benefits of this kind of knowledge are present throughout the clinical assessment literature. A good way to appreciate the rationale for the use of factor analysis in clinical research is to consider some of the examples that follow.

We begin with one of the most well-known examples, which is the factor analysis-based finding that positive affect and negative affect do not covary highly (that is, they are not opposite poles on a single dimension but rather fall on separate dimensions; Clark & Watson, 1991). What that means is that being high on negative affectivity is largely unrelated to one's level of positive affectivity. Individuals can experience both intense negative affect and intense positive affect, they can be high in negative affect and unremarkable in positive affect, and they can be anhedonic (experience an absence of positive affect) and be unremarkable in negative affect, among other possibilities. This finding is important for clinical assessment and intervention. An evaluation of negative affectivity (which might include an assessment of nervousness, distress, irritability, jitteriness, and shame) of course provides useful information, but such an evaluation provides the clinician with no information concerning the client's positive affectivity (perhaps assessed with items measuring enthusiasm, excitement, happiness, and pride). The clinician must assess each dimension of affect separately.

Proper assessment of the two affect dimensions has important implications for clinical case formulation, treatment design, and treatment outcome evaluation. Low levels of positive affect can often be treated with behavioral interventions emphasizing participation in previously rewarding activities; such participation often leads to increased positive mood (Dimidjian et al., 2006). High levels of negative affect are likely not reduced by engaging in rewarding activities; rather, cognitive behavioral therapy or pharmacotherapy may be indicated.

When you as a clinician assess dysfunction and plan appropriate treatment, you must be aware of research that identifies the dimensions of the dysfunction about which you are concerned. As discussed in Chapter 1, there is considerable evidence that many diagnoses based on the *Diagnostic and Statistical Manual of Mental Disorders* (American Psychiatric Association, 2000) are multidimensional, and that the different dimensions require different treatments (Smith & Combs, 2010, provide a more detailed discussion of this literature). Recent factor analysis research suggest multidimensionality to be true even of psychosis. Typical dimensions of psychosis have been described as (a) degree of conviction about the reality of the psychotic experience; (b) the degree of cognitive preoccupation with the psychotic experience; (c) the impact of the psychotic experience on the patient's daily functioning; (d) the degree of emotional involvement with the psychotic experience; and (e) how well a patient can adopt an external perspective about the psychotic experience. A form of factor analysis that enables one to compare alternative factor analysis solutions (we say more about this in this chapter) compared this five-factor structure to a traditional, single factor of psychosis. The five factors explained the correlations among psychosis items more accurately (see Mizrahi et al., 2006, for a review). For clinical assessment purposes, these findings suggest that the clinician can make better judgments about the client if he or she considers data on these five factors compared to considering data only on a single dimension, such as "level of psychosis."

Further strengthening the importance of a multidimensional approach to psychosis, antipsychotic medications appear to influence different dimensions of psychosis differently: Medication produced only a 6% improvement in the degree of conviction about the psychotic experience and no improvement in external perspective about the experience but produced a 32% improvement on the behavioral impact of the psychotic experience (Mizrahi et al., 2006). Notice the incremental utility of focusing on more specific aspects of psychosis that have been identified in factor analytic research. Antipsychotic medications do not appear to influence psychosis when it is measured as a single higher-order construct; they only influence certain dimensions of the problem. To generalize from this finding, clinical assessment of each of the five dimensions is necessary to characterize the psychotic experience specifically for a patient, develop an individualized case formulation, choose the appropriate intervention for each dimension (or develop new interventions, as necessary), and monitor specific intervention effects.*

We briefly mention one more example. Numerous research laboratories have identified four factors within the posttraumatic stress disorder (PTSD) symptom set; the four factors have been labeled intrusions, avoidance, dysphoria, and hyperarousal (Simms, Watson, & Doebbeling, 2002). Attending to this set of factor analytic findings can lead to significantly improved care. These four dimensions are quite different from each other; it does not make sense either to derive a single score for

---

* As also discussed in Chapter 2, psychometric evaluations such as factor analysis are relevant to the specific assessment instruments and measures evaluated. The results of these evaluations can differ across different instruments that target the same phenomenon. Confidence in the meaning of factor analysis or other sources of psychometric evidence for the construct evaluated (in this case, psychosis) increases when the results from different assessment instruments are consistent (e.g., this is the case with multiple ways of measuring positive and negative affect).

PTSD (which is likely to mask important differences across the dimensions for a client) or to try to treat PTSD as a whole. Fortunately, there are reasonably well validated and distinct treatments for dysphoria/ anhedonia, avoidance of stressful stimuli, excessively heightened arousal system, and intrusive, unwanted thoughts. The factor analytic findings have made it possible for clinicians to assess each dimension (recall that we discussed in Chapter 1 how the importance of different aspects of a behavior problem can vary across clients) and provide treatment focused on the dimensions that are most relevant for any one client.

In addition to identifying separate dimensions within instruments and within disorders, factor analysis research has also contributed to the identification of common dimensions shared by many disorders. For example, the internalizing and externalizing dimensions that were first identified with respect to childhood dysfunction (Achenbach & Edelbrock, 1978) have also been identified in factor analyses of measures of adult disorders (Krueger & Markon, 2006). Because these and similar findings indicated that many different forms of psychopathology tend to covary, they have led to the hypothesis that there are actually core pathological processes contributing to many different specific types of dysfunction. This possibility has led to efforts to identify common treatment approaches for related disorders (Brown & Barlow, 2009).

So far, this discussion has not considered the distinction between factor analysis conducted in an exploratory way (i.e., without a prior dimensional model in mind) and factor analysis designed to test a dimensional model or compare two possible dimensional models. We next describe exploratory factor analysis (EFA), including variants of the technique. We introduce and explain terms and statistics encountered when reading EFA reports.

EXPLORATORY FACTOR ANALYSIS

Exploratory factor analysis, as implied by the name, does not begin with any model of the dimensional structure of the data set to be analyzed. Instead, the clinical researcher begins with a matrix containing the correlations between each pair of scores (correlations between items, behavioral observations, physiological measures, or whatever one wants to study) and conducts a mathematical analysis to identify underlying dimensions to the set of scores.

Although we do not attempt to describe the mathematics underlying this process, it is important that you have a basic sense of how this works. One begins with a matrix containing the correlations between each pair of variables. (Two caveats: first, we use *variables* generically. In this use, the term could refer to behavioral observations of a child's interactions with peers, observer ratings of subjects' performance on various social skills tasks, measures of multiple physiological responses to a stressful stimulus, self-reports of panic-related symptoms, scale scores from various instruments, and so on. Second, factor analyses can be conducted on data other than correlations, but that complexity is not necessary for us to address here.) When variables are significantly correlated with one another (such as the verbal and the visual/spatial measures in Table 6.1), the set of related variables is described as sharing variance. What that means is that variation in responses to one variable is predictable from variation in responses to other variables.

A factor that is derived from factor analysis is a new variable that, to use common metaphors employed in the field, "captures" or "holds" the variance shared by the set of items. The factor is constructed as a weighted composite of the items, and the weights reflect how much variance in the item is shared with variance in the underlying factor. If we were to factor analyze the correlation matrix in Table 6.1, presumably we would get two factors. Both factors would be linear composites of the six scales. One factor would be constructed with high weights on the three verbal scales and low weights on the three visual/spatial scales, and the second factor would consist of high weights on the visual/spatial scales and low weights on the verbal scales.

By looking at the weights of the variables on a factor, we can understand which variables contribute to each factor/dimension and thus form hypotheses about the nature of each underlying dimension. So, we would look at, say, Factor 1 and note that it is a composite of three highly weighted verbal tests and three low-weighted visual/spatial tests. That observation would lead us to conclude that there is an underlying dimension shared by the verbal tests but not by the visual/spatial tests. The idea of a dimension means that people who do well on one of those verbal tests tend to do well on the others (and the same is true for doing poorly). If that is true, we might well consider whether there is some common process or some common ability measured by the verbal tests. Such an observation might lead us to hypothesize the existence of a verbal reasoning dimension of intellectual functioning. An analogous set of observations might also lead us to hypothesize the existence of a visual/spatial dimension of intellectual functioning. If these hypotheses are well supported by the empirical literature, that is, if these findings are replicated in other studies, then you, as a clinician, are in a strong position to give clients feedback and make clinical decisions concerning their verbal reasoning and their visual/spatial reasoning. You can see how a factor analysis of this kind clarifies patterns of performance, facilitates clinical judgments, and can readily lead to advances in theory and understanding of complex psychological constructs.

This type of factor analysis is called exploratory because we did not start with a theoretical model that we then tested; instead, we arrived at a model inductively. In the example of intellectual functioning, we did not begin with the supposition that these two dimensions would be identified. We observed the pattern of covariance within a specific sample, which led us to formulate, essentially, a model of aspects of intellectual functioning. As you might imagine, so far we have glossed over numerous complexities and details to provide this summary. Next, we fill in some of the detail and address some of the complexities so that you will be in a position to understand EFA reports, draw accurate conclusions from them, and use these data to help you make valid and useful clinical judgments.

Rotated and Unrotated Factor Solutions

The first complexity is the distinction between an unrotated and a rotated factor solution. The typical procedure by which an EFA works is that the first factor extracted from the data is the one that explains the most possible shared variance in the data set as a whole (in the matrix of correlations). The second factor extracted is the one that explains the most variance remaining after the shared variance from the first factor is removed, and each subsequent factor is derived to explain the most variance of what is left (called *residual variance*). As you might imagine, using this procedure, the first factor tends to explain the bulk of the variance, and it tends to be constructed by loadings on all the variables in the correlation matrix. Thus, in Table 6.1, because the correlations between the verbal subtests and the visual/spatial subtests were not zero, a first factor would include the variance shared by all six subtests. Each subsequent factor also includes variance shared by all six subtests.

This approach is not always judged to be most helpful. Because each factor is constructed with contributions from each of the variables in the correlation matrix, it is not always clear how to interpret the factors (dimensions) as different from each other. For both researchers and the clinicians who use the research, it is often more helpful if the dimensions are more clearly distinct from each other. To clarify this idea further, we now introduce the idea of simple structure. Simple structure refers to the structure of factor loadings, and a structure of loadings is simple to the degree that a set of variables loads highly on only one factor; for that set of variables, loadings on other factors are near zero. You can see why simple structure is desirable: If a factor is primarily defined by one subset of items, a second factor is primarily defined by a second subset of items, and so on, then the meaning of each factor is easier to understand.

Typically, the original factor analysis, developed to explain the maximum possible shared variance in the correlation matrix, does not have very good simple structure. Factors developed in this way are not easily interpretable. Consider Figure 6.1 and Table 6.2. The figure and the table represent the results of a factor analysis conducted on 12 variables administered to a sample of individuals. In Figure 6.1, the solid lines depict the two original factors, derived to explain the most shared variance in the set of 12 variables. As you can see, the loadings of the 12 variables range from high to low on Factor 1, and they also range from high to low on Factor 2. The points representing the 12 scales are based on the scale loadings on the two factors; those loadings are given on the left side of Table 6.2. As you can see from the table, this

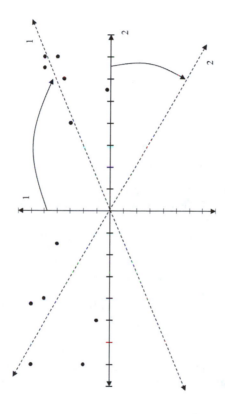

Figure 6.1   The horizontal and vertical axes represent unrotated factors derived to explain the covariances among the variables plotted as single points. The dotted, straight lines represent rotated factors, and the curved arrow depicts the nature of the rotation.

TABLE 6.2 Loadings on Unrotated and Rotated Factor Solutions

	Unrotated Factor Solution		Rotated Factor Solution	
	Factor 1	Factor 2	Factor 1	Factor 2
X1	−.48	.58	.12	**.78**
X2	−.50	.14	−.41	**.37**
X3	−.64	.54	−.07	**.82**
X4	−.63	.41	−.07	**.70**
X5	−.19	.46	.13	**.51**
X6	−.68	.28	−.27	**.61**
X7	.74	.49	**.94**	.06
X8	.64	.40	**.74**	.04
X9	.52	.02	.13	−.27
X10	.44	.27	**.40**	.01
X11	.60	.35	**.67**	.01
X12	.74	.37	**.84**	−.04

Bold indicates high loadings of a variable on one factor.

X refers to a scale on an instrument, as described in the text.

two-factor solution does not have good simple structure. Each factor is a composite of all 12 variables, and it is hard to perceive the distinction in meaning between the two factors.

To address this problem, analysts rotate the factors in space so that each factor is maximally collinear with a distinct cluster of variables. The two dotted lines represent the rotated factors. As you can see, Factor 1 now overlaps with one cluster of six variables, and Factor 2 now overlaps with the other cluster of six variables. Once the factors are rotated, one can then present the loadings of each variable on the rotated factors. The right side of Table 6.2 presents those new loadings. As you can see, there is a much more understandable simple structure. Factor 1 is characterized by high loadings on the second six variables in the table, and for the most part, relatively inconsequential loadings on the first six variables in the table. This new, rotated factor is more readily interpretable; it largely comprises the variance shared by the second six variables. Similarly, Factor 2 is largely characterized by high loadings on the first six variables and relatively low loadings on the second six variables. It also, then, is more easily interpreted; it largely captures the variance shared by the first six variables in the table. The "meaning" of the factors (how they are labeled) is then inferred by the meaning of the variables that compose them.

There are no hard-and-fast rules for determining what counts as a high loading and what should be viewed as an inconsequential loading. Like correlations, loadings can theoretically vary from .00 to 1.0 and be either positive or negative (if a loading is negative, high scores on the variable are associated with low scores on the factor). In the rotated factor solution portion of Table 6.2, we have followed a common practice of placing reasonably high loadings that also reflect simple structure in bold type. As you can see, we bolded loadings of .40 or greater when they also reflected simple structure (which we considered present when the primary loading was more than .30 higher than the secondary loading). The absence of clear rules for identifying important variables in a factor analysis solution indicates how important it is that clinical scientists and clinicians examine factor analysis results carefully. There are many cases in the literature for which the results of factor analyses are "overinterpreted": (a) The factor solution does not explain much of the variance in the data matrix, suggesting a poorly constructed assessment instrument; (b) factors are composed of items that only load weakly on them, suggesting that they are not good markers of the targeted construct; (c) many items load strongly on several factors, indicating a lack of discriminant validity among the factors; and (d) items loading on a factor do not fit within a conceptually homogeneous construct, making it difficult to interpret the meaning of the factor/scale score. In these cases, it is difficult to draw clinically useful inferences from the factor analysis.

To help you appreciate the substance of the improved interpretability, we tell you what each scale represents. The first six scales (X1 through X6) are the six subscales of the Neuroticism domain of the NEO PI-R version of the five-factor model of personality (Costa & McCrae, 1992). The six subscales are understood to measure anxiety, self-consciousness, depression, vulnerability, impulsiveness, and angry hostility. The second six scales (X7 through X12) are the six subscales of the Extraversion domain of the NEO PI-R. They are thought to measure gregariousness, activity level, assertiveness, excitement seeking, positive emotions, and warmth. Thus, Factor 1 for the most part represents variance shared across the six Extraversion scales, with little contribution from Neuroticism, and Factor 2 largely represents variance shared across the six Neuroticism scales, with little contribution from Extraversion. As you can see, the rotated factor solution results are readily interpretable.

As is implied by Figure 6.1, the original factors are relatively independent of each other, or orthogonal. As we said, each new factor only explains residual variance—that variance not explained by preceding factors, so each new factor is independent of those preceding factors. However, there are different approaches to rotating factor solutions. One approach is to preserve the orthogonality (independence) of the factors. One does an orthogonal rotation so that the factors can be interpreted independently of each other. If they are independent, variation on Factor 1 is unrelated to variation on Factor 2.

This advantage is important, but orthogonal rotation also has a downside. If, "in nature," the two dimensions are not truly independent (in the case of Neuroticism and Extraversion, the two factors correlate significantly and negatively: $r = -.27$ in the sample used for the factor analysis), then an orthogonal rotation will not accurately represent one or both of the dimensions. It is often the case that dimensions of functioning are related to each other (the relation between measures of "anxiety" and "depression" is a well-known example). When that is true, an alternative analytic strategy is to use what is called an oblique rotation (a rotation that does not preserve the independence of the factors). An oblique rotation has the advantage of permitting a more accurate representation of the underlying dimensions, along with the disadvantage that inter-pretive statements about the factors are not independent of each other. Using our example, if we were to say something about being high on the Neuroticism factor, what we said would apply to a small degree to being low on the Extraversion factor (because the two are negatively correlated). To the degree that is true, then inferences we draw in the future about the influence of Neuroticism could in part partially reflect the influence of low Extraversion.

To understand factor analysis reports accurately and to know how to use these results in your clinical practice, it will be important for you to know whether factors were rotated to be orthogonal or were allowed to be correlated with each other. Our factor analysis example involved the study of personality functioning, for which it is widely understood that the different dimensions of personality are related to each other. For that reason, we used an oblique rotation to gain the advantage of more accurately capturing underlying personality dimen-sions. There is a variety of types of factor rotations, and in your reading, you will come across a number of different terms. Among the most common orthogonal rotations is varimax, and among the most common oblique rotations is direct oblimin.

Factor Analysis and Component Analysis

There is another distinction we have not yet mentioned: There is a dif-ference between factor analysis and what is called principle component analysis. In our made-up correlation matrix given in Table 6.1, note that we put dashes in the spaces for the correlation of a variable with itself. In factor analysis (or principal factor analysis), what is typically put there is some measure of how predictable a variable is from the combination of all other variables in the data set (i.e., a coefficient that reflects how much of the variance is shared with the other variables to be analyzed). The idea is that factor analysis seeks to identify underlying dimensions for the shared variance among the variables. Thus, only the variance in a vari-able that is shared with the other variables is analyzed in factor analysis. Principle component analysis is different. For component analysis, one analyzes all the variance of each variable whether that variance is shared with other variables or not. Accordingly, one places 1.0 in the correlation matrix for the correlation between a variable and itself. The idea behind the name *component analysis* is that one is seeking merely to identify a smaller set of components to a large data set. The terminology is used to attempt to communicate that analyzing components is different from analyzing factors; in the latter case, one is determining the dimensions that underlie what the variables have in common. In the former case, one is not restricted to what the variables have in common; instead, one is trying to reduce the data set to a smaller number of components without leaving out any of the variance on each of the variables.

When you read reports of factor analyses, you should determine whether the analysis was actually a factor analysis or was, instead, a components analysis. If it was a factor analysis, then you can understand the factors as representations of the underlying communality in a set of variables or constructs. If it was a component analysis, you should view the components as convenient summaries of the set of variables or constructs. In practice, the two methods often (but not always) produce similar results.

Guidelines for Determining the Number of Factors in a Factor Analysis

Until now, we have said nothing about how to determine how many factors are present in a data set. There is judgment involved, and to be an informed reader of factor analysis results, you must understand the nature of the judgment process. We next provide an overview of this process so you can understand the basis for decisions researchers have made in the assessment articles. Later, we review limitations of this procedure. Your knowledge of limitations of factor analysis is likely to be useful in helping you draw appropriate clinical inferences from factor analysis studies.

One important piece of information that is provided for each factor is how much variance the factor explains. Using standard scores, the total variance explained by a single variable in the analysis is 1.0. For a factor to reflect an underlying dimension, presumably it should explain more variance than that explained by a single variable. Thus, one statistic researchers consider in deciding whether a factor can be understood to reflect an underlying dimension is how much variance the factor explains. Now, it is time to introduce another term: eigenvalue. An eigenvalue is the amount of variance explained by a factor. Mathematically, the eigenvalue of a factor is the sum of the column of the squared loadings for the factor (the proportion of variance explained). The amount of variance explained changes when the factors are rotated, so researchers consider both unrotated and rotated eigenvalues. Table 6.3 provides the eigenvalues for the factor analysis conducted on the 12 personality scales.

As you can see from Table 6.3, the first factor had a much higher eigenvalue (i.e., explained more variance) than did the second factor and so on. That pattern is always true because each factor is defined to explain the most possible available variance. Another thing to notice is that the eigenvalues for the rotated solution are slightly lower; this

TABLE 6.3   Factor Analysis Eigenvalues

Factor	Unrotated Solution	Rotated Solution
1	4.50	4.12
2	2.27	1.85
3	1.27	0.86
4	.82	
5	.64	
6	.56	
7	.49	
8	.41	
9	.30	
10	.28	
11	.26	
12	.20	

will also always be true because the rotated solution is not designed to explain the maximum amount of variance in the variable set but rather to overlap with one cluster of variables to improve the simple structure of the factors.

The third thing to notice is that most of the factors had unrotated eigenvalues less than 1.0. Since 1.0 is the amount of variance explained by an individual variable, any factor with an eigenvalue less than 1.0 is actually explaining less variance than is a single variable. Such factors can hardly be construed to reflect underlying, common dimensions across the item set. For that reason, one EFA guideline is only to consider factors with eigenvalues greater than 1.0 (as you can see, we only rotated the factors with unrotated eigenvalues greater than 1.0). The guideline only means that any prospective underlying factor must explain more variance than that explained by a single variable.

Although it is hard to imagine a situation in which one would want to retain a factor with an eigenvalue less than 1.0, it is not the case that all factors with eigenvalues greater than 1.0 merit inclusion in a factor solution that identifies underlying dimensions in a data set. There are two reasons why a factor with an eigenvalue greater than 1.0 might not be retained in a factor solution.

The first reason is that the factor does not make conceptual sense. Notice that our factor analysis did produce a third unrotated factor with an eigenvalue greater than 1.0. Its rotated eigenvalue was less than 1.0, so the factor would probably not have been included in any case, but considering the nature of the factor is instructive. Factor 3 had high loadings on assertiveness from the Extraversion domain (.66) and self-consciousness (.45) from the Neuroticism domain. It had minor loadings (between .20 and .27) on excitement seeking from Extraversion and impulsiveness from Neuroticism; all other loadings were near zero. Remember also that Factor 3 concerns only variance not explained by Factors 1 and 2. So, Factor 3 involves that part of assertiveness that is not explained by Factor 1, that part of self-consciousness that is not explained by Factor 2, along with those parts of excitement seeking and impulsiveness that are not explained by the first two factors. It is hard to assign any coherent conceptual meaning to this pattern of loadings, and it is even harder when one considers that we do not know what the substantive meaning is of "that part of assertiveness not explained by Factor 1," and so on. For these reasons, even if the rotated solution had an eigenvalue greater than 1.0, we would not have described the factor as representing a meaningful underlying dimension in the data set.

The second reason researchers may not include a factor with an eigenvalue greater than 1.0 is that sometimes there are numerous factors with eigenvalues just over and just under 1.0. One often sees solutions in which, for example, Factors 4 through 7 have eigenvalues like these: 1.11, 1.07, .98, .96, respectively. Given the relative equality of the four factors in terms of variance explained, there is little justification for selecting the first two factors and discarding the second two. For this reason, researchers developed what is called the scree plot, which plots the eigenvalues for each factor (the term comes from the word *scree*, which refers to the rock junk at the base of a cliff or mountain face you are trying to climb). There can be a pronounced bend in the line connecting the eigenvalues, sometimes described as an elbow in the eigenvalue distribution. That is, if factor solution eigenvalues were 3.71, 3.32, 2.95, 1.11, 1.09, .98, and .96, you can see that the line connecting those values would drop steadily until the fourth factor, when it would essentially level off and not change much from Factor 4 through Factor 7. When that is the case, one tends to consider only those factors with eigenvalues above the bend in the distribution. In this example, that would mean the first three factors would be examined for conceptual coherence and considered for inclusion in a factor solution designed to describe the underlying dimensions of the data set.

This information can help you read clinical assessment articles accurately and carefully. You can recognize that factors with eigenvalues lower than 1.0 lack empirical meaning and should not influence how you view scores on a set of scales. On the other side of the coin, careful examination of some factors with eigenvalues greater than 1.0 might reveal that they lack conceptual coherence and so should not be interpreted. The value of the scree plot perspective is that it can provide guidance to you, as a reader, about which dimensions appear to be most important in explaining covariation among a set of items or scales.

You may be struck by the subjectivity apparent in this process. We refer to this concern more in the following discussion when we talk about limitations to EFA. But, you should also appreciate that researchers have worked on this problem and have sought more rigorous ways to determine factor structure. We do not go into specifics of these methods here except to note that they include means of testing whether factor solutions replicate on independent samples and means of determining that a factor solution would not likely have been generated by chance. Another term to be aware of is communality. The communality of a variable is the proportion of its total variance that is explained by the factors. You can easily calculate the communality of a variable; it is the sum of the squared loadings for a variable on each factor (typically, as in Table 6.2, the sum of the squared loadings across the row). For example, X1 in Table 6.2 has rotated factor loadings of .12 and .78 on the two factors. Its communality is $(.12)^2 + (.78)^2 = .63$; this means that 63% of the variance in X1 is explained by the two factors we retained from the factor analysis.

Limitations to EFA

You can see how valuable factor analysis is as a mathematical technique for examining the underlying dimensionality of assessment instruments, the constructs they are intended to measure, and the relations among the measured constructs. The capacity to understand which constructs covary in individuals can clarify our understanding of psychological functioning, can improve theoretical and explanatory models, and can inform assessment decisions. The finding noted above, which has been demonstrated numerous times by numerous researchers (e.g., Costa & McCrae, 1992), suggests that anxiety, depression, self-consciousness, angry hostility, vulnerability, and impulsiveness all share a substantial amount of variance: Individuals high on a measure of one of those constructs are likely to be high on measures of others of those constructs. Researchers labeled that domain "Neuroticism" to reflect the subjective distress and affective lability that the six constructs appear to share. The finding that these traits share variance can be useful for clinical assessment. In many places in this book, we emphasize the need for precise assessment of specific constructs to best guide intervention efforts and best assess change over time. It is also true, though, that knowing that the presence of one Neuroticism-type trait increases the likelihood that others are present that can inform the assessment process. Although there are important advantages to factor analysis, there are also important limitations to the procedure of which clinicians, and clinical researchers, need to be aware. Some of them may already be apparent to you.

First, it is important to appreciate that the results of a factor analysis depend on which assessment instruments, measures, and variables are available for the analysis. EFA helps identify underlying dimensions in a variable set; it does not help identify underlying dimensions in nature or even underlying dimensions in a phenomenon of interest. Suppose we seek to identify the underlying dimensions of intellectual functioning, and then suppose the intellectual functioning variables we measure are word definitions, analogies, and general fund of information, which are three verbal skills. We could then factor analyze those three measures, get one factor, and report that we have found that intellectual functioning exists on a single dimension. But, our research design did not include any visual/spatial tests. Without those tests in the study, they could hardly have emerged in a factor analysis. Assume that, as indicated in our previous, made-up factor analysis example, visual/spatial functioning falls on a different factor from verbal functioning. You can see that our conclusion, with respect to the dimensions of intellectual functioning, was flawed; what we really had learned was something about the dimensionality of verbal functioning. Our starting assumption that word definitions, analogies, and general fund of information reflected the full range of intellectual functioning was a mistake. It is of course the case that the results of the factor analysis reflected that mistake in our research design. Truly, what we are describing is not really a limitation of factor analysis at all; we are simply noting that nothing about factor analysis can correct for errors in research design and the concepts that underlie the strategy.

This reality has important implications for clinicians. It is important that you not mistake the results of a factor analysis of a set of variables for a necessarily accurate description of the underlying dimensions in some phenomenon of clinical interest. To use the results of factor analytic studies accurately, you must consider which variables were analyzed and whether that set of variables is an accurate, empirically informed representation of the construct domain of interest. You may sometimes find that researchers describe their results as though they reflect the dimensionality of an entire phenomenon, even though such a conclusion is not warranted by the instrument content or the results of the factor analysis. A second difficulty, again with how factor analysis is used rather than with the technique itself, concerns how factors are labeled. You will notice that researchers give labels to their factors (examples include "Neuroticism," "Extraversion," and "Visual/Spatial Functioning"), and at this point, you can appreciate that researchers decide on their labels by studying the pattern of factor loadings and the content of the items within a factor. There is, of course, subjective judgment that goes into labeling the factors. One problem that can come up is that those labels can be reified (i.e., viewed as a real, concrete thing). Over time, clinicians and researchers can come to believe the factor label is an objective label for an established, real process. Remember our discussion of construct validity in Chapter 3: The results of any factor analysis should be viewed just like the results of any empirical study, that is, as provisional evidence in support of, or counter to, some theory, model, or perspective. When clinicians use scales that were developed and labeled from factor analysis, they should keep that in mind.

A third difficulty with how factor analysis is used is that researchers sometimes report factor analytic results, perhaps along with internal consistency estimates, as the sole evidence in support of the validity of an instrument. In the absence of evidence that the different factors predict external criteria of interest differently (e.g., the dysphoria factor within the PTSD symptom set predicts anxious and depressed behavior, whereas the hyperarousal factor within PTSD predicts heightened vigilance and autonomic nervous system activation), clinical scientists should regard factor analysis-based validity claims with caution. Recall from Chapter 3 that part of validating a measure is the process of determining the relationship between scores on the measure and other important, relevant indicators of life functioning. The validation of factor analysis results should follow the same principles.

A fourth difficulty is that there is no mathematical or statistical rule for determining how many factors best summarize a variable set. As you saw, researchers make judgments based on eigenvalues, scree plots, and factor interpretability. This decision-making process has two implications. The first is that different researchers draw different conclusions, even retaining different numbers of factors, from similar data; it sometimes occurs that debates in the literature are less based on the results of two different EFAs and more on how different researchers, with different theoretical perspectives, view the same factor analytic results. The second, as we noted, is that clinicians should avoid the reification of factor analytic results; these results should be viewed with the same informed, skeptical eye used by clinical scientists to view all empirical reports.

Fifth, the validity and utility of EFA analyses are a function of the quality of the variables, observations, or scales that go into the factor analysis. Researchers sometimes factor analyze variables or scales for which there is low reliability or limited evidence of validity. Obviously, a factor analysis of nonvalid variables should not be the basis for clinical decision making.

Last, you should also be aware that the size and nature of the samples used are important for evaluating factor analytic results. Concerning size, there are no firm guidelines for the size of the sample necessary for EFA analyses, but one recent study found that analyses with at least 20 participants for each variable were far more accurate than analyses with smaller participant-to-variable ratios (Costello & Osborne, 2005). Also, a minimum of 200 participants overall in a sample is a common guideline. Concerning the nature of the sample, a factor analytic solution in a sample with one set of characteristics may not replicate in a different sample with different characteristics. For example, results from a largely middle-class, European American sample may not generalize to an impoverished, predominantly minority population. To reiterate a point made in many ways throughout this chapter, it is important that you read factor analytic reports carefully; it is incumbent on you to decide how much confidence to place in the results of factor analytic studies and to determine whether the results of such studies can help or hinder your clinical decision making.

CONFIRMATORY FACTOR ANALYSIS

We next turn to confirmatory factor analysis (CFA). As noted, CFA is typically used to test hypotheses about factor structures or to compare competing dimensional theories about an assessment instrument and construct. Perhaps even more so than EFA, CFA is a complex set of mathematical techniques and procedures. We do not address the underlying mathematics of CFA; instead, we give an intuitive feel for how it works, provide basic information concerning how to interpret CFA results, and review some of the typical pitfalls of using CFA. These topics will help you understand how the results of CFA can assist with clinical assessments.

Typical CFA use begins with a theory about the dimensionality of a variable set and seeks to test whether the correlations among the variables in a sample are consistent with a theory, usually based on previous factor analytic research or theories about the measured construct. Returning to our first example, we might hypothesize that there are two dimensions of intellectual functioning (verbal and visual/spatial); we might then give several measures of each dimension to participants in a sample, and we might then want to test whether our hypothesis was correct.

To understand the essence of how this procedure works, suppose we use the six intellectual functioning variables referred to in our initial example in this chapter. Once we have scores on the six variables from all the members of our sample, we would then correlate each variable with every other variable. We could present the results of that analysis as a 6 × 6 correlation matrix. We also have a theory concerning how the six variables should relate to each other; suppose we believe variables 1 through 3 should relate highly because they all reflect verbal functioning; variables 4 through 6 should all relate highly because they reflect visual/spatial functioning, and there should be close to no relationship between the verbal and the visual/spatial tests. Our theory thus specifies a pattern of correlations among the six variables: Variables 1 through 3 should have high correlations, 4 through 6 should have high correlations, and there should be near-zero correlations across the two domains.

Thus, in contrast to EFA, we have a theory that implies a certain pattern of correlations among the six variables. Imagine a matrix of the correlations implied by the theory and then imagine laying this matrix on top of the matrix containing the actual correlations from the data set. In each cell, we would have two values: the actual correlation in the sample and the correlation implied by our theory. If our theory is accurate, there should be little difference between the two values. To determine how well our theory fits the data, we can subtract each theory-based correlation from each actual correlation and can then average those differences. If the average difference is small, the theoretical correlations were similar to the actual correlations: The theory fit the data well and is supported. If the average difference is large, or large for some correlations, then the theory did not capture what actually happened and is not fully accurate.

You can see how this idea can be readily extended to compare two alternative, competing dimensional models for a set of data. If two different models specify two different patterns of correlations among the variables, one can compare how well each of the two models fits the obtained matrix of correlations and thus decide which model is preferred. Because CFA permits theory testing and theory comparison, it has become increasingly popular. Often, CFA is used to test the stability of results obtained from an EFA on a different sample (see discussion of equivalence in Chapter 7). It is also used in cross-cultural research. One cannot presume that a factor structure developed in one population fits well in other populations. Accordingly, researchers often use CFA both to test whether factor structures are consistent across populations and to test competing models in different cultural groups.

In contrast to EFA, there is a variety of statistics that provide information concerning how well a model fits obtained data. One way to understand the different types of statistics available is to contrast what are called absolute fit indices with what are called relative, or incremental, fit indices (Hu & Bentler, 1995). The standardized root mean square residual (SRMR) is considered an absolute fit index in that it provides a direct comparison of the covariance matrix implied by the model and the actual covariance matrix obtained in the study. It represents the average deviation between the implied and obtained values for a given covariance. The root mean square error of approximation (RMSEA) is closely related but adjusts for the complexity of a model; it produces more favorable values for simpler, parsimonious models. SRMR values of approximately .09 and lower are thought to indicate good model fit (Hu & Bentler, 1999), and RMSEA values of .06 are thought to indicate a close fit, .08 a fair fit, and .10 a marginal fit (Browne & Cudeck, 1993; Hu & Bentler, 1999).

Two widely used examples of incremental fit indices are the comparative fit index (CFI) and the Tucker-Lewis index (TLI), also known as the nonnormed fit index (NNFI). R. B. Kline (2005), discusses these and other indices in detail. Essentially, these and similar indices report on the amount of improvement one's model provides over a null model (typically, the null model is that none of the variables are related to each other). CFI and NNFI values of .90 or .95 are thought to indicate good fit (Hu & Bentler, 1999; R. B. Kline, 2005). It is important to appreciate that these values are guidelines, and that the degree of model fit is influenced by many factors. Researchers typically rely on convergence across several fit indices to conclude that a model fits the data well. As a clinical scientist, you may often read reports of CFA studies. For that reason, you should be aware of the nature of these fit indices and commonly accepted values indicative of good fit; this awareness will help you read those reports carefully.

Limitations to CFA

As it is typically used, CFA tests certain kinds of dimensional models, that is, models in which each variable that loads on the same factor is thought to be a parallel, alternative indicator of that factor. When that is the case, it makes sense to allow a given variable to load on only one factor; in one's theory, it is an indicator of that factor but not of any other, separate factor. CFA often provides useful information about how well such a model fits a data set. But, there is a different circumstance to which factor analysis is often applied. Frequently, one does not have parallel, alternative indicators of single factors; rather, one has measures of a variety of constructs and wants to see which sets of constructs tend to go together. When that is the case, it is much more typical that a variable has loadings on more than one factor; a variable might load predominantly on a single factor, but it might also have nontrivial loadings on other factors.

CFA models, which typically specify a variable to have zero loadings on all but one factor, cannot replicate the correlation matrix from such a situation well. Modifications of CFA, such as specifying multiple loadings across factors, have not worked well for reasons that, though clear, go beyond our purposes in this chapter. To summarize this point, CFA is better used when one has parallel or equivalent indicators and not when one is measuring several constructs that may load on multiple underlying dimensions. In the latter case, CFA fit indices are likely to indicate poor fit; as a clinical scientist, you should understand when poor fit occurs due to using CFA incorrectly rather than to inadequacy of the model.

As we have described it, CFA is a theory-driven, hypothesis-testing approach. You should be aware that sometimes researchers modify their theoretical models based on results from initial CFAs. For example, we might have started with a model that identified X1 through X3 as measures of verbal functioning and X4 through X6 as measures of visual/spatial functioning and then learned, based on output from the analyses, that our model would fit the data better if we specified a third factor, perhaps measuring memory functioning, that included V3 and V6. If we then report a three-factor model, it is important to understand that we are not reporting a test of our initial hypothesis (i.e., we are not "confirming" our original hypothesis). Rather, we are reporting the results of a modification of our model based on the results of our factor analysis. Because model modifications that are made based on data often do not replicate (MacCallum, Roznowski, & Necowitz, 1992), you should view results of this kind with greater caution.

Because CFA is a theory-testing approach, one should view the findings as one piece of evidence concerning the theory. As a reader of a CFA report, you may have good, empirical reasons for questioning a theory, even though the CFA results look good. Successful CFA results do not constitute proof of a theory; rather, they are one piece of evidence among many.

We again want to mention two sets of concerns that we raised with respect to EFA. First, a CFA conducted on variables that lack reliability and validity should be viewed skeptically, and factor analytic results involving such variables are likely to be unreliable. Second, an accurate reading of CFA results includes consideration of the nature of the sample used in the study. Does the sample share characteristics with the client or samples to which one wants to apply the results? How are the study samples and one's clinical population similar? How are they different? Concerning the size of CFA samples, the issue is complex, but guidelines such as 20 participants per variable and a minimum of 200 participants overall are reasonable.

In summary, both inductive-based EFA and deductive-based CFA are valuable analytic strategies for understanding the dimensionality of psychological constructs. Both techniques are frequently used for that reason. Although the specifics of these tools are mathematically complex, we hope you now have a strong intuitive feel for what these techniques can provide to clinical scientists. As a result of reading this chapter, we hope that you can read factor analytic reports accurately, read them critically, and recognize the important strengths and limitations in the technique as you consider factor analytic findings.

SUMMARY AND RECOMMENDATIONS

1. Factor analysis is one mathematical procedure for determining which sets of variables tend to co-occur in a sample of subjects. Identification of patterns of covariation in clinical phenomena can lead to more accurate assessments, better treatment planning, and thus more effective treatment.
2. EFA is often used to identify underlying dimensions in a data set. Principal component analysis is closely related to factor analysis; it is used to reduce a large number of variables to a smaller, more manageable number of underlying components. CFA is typically used to test hypotheses concerning the structure of a set of variables or to compare competing structural hypotheses.
3. It is incumbent on clinicians to read factor analytic reports carefully. Readers should consider a number of things, including each of the following, before applying the results of a factor analysis in clinical decision making:
   a. Aspects of the method (e.g., How are the study participants similar to, or different from, the population to which one wants to apply the results? What content was included in the variables to be analyzed? Is there evidence that the variables to be analyzed are reliable and valid?)
   b. Aspects of the data analytic procedure (e.g., How was the number of factors determined? Was the sample large enough? For CFA, was the original model modified to fit the data better?)

   c. Aspects of the results (e.g., How much variance did each factor account for? How simple was the structure? For CFA, how good is the model fit?)
4. When approached with the careful, critical scrutiny characteristic of clinical science, factor analytic findings can provide invaluable information to the clinician.

RECOMMENDED SOURCES

Costello, A. B., & Osborne, J. W. (2005). Best practices in exploratory factor analysis: Four recommendations for getting the most from your analysis. *Practical Assessment, Research and Evaluation, 10,* 1–9.

Floyd, F. J., & Widaman, K. F. (1995). Factor analysis in the development and refinement of clinical assessment instruments. *Psychological Assessment, 7,* 286–299.

Kline, R. B. (2005). *Principles and practice of structural equation modeling.* New York: Guilford Press.

Rummel, R. J. (1988). *Applied factor analysis.* Chicago: Northwestern University Press.

7

The Conditional Nature of Psychometric Evidence

INTRODUCTION

The first six chapters introduced psychometric concepts and methods of analyzing measures that contribute to the scientific foundations of clinical assessment. We discussed the evolution of the concept of construct validity and the meaning and importance of psychometric dimensions such as temporal stability, internal consistency, content validity, convergent and discriminant validity, construct validity, and factor structure. We discussed the importance of these dimensions of psychometric evidence for the judgments and decisions made by the clinician—judgments about diagnosis, clinical case formulation, and treatment process and outcome evaluation. All dimensions of psychometric evidence are important when developing, selecting, applying, and interpreting clinical assessment instruments and the measures derived from them. In this chapter, we consider more closely an additional aspect of the scientific foundations of clinical assessment: the conditional nature of the psychometric evidence.

The main thesis of the chapter is that the psychometric properties of an assessment instrument (more specifically, of the measures derived from an assessment instrument) are conditional and unstable. We emphasize that validity, reliability, and factor structure are not unconditional and stable properties of measures; they can vary as a function of the characteristics of an assessment occasion, the context of assessment, and the persons from whom the measures are derived. Further, the elements of some clinical assessment instruments can diminish in their relevance and representativeness over time as we gain a better understanding of the phenomenon that they are intended to measure.

As an example of the conditional nature of psychometric evidence, a behavior-problem checklist might provide more accurate measures of aggressive behaviors for younger than for older children, for severe more than for mild forms of aggression, or for children of northern European ethnic backgrounds than for children of Southeast Asian ethnic backgrounds. Also, the accuracy and clinical utility of the measures might depend on the psychological state of the child (such as his or her level of fatigue or medication status when the instrument is applied) and on who provides the information (for example, child, mother, father, teacher). Further, the measures might be more useful for evaluating treatment outcome than for contributing to a clinical case formulation.

Haynes and Lench (2003) discussed how the incremental validity and utility of new assessment measures can be conditional. Recall from Chapters 4 and 5 that incremental validity is the degree to which a measure explains or predicts some phenomenon relative to other measures of the same phenomenon. Incremental validity and utility are particularly important considerations when developing a new assessment instrument. They address the question: Are measures from the new instrument better (i.e., more reliable, accurate, clinically useful, cost-beneficial) than those from already existing instruments?

There are multiple answers to the question of whether a new instrument is better than an existing instrument; thus, the incremental validity of a new measure can be evaluated in multiple ways. That is, estimates of incremental validity of a new measure can vary depending on the comparison measures used and the goals of assessment. For example, there are multiple ways in which the incremental validity of a new self-report measure of manic episodes could be evaluated. One way to compare the new instrument with others would be its degree of incremental sensitivity to change. Because the mood and activity of persons with hypomania or bipolar disorders can change quickly, a measure that accurately tracks those changes would be helpful for monitoring response to treatment and for identifying factors that trigger or maintain those changes (for more discussion of sensitivity to change, see Santor, Debrota, Engelhardt, & Gelwicks, 2008). As we discussed in Chapters 1 and 5, sensitivity to change in self-report measures can be enhanced with shorter time frames for the items and more specifically defined markers.

The new instrument could also be compared to others on its degree of incremental content validity. Recall that content validity is the degree to which the elements of an assessment instrument accurately reflect all aspects (representativeness) and only relevant aspects (relevance) of the measured phenomenon. For a manic episode, content validity would be the degree to which the items on a questionnaire (or queries in an electronic diary or codes in an observation system) provided measures of irritable, elevated, and expansive moods; self-esteem; thoughts of grandiosity; time sleeping; distractibility; and other symptoms that currently define manic episodes (i.e., the representativeness of items in an assessment instrument; *Diagnostic and Statistical Manual of Mental Disorders, Fourth Edition, Text Revision* [*DSM-IV-TR*], American Psychiatric Association [APA], 2000, p. 362). Content validity of the new instrument would also reflect the degree to which it did not include items (such as diminished interest in activities, feelings of guilt, suicidal ideation) that measured other phenomena (i.e., the relevance of the elements of the assessment instrument).

Content validity is an important dimension of psychometric evidence, but indices of validity for a measure can also differ across other psychometric evaluative dimensions. For example, indices of incremental validity of a new assessment instrument measure could vary depending on whether one considers its positive predictive power, sensitivity or specificity, predictive efficacy, convergent or discriminant validity, or discriminative validity (see Chapters 3 and 4 for more details). Or, a measure might be more valid and sensitive when used with clients who experience more extreme forms of mania than with clients who experience less-extreme forms of mania.

Measures of the validity of a new instrument could also depend on the goals of assessment—the inferences that are to be drawn from the measures. Indices of incremental validity could vary depending on whether the instrument is to be used as a brief screening instrument, for formal diagnosis, as a treatment outcome measure, or to help identify causal factors for manic episodes. For example, a measure of specific aspects of mania symptom experience over the last week may have incremental validity over other measures for assessing treatment outcome but not for brief screening.

These are just a few examples of the conditional nature of validity evaluations. In many cases, the answer to the question, Is this measure better than others? is, It depends! Table 7.1 summarizes many aspects of the conditional nature of reliability and validity. The selection of measures and measurement strategies as a function of the purpose of assessment, the characteristics of the assessment occasion, and other factors listed in Table 7.1 are consistent with a functional approach to assessment: To obtain information that is most useful in clinical decision making, the measurement strategy in clinical assessment should be congruent with the goals of the assessment and the characteristics of the client.

A further challenge in the complex conditional nature of psychometric indices is the multifaceted nature of many clinical phenomena and assessment instruments. Recall from Chapters 1–6 that many assessment instruments provide scores on multiple measures that can differ in their levels of supporting validity evidence. For example, it

TABLE 7.1   Aspects of the Conditional Nature of Reliability, Validity, and Utility of Clinical Assessment Measures

Aspect	Examples
Clinical population	A questionnaire measure of manic episodes may be more valid for adults than for adolescents. A questionnaire measure of couple satisfaction may be more valid for British, European Americans, and Canadians than for African- or Asian American or immigrants to Britain, Canada, and Australia.
Emotional or physiological state of the client	The *ecological validity* and utility for clinical case formulation of an analog observation measure of couple communication might vary as a function of the emotional state of one or both participants during the communication assessment. The validity of responses to a clinical interview about a client's use of alcohol may depend on the client's alcohol intake just before the interview.
Psychometric dimension used for evaluation	Measures from questionnaire measuring depressed mood may exhibit better discriminative than predictive validity. An observation measure of social anxiety in a clinic setting may exhibit better internal consistency and temporal stability than convergent validity.
Aspect of a disorder or phenomenon	An analog behavioral observation measure of obsessive-compulsive disorder may be more valid and clinically useful for measuring a client's actions than his or her thoughts. A questionnaire measure of generalized anxiety may be more valid for measuring the cognitive than the overt behavioral components of anxiety.
Severity of a disorder	A hospital staff behavior rating of verbal aggression may be more valid for extreme than for milder forms of aggression. A questionnaire measure of anxiety may be more valid for low and moderate than for high levels of anxiety (i.e., the questionnaire may exhibit a ceiling effect).
Setting in which assessment occurs	An ambulatory measure of eating and exercise (such as with a handheld computer) may be more useful in home than in work settings. An observation measure of parent-child interaction in the home may be more likely to identify clinically useful parent-child interactions during dinnertime than right after school.

TABLE 7.1 (continued)   Aspects of the Conditional Nature of Reliability, Validity, and Utility of Clinical Assessment Measures

Aspect	Examples
Goals of assessment and inferences to be derived from the measures	A structured clinical interview for schizophrenia may be more valid and useful for diagnosis than for treatment planning. A self-monitoring measure of social interactions may be more useful for clinical case formulation and treatment outcome evaluation than for diagnosis.
Temporal aspects of validity evaluation	The convergent validity of a measure of couple problem-solving skills may be different depending on whether concurrent or future measures of couple satisfaction are used for comparison. The predictive validity of a self-report measure of self-injurious thoughts may be different depending on the time frame of measurement.
Measures that are derived from an assessment instrument	With assessment instruments that provide multiple measures (such as the MMPI, Conflict Tactics Scale, Marital Interaction Coding System, Rorschach Inkblot Test), the measures can differ in their reliability, validity, and clinical utility.
How an assessment instrument is scored	Measures from a multi-item questionnaire of quality of life might vary in their clinical utility and validity depending on which factors or scales were used to derive the measures. Items from a questionnaire measure of depressed mood can be weighted in different ways to provide different measures of the same construct, which can differ in their psychometric properties.
Temporal focus and aspects of assessment	A clinic-based observation of parent-child interactions may be more useful for identifying important immediate response contingencies that maintain a child's oppositional behavior than for identifying less-immediate or delayed-response contingencies. A self-monitoring measure of life stressors and their effects on a client may provide different indices of functional relations depending on how often during a day or week responses are recorded.
The context of assessment	The validity of a computerized measure of working memory might vary depending on the amount of time the respondent has spent in the testing situation prior to testing. The validity of responses to an interview query about domestic violence may depend on whether the perpetrator is present.

is possible that, compared to other instruments, our new assessment instrument to measure manic episodes could provide more sensitive-to-change and content-valid measures of cognitive aspects of manic episodes (e.g., elevated self-esteem and ideas of grandiosity) but less-valid and less-sensitive measures of behavioral aspects of manic episodes (e.g., increased talkativeness and involvement in pleasurable activities).

In Table 7.1 and the following sections of this chapter, we consider more closely several aspects of the conditional nature of reliability and validity. First, we present a psychometric context for evaluating some aspects of the conditional and dynamic nature of psychometric attributes: measurement equivalence and measurement invariance.

MEASUREMENT EQUIVALENCE AND INVARIANCE AS CONTEXTS FOR CONSIDERING THE CONDITIONAL NATURE OF PSYCHOMETRIC ATTRIBUTES

The conditional nature of psychometric evidence invokes two inter-related psychometric concepts: *measurement equivalence* and *measurement invariance*. Measurement equivalence and invariance (these two terms are often used interchangeably) most often refer to the degree of congruence between measures from the same instrument derived from different groups, assessment contexts, methods, or strategies (see Glossary). In reference to data obtained from different ethnic or cultural groups, for example, equivalence is the degree to which a measure derived from culturally different groups shares a common meaning and relevance (Chin & Kameoka, 2006).

In clinical assessment, measurement equivalence and measurement invariance encompass both the construct that is measured and the measures of the construct (Knight, Roosa, & Umaña-Taylor, 2009). For example, does a score of 15 on a depression inventory mean the same thing for clients from Cairo, Chicago, and Hong Kong? Or, considering within-country and -region variance, does this score mean the same thing for clients from the United States or Canada or persons of Mexican, Japanese, and northern European descent? Are the meanings of *depression*, of the individual items in the questionnaire (does the term *sad* have the same meaning across these groups?), and of a particular score from a depression questionnaire similar for persons from these different groups? Going further, should the same cutoff scores be used for diagnosis and screening, and are all of the items on the scale relevant across these three groups?

The concepts of measurement equivalence and invariance address important issues when researchers want to compare groups because comparisons can only be made if measures are equivalent (see our brief discussion of etic and emic research strategies in this chapter). A measure must have the same meaning in the groups if we wish to compare groups on that measure.

These concepts are also important in clinical assessment with individual clients because the clinician must understand what a measure means for a person in a given assessment context. Does the score of 15 on the depression inventory for a client mean the same thing as suggested by the normative data on that instrument? How does that score compare with the scores of others from the same population? Does that score reflect the expressions of depression that are characteristics of the client's culture? Does the meaning of the measure change if the client is measured in a different assessment context (for example, in an outpatient mental health clinic vs. an inpatient psychiatric setting), if the client was in a different physiological or emotional state, or if the client was from a cultural group that differs from that used in the development and validation of a measure? These are important considerations because the meaning of a measure affects the validity of the clinician's inferences about a client's diagnosis, treatment effects, and case formulation.

Evaluation of Measurement Equivalence and Invariance

There are several ways to evaluate measurement equivalence and invariance. For multi-item questionnaires, multigroup confirmatory factor analysis (CFA; see Chapter 6) can be used. Equivalence is indicated by the degree to which the factor structures from the compared groups are similar. Are similar factors found in the groups (or are similar factors found across assessment contexts or settings?)? Does the number of factors obtained differ between groups? Are the same items associated with the same latent factors in each group? Are there significant differences in item loadings? This aspect of measurement equivalence is sometimes called factorial or configural invariance (for an example, see Nair, White, Knight, & Roosa, 2009).

Differences between groups in the factor structure and factor loadings for an assessment instrument suggest between-group differences in the meaning of the latent factor or in the indicators (i.e., items, in the case of a questionnaire) that are supposed to measure that factor. Similarities in meaning and markers of a construct, which are often reflected in the items of a questionnaire, are referred to as *conceptual* or *functional equivalence.* Differences between groups in the factor structure of our depression measure could mean that the concept of depression differs across the two groups. It could also mean that the indicators for the construct are different—that people from the two groups act, feel, or think in different ways when they are depressed. The degree to which the same set of behaviors is used and combined to generate meaning for a construct is sometimes referred to as *operational equivalence.*

A common practice in multicultural psychological assessment is simply to translate an instrument developed in one culture into a different language and apply it in the second culture. The problem is that this approach imports a construct from one culture to another without examining the degree to which the construct is defined in a similar manner in the new culture. In effect, the content validity of the instrument may be diminished when applied in a different culture. Higher-level (i.e., more heterogeneous, multifaceted) constructs such as depression, anxiety, schizophrenia, assertion, and marital satisfaction are especially likely to have different meanings across cultures. Further complicating this approach to multicultural assessment, the meaning of items can change with their translations. Nair et al. (2009) emphasized this point when they noted that careful translation of an instrument does not ensure that the translated version measures the same construct in the same way as the original version.[*] Finding support for measurement equivalence through CFA procedures, and through other reliability comparative evaluations such as test-retest stability and internal consistency, is necessary to establish the meaning of a measure used in clinical assessment. Failure to find a satisfactory degree of measurement equivalence indicates that the clinician should be cautious in drawing inferences about a client from the obtained measures (see our discussion of multimethod and multisource assessment in Chapter 9).

However, finding measurement equivalence through standard psychometric comparison is insufficient to assert that a measure is equivalent across groups (see discussion by Bingenheimer, Raudenbush, Leventhal, & Brooks-Gunn, 2005, and the example provided by Warren et al., 2008). CFA and all reliability evaluation procedures only examine patterns of covariance among items, not whether the instrument includes markers for important elements of a construct in a different group. The meanings and interrelations of the items included in the instrument might overlap in two cultures, but there might also be important aspects of the construct in the other culture that are not tapped by the instrument. In content validity terms, we would say that the items are relevant, but the instrument is insufficiently representative in the other culture.

Van de Vijver and Tanaka-Matsumi (2007) discussed the challenges of adapting a cognitive test to different cultures. The authors examined the application of the second edition of the Kaufman Assessment Battery for Children (KABC-II) with children of low socioeconomic status (SES) in Bangalore, India. The authors found that to strengthen the reliability of the KABC-II for the sample in India, changes were needed in the wording of the items, instructions for the application of the subtests, and the order in which items were presented. A straight translation into the Kannada language would have resulted in significant nonequivalence. Chen (2008) provided another example of a "feeling

---

[*] Fernandez, Boccaccini, and Noland (2007) recommended four steps in selecting translated tests: (a) review catalogues and Web sites of test publishing companies to identify the set of translated tests; (b) examine the psychometric evidence for the translated test (not just evidence for the test in its original language); (c) consider the relevance of the samples used for psychometric evidence for the client (e.g., are data from samples from Spain relevant to recent immigrants from South America?); (d) evaluate the strength of the psychometric evidence to determine the degree to which the test is appropriate and useful in the assessment context.

blue" item on a depression questionnaire. Chen noted that such an item would be interpreted differently by Chinese and American respondents (one recommendation is that cross-cultural assessment never should try to import metaphors, such as "blue").

Nonequivalence can also occur when an assessment instrument is adapted across relatively similar cultures. For example, norms for frequently used measures of intelligence and cognitive functioning can differ for children from the United States, Canada, Australia, and other predominantly English-speaking countries (for an example of equivalence testing of a child behavior checklist across dimensions of language, ethnicity, and economic status, see Gross et al., 2006).

The consequence of between-group differences in the way an item is interpreted could yield differences in scale scores, correlations between the item and convergent measures, factor loadings, and test-retest reliabilities. Ultimately, those differences affect the validity of inferences drawn by the clinician, such as judgments about the specific aspects of a client's behavior problems and treatment goals, clinical case formulation, how well an intervention is working, and the specific effects of an intervention.

As another example, Bingenheimer et al. (2005) discussed group differences in the meaning of the construct "authoritarian parenting," used frequently in studies of family functioning in the United States. Citing other sources, they noted that this construct might not be useful in evaluating the child-rearing styles of Chinese parents. Instead, concepts such as *chiao shun* ("training") and *guan* ("governing," "loving") may demonstrate higher levels of validity and clinical utility. Note how a measure such as authoritarian parenting could perform well in multicultural CFA studies (i.e., could show equivalence in factor structure across cultures) yet omit markers of constructs such as governing and loving that are clinically useful in different groups.

Scalar equivalence is also an important consideration in interpreting measures from different groups. Scalar equivalence poses the question: Do the same numbers from different groups mean the same thing? Groups can differ in their tendencies to overreport or underreport, which affects the meaning of a measure. Chen (2008) noted that Chinese respondents tend to mark toward the middle of scales, whereas North American respondents tend to mark more often at either extreme. He also noted that Chinese respondents might be more strongly influenced by social desirability. In such a case, note how a 4 on a 5-point scale of depressed mood, relationship satisfaction, or substance use could have a different meaning for a Chinese than a North American respondent (i.e., in this example, a 4 would probably represent a more extreme score, based on standard deviations, for the Chinese respondent).

Item response theory (IRT) can also be used to examine equivalence. Within an IRT framework (see Chapters 1 and 2), equivalence is the degree to which the item parameters hold across groups. In between-group comparisons, IRT statistics examines the degree to which item responses are related to the target construct, equivalently, for different groups. *Differential item functioning* suggests measurement nonequivalence. See the work of Bingenheimer et al. (2005) and Gorin and Embretson (2008) for extended discussions of IRT and equivalence.[*]

These examples point to the need for careful scale development and transposition of instruments and constructs from one culture to another (for an example of these procedures, also see Malda et al., 2008). These findings also point to the need for multimethod convergent validation within and across cultures to evaluate measurement equivalence. Assuming satisfactory cross-group factor structure or the development of a new instrument in the second culture or assessment context, is the measure related to important criteria in the same manner? When an existing instrument is applied to a different group or in a different context, are there differences between groups or contexts in the positive predictive power, negative predictive power, reliability, or criterion-related validity of the measure?

In summary, the concepts of measurement equivalence and measurement invariance are fundamental to our emphasis on the conditional nature of psychometric evidence in clinical assessment. Several recommendations for clinical assessment follow from this discussion:

1. Be cautious in drawing clinical judgments from measures derived from assessment instruments that have only been translated for use with persons within a culture different from that used for the original instrument development.
2. Consider if measures from an instrument have been shown to be valid for persons with your client's characteristics and administered in this assessment context.
3. Consider if published norms and validity studies are relevant for this person and this assessment context.
4. Look for evidence of validity and utility in addition to factorial invariance and reliability.
5. Use multimethod and multimeasurement assessment strategies (see Chapter 9) to reduce the measurement and judgment errors associated with an assessment instrument applied in a new assessment context.

This section reviewed the concepts of measurement equivalence and invariance, focusing on the differences between cultures in the meaning of measures. In the following sections, we discuss other factors associated with the conditional nature of psychometric indices.

---

[*] Within IRT measurement models, equivalence can also refer to the process of equating different measures of the same construct (e.g., what would a score on the Center for Epidemiological Studies-Depression [CES-D] be equivalent to on the Beck Depression Inventory II [BDI-II]?).

ASPECTS OF THE CONDITIONAL NATURE OF RELIABILITY, VALIDITY, AND UTILITY OF MEASURES FROM AN ASSESSMENT INSTRUMENT

Table 7.1 summarizes some of the factors that are associated with the conditional nature of validity and utility of a measure. We discuss several of these in more detail in the following sections.

Sources of Variance in Psychometric Evidence

As a Function of Population, Client Diagnostic Status and State, and Individual Differences

As mentioned in this chapter, a clinical assessment instrument may provide data that are more valid and useful for some populations than for others. Many studies have noted that patterns of social interactions, beliefs, attitudes, traditions, family and couple relations, values, physical activities, and the meanings, characteristics, and causes of behavior problems can vary as a function of dimensions of individual differences, such as age, sex, religious affiliation, SES, and ethnicity.

Individual differences associated with culture and ethnicity have been discussed in articles by Chin and Kameoka (2006), Tanaka-Matsumi (2004), and many others. This extensive research literature has included emic strategies, which focus on aspects of behavior within a culture, etic strategies, which focus on aspects of behavior across cultures, and more recently the integration of these two strategies (Draguns & Tanaka-Matsumi, 2003).

Another important finding from the literature on individual differences in psychological assessment is that the validity and utility of measures can vary as a function of the clinical status of clients. For example, Bellack, Mueser, Gingerich, and Agresta (1997) discussed differences as a function of recency of symptom onset in the validity and utility of analog behavioral observations (ABOs) of the social skills of patients diagnosed with schizophrenia. These authors suggested that brief assessments are less useful with patients with recent-onset symptoms than with patients who have been experiencing symptoms for longer periods. Patients with recent-onset symptoms often have more difficulty staying on task during the assessment and sustaining social interactions sufficiently to allow the collection of useful data. In this case, inferences about the validity and utility of analog measures of social skills for patients with a schizophrenia diagnosis depend on the clinical status of the patient.

As we noted in Chapters 2 and 3, the reliability and validity of a measure can differ as a function of the diagnostic status of the person, such as whether a client presents with multiple behavior problems. For example, in a meta-analysis of 90 studies on depression that used the Beck Depression Inventory (BDI), Yin and Fan (2000) reported significantly lower reliability estimates for samples of adults who were "substance addicts" compared to other samples (the authors suggested that this may be due to a restricted range of scores associated with the substance-abusing samples).

Haynes and Yoshioka (2007) discussed the conditional validity and utility of ambulatory biosensor measures. For example, Terbizan, Dolezal, and Albano (2002) examined the accuracy of measures from seven commercially available heart rate monitors that had been frequently used in exercise programs. The authors compared heart rate measures from the monitors with measures from standardized chest electrocardiographic (ECG) electrodes during rest and increasing levels of treadmill exercise. Four of the monitors were reasonably accurate during rest (average correlation .92 between the monitor and criterion measures). However, the reliability and validity correlations decreased as exercise levels increased (e.g., correlations of −.26, .23, .38, .64 for four of the monitors during strenuous exercise).

In summary, modern research on behavior disorders, culture, personality, and other dimensions of individual difference indicates that there are both universally applicable (e.g., the personality trait concept of "extraversion") and population-specific aspects of behavior and behavior problems (Smith, Spillane, & Annus, 2006). The implication for clinical assessment is that the reliability, validity, and utility of a measure can vary depending on the characteristics of the population. In selecting and interpreting measures, the clinician should consider the degree to which the measure has been shown to be valid with subjects who resemble the client.

As a Function of Disorder Severity

An important consideration in evaluating the psychometric evidence for a measure from clinical assessment instruments is its validity across the range of behavior problem severities or, more specifically in a clinical assessment context, whether the measure captures the phenomenon across the range of severities most important for the assessment context. Stated differently, does a measure discriminate among persons who differ across a range of the measured phenomenon, and is it sensitive to all expected changes across time in severity in the phenomenon for a patient? A measure that accurately tracks changes in the target phenomenon is said to exhibit a *monotonic functional relation* with changes in the target phenomenon.

Consider a measure of generalized anxiety that accurately reflects changes in a client's symptoms within the severe and moderate range but not within the mild range. The effect on clinical assessment inferences would be that, at low levels of severity, true changes in anxiety symptoms would not be reflected in changes in the measure. That is, at low levels of symptom severity the measure would provide misleading indicators of treatment effects, of factors associated with change, or of relapse likelihood. This *floor effect* of a measure is an important consideration because it could impair our ability to detect some treatment-related changes and to identify the triggers and maintaining factors for some generalized anxiety disorder (GAD) symptoms. Also, residual symptoms following successful treatment have been found in some studies to predict the likelihood of, and latency to, relapse (for example, see Fava, 2006).

There are several ways to examine the validity of a measure across levels of severity of a construct. For example, Santor et al. (2008) reviewed the extensive history of problems, and the multiple modifications, in the Hamilton Rating Scale for Depression (HRSD). The authors reviewed the evidence showing that some items were better than other items at discriminating among persons who differed in their severity of depression. They then used individual item response curves to select from the 17 items of the HRSD those that best discriminated among individuals across different degrees of depressive severity.[*] Santor et al. evaluated the performance of individual items on the basis of a response characteristic curve, a curve that reflects the probability that, across the range of depressive severities, a respondent will endorse a response option (by means of measuring the area under the curve, or AUC).[†] The authors then examined the incremental convergent validity and sensitivity to change of the new, shorter measure (the HRSD-6) compared to other measures of depression, on a sample of about 1,000 patients who were receiving either drug or placebo interventions for depression. They found that the six items selected on the basis of their item response curves were incrementally better than the comparison measures at detecting change in depressed mood across the range of depressive severities—a nice illustration that the validity of a measure can be enhanced when underperforming items from the instrument are removed.

Another strategy, exemplified by the work of Takegami et al. (2009), is to compare the *receiver operating characteristics (ROCs)* (see Text Box 7.1) of a measure at different levels of severity of the measured construct. Takegami and his coauthors examined the degree to which a four-item (body mass index, sex, blood pressure, and snoring) questionnaire could identify persons with sleep-disordered breathing (e.g., sleep apnea) within clinic and community-based samples.

---

[*] In also examining a maximum likelihood analytic strategy for item selection, the authors retained all 17 items in the HRSD but, using maximum likelihood estimates, constructed an optimal depressive severity score that weighted highly discriminating items more heavily than poorly discriminating items.

[†] Examples of AUC and receiver operating characteristic (ROC), applied for diagnostic purposes can be seen at: http://www.mlahanas.de/MOEA/Med/ROC21.htm. A Web-based software program for calculating ROC and AUC is available from John Eng at Johns Hopkins University at http://www.rad.jhmi.edu/jeng/javarad/roc/JROCFITi.html

---

**TEXT BOX 7.1   RECEIVER OPERATING
CHARACTERISTICS**

Receiver operating characteristics (ROCs) can be used to evaluate the performance of a measure (usually in terms of predictive accuracy with a dichotomous criterion such as medical or psychiatric diagnosis) across a range of cut scores. True positive rates are plotted against true negative rates (1 – Sensitivity) for the difference score to obtain an ROC curve. ROC curves can range from .5 (the discriminative validity of the measure that is not different from chance) to 1.0 (perfect discrimination between categories or populations).

The AUC provides an estimate of the overall predictive efficacy of the measure. AUCs can be used to compare different instruments used to measure the same phenomenon, to compare the efficacy of one measure applied to different groups or clinical populations, or to compare the efficacy of one measure applied with persons who differ in the severity of a disorder (such as persons with a formal diagnosis of GAD compared to those with "subclinical" symptomology). Essentially, ROC strategies can be used to address the relative predictive efficacy of a measure across multiple dimensions of interest.

With a sample of several hundred Japanese participants, Takegami et al. (2009) found that a measure based on these four items provided good diagnostic accuracy (AUC = .9) across the range of breathing problem severities (sensitivity was .93, and specificity was .66, using a cut score of 11). Recalling our previous discussion of incremental validity, the authors found that these four simple measures, commonly obtained in most medical settings, performed as well as more complex measures in identifying patients with sleep-related breathing difficulties, especially in the moderate-to-severe difficulty range.

In sum, validity evidence for a measure can vary as a function of severity of the measured phenomenon. In selecting and interpreting measures in clinical assessment, the clinician must consider the degree to which the psychometric evidence for the measure pertains to the level of severity characteristic of clients in the assessment context and the level of severity that might be associated with treatment effects.

As a Function of the Psychometric Dimension Used for Evaluation

An important goal of a functional approach to clinical assessment is to consider which dimension of psychometric evaluation is most relevant for the intended use of the measure. For example, if a measure were going to be used for brief screening or diagnostic purposes, the *positive predictive power* of the measure would be an especially important dimension of psychometric evaluation. Alternatively, if a measure is going to be used to document changes in symptoms in response to treatment, *content validity* and *precision* (i.e., validity and sensitivity to change) would be especially important dimensions of evaluation. These examples highlight the conditional importance of various dimensions of psychometric evidence.

Closely associated with the concept of the conditional importance of various psychometric dimensions is the idea that the psychometric support for a measure can differ across evaluative dimensions. A measure can vary in its degree of empirical support depending on which dimensions of validity, reliability, and utility are considered. As noted, a self-report measure of social anxiety in children may demonstrate excellent internal consistency and temporal stability and concurrently demonstrate low levels of content and predictive validity.

Contributors to a book on evidence-based approaches to clinical assessment by Hunsley and Mash (2008b) provided many examples of the conditional nature of empirical support for clinical assessment measures across dimensions of psychometric evaluation. The chapters in the work of Hunsley and Mash (2008b) review the psychometric evidence for clinical assessment measures used in 25 behavior disorders, such as alcohol use; chronic pain; obsessive-compulsive disorder (OCD); depression in children, adolescents, and adults; bipolar disorders; GAD; couple distress; and others. For each of the disorders, and within the context of the purpose of the measure (such as brief screening, diagnosis, case formulation, treatment outcome evaluation), measures from frequently used assessment instruments were evaluated on multiple psychometric dimensions, including internal consistency, interrater reliability, test-retest reliability, content validity, construct validity, treatment sensitivity, validity generalization (the applicability of a measure across different groups or assessment contexts), and clinical utility.

All chapters in the book by Hunsley and Mash support our main point: A measure can perform well on some psychometric dimensions and less well on others. Examples include (a) for monitoring treatment outcome with child and adolescent depression, the Kiddie Schedule for Affective Disorders and Schizophrenia (K-SADS) was rated as excellent on the dimension of treatment sensitivity but only adequate on test-retest reliability (Dougherty, Klein, Olino, & Laptook, 2008); (b) for monitoring treatment outcome with panic and agoraphobia, the Anxiety Sensitivity Index was rated as excellent on validity generalization but only adequate on content validity (Keller & Craske, 2008); and (c) for aiding in case formulation, the Trauma-Related Events Questionnaire was rated as excellent for validity generalization, but only adequate for clinical utility (Keane, Silberbogen, & Seierich, 2008).

Hunsley and Mash's book (2008b) and many other books and articles (e.g., see Wiley's four-volume series on *Psychological Assessment* [Hersen, 2004] and Butcher, 2009) also emphasize how the most important dimensions of psychometric evidence for a measure can vary depending on the purpose of assessment. For example, Haynes (2001) noted in a discussion of ABO that if the goal of an assessment occasion is to estimate a psychiatric patient's social skills (for example, to see if social skills training might be helpful), the degree to which measures of the rate of positive and negative social behaviors observed in the ABO correlate with the rate of those behaviors at home (generalizability across settings or ecological validity of behavior rate) may not be an important indicator of validity or utility of the analog measures. For this assessment purpose, the ABO may be more useful as a measure of social *skills* rather than typical social *performance* of the patient (which is also important, but a different aspect of social skills). Consequently, in this case, temporal stability and covariance with other measures of social skill (rather than performance) would be especially important evaluative dimensions to consider.

As a Function of Assessment Purpose

The chapters in the book by Hunsley and Mash (2008b) illustrate another aspect of the conditional nature of psychometric evidence: Psychometric evidence for a measure may not generalize across purposes of assessment. For example, based on psychometric evidence: (a) the Anxiety Disorders Interview Schedule (of the *Diagnostic and Statistical Manual of Mental Disorders, Fourth Edition* [*DSM-IV*], American Psychiatric Association, 2000) was highly recommended for diagnosis but not for treatment planning in the assessment of phobias (Rowa, McCabe, & Antony, 2008); (b) the Diagnostic Interview for Personality Disorders was highly recommended for diagnosis but not for treatment planning in the assessment of personality disorders (Widiger, 2008); and (c) the Positive and Negative Syndrome scale was highly recommended for case conceptualization but not for diagnosis in the assessment of schizophrenia (Mueser & Glynn, 2008).

As a Function of the Aspect of the Measured Phenomenon

Different measures of the same phenomenon can vary in the degree to which they provide reliable and valid measures of the various aspects of the phenomenon. Most constructs measured in clinical assessment are complex and have multiple facets. Consider the multiple aspects of anger and aggression (e.g., verbal aggression, throwing objects, severe physical aggression, psychophysiological and emotional responses, cognitive aspects) and social assertion skills (e.g., initiating conversations with strangers, social anxiety and avoidance, appropriately refusing unreasonable requests, emotional responses during social interactions).

An assessment instrument may provide a valid measure of some but not other aspects and response modes of a phenomenon. For example, one measure of depression can more validly reflect the cognitive aspects of depression (e.g., negative thoughts about oneself) than of the activity aspects of depression (e.g., a reduction in motor activity), whereas another measure can more validly reflect somatic aspects of depression (such as fatigue and sleeping). Similarly, one ABO instrument, compared to another, may provide more valid indices of subjective distress and social skill and less-valid indices of psychophysiological aspects of social anxiety. As another example, Turk and Melzack, in their 2001 book on pain measurement, noted how different assessment instruments and strategies focus on different aspects of pain, such as self-reports of pain intensity, functional impairment and performance of daily activities by pain patients, pain-related facial and postural movements, expectations by pain patients about their capabilities, psychophysiological correlates of pain reports, motivational aspects of pain, and pain-related thoughts and beliefs.

SUMMARY AND RECOMMENDATIONS AND THE DYNAMIC CHARACTERISTICS OF PSYCHOMETRIC EVIDENCE

Measurement considerations outlined in Table 7.1 emphasize our main point: Inferences about the psychometric characteristics of measures obtained from a clinical assessment instrument are always conditional. Psychometric support for a measure can vary with sample composition used for evaluation, the purpose of assessment, the psychometric dimension considered, and many other aspects. Thus, underscoring the message in previous chapters, psychometric characteristics do not "reside" with an instrument or with scores from that instrument.

In summarizing, we make one more point, about the dynamic nature of psychometric evidence: The validity of a measure can erode over time, and past validity indices, even when their conditional nature is appropriately considered, may not be generalizable to contemporaneous applications of the instrument. The primary threat to the temporal generalizability of psychometric evidence is our growing, science-based understanding of the phenomena they measure. Consider the evolution of our understanding of the nature and causal factors associated with couple distress, childhood depression, antisocial behavior, and posttraumatic stress disorder (PTSD). For example, modern concepts of couple distress (Snyder, Heyman, & Haynes, 2008) now include paralinguistic, emotional, values, and psychophysiological aspects that were not part of the couple distress construct several decades ago. Assessment instruments constructed prior to a more sophisticated understanding of a phenomenon are likely to contain some elements that are irrelevant to the phenomenon and to omit elements that are relevant (i.e., to demonstrate decreased content validity over time).

There are several implications for clinical assessment associated with the conditional and dynamic nature of psychometric evidence. First, unconditional assumptions and statements regarding the validity and reliability of an instrument are unwarranted. As editor of *Psychological Assessment* from 1997 to 2003, one of us (S.H.) evaluated the content of about 2,000 manuscripts submitted for publication. To support their use of a particular assessment instrument, about 75% of empirically based submissions included unconditional statements of their validity such as "Measure A has been shown in previous research to be a reliable and valid measure of Construct A." These statements failed to acknowledge the variability of psychological evidence across the many aspects reviewed in this chapter.

Second, and perhaps most obvious, is the mandate that clinicians carefully consider the degree to which the psychometric evidence associated with a potential assessment instrument is congruent with the context of the assessment occasion. Does the instrument provide data that are likely to be valid for this client, for this assessment purpose, in this assessment context?

Third, given that appropriately conditional psychometric evidence will not always be available, the clinician should be cautious when drawing inferences from the measures they use. The clinician should consider that the measure might reflect sources of measurement and judgment error and approach the assessment task cautiously within a problem-solving framework. Perhaps the most useful assessment strategy is to include multiple methods, instruments, and sources to reduce judgment errors that can result from placing too much emphasis on one measure in making clinical judgments.

Fourth, the conditional nature of psychometric evidence suggests that the validity and utility of clinical judgments can be strengthened by an assessment strategy that includes multiple methods of assessment, in multiple contexts, using multiple sources of information. The benefits and limitations of multimethod assessment are discussed in Chapter 9.

RECOMMENDED SOURCES

Measurement Models in Psychological Assessment

Gorin, J. S., & Embretson, S. E. (2008). Item response theory and Rasch models. In D. McKay (Ed.), *Handbook of research methods in abnormal and clinical psychology* (pp. 271–292). Los Angeles: Sage.

The Conditional Nature of Psychometric Evidence

Hunsley, J., & Mash, E. J. (Eds.). (2008). *A guide to assessments that work*. New York: Oxford University Press.

8

How to Evaluate Commonly Used Statistical Methods in Clinical Assessment Research

INTRODUCTION

In Chapter 6, we introduced you to factor analysis, in part to prepare you to read research reports using factor analysis to examine psychometric evidence for a measure with an informed and critical eye. We devoted a chapter to that statistical technique because it is used so frequently and because identification of patterns of covariation in clinical phenomena is a central concern for clinical scientists and practitioners. In this chapter, we continue with the same theme by describing a series of statistical procedures that are used as part of the construct validation process.

Two of the central assessment tasks you face as clinicians are to select the best available measures to use for each assessment occasion and to evaluate the results of clinical assessments accurately. To do so, you must be able to critically evaluate published research regarding the psychometric evidence for multiple alternative measures of constructs. The aim of this chapter is to provide some of the tools necessary for this task. Of course, this task can be overwhelming; fortunately, for many disorders, measures, and assessment contexts, others have evaluated the research critically for the field (e.g., Hunsley & Mash, 2008b).

Nonetheless, because the validation process is ongoing and because new assessment challenges, along with new tools, become available all the time, you will often need to evaluate measures yourself.

An accurate understanding of statistical procedures enables good judgments regarding when to place confidence in a set of findings, when to remain skeptical of findings, and how to understand both the strengths and limitations of empirical reports. As we hope you have come to appreciate as you read this book, construct validation and theory testing are ongoing and interrelated enterprises characterized by uncertainty and incompletely answered questions. For you to use the empirical literature to guide practice, it is important to bring an appropriate level of scientific skepticism to what you read, and that you read the literature in an active way (i.e., you make judgments concerning the validity, relevance, and generalizability of reported findings as you read).

First, we discuss how to determine whether an empirical effect is present and of sufficient magnitude to be important. Typically, it is crucial for the assessment process to know the magnitude of predictive effects for measures. You will use that knowledge both to choose the best instruments for your purpose and to decide how much confidence to place in the inferences to be drawn from assessment results. We then consider statistical procedures commonly used to address different facets of the validation enterprise, such as convergent validity and discriminant validity.

STATISTICAL SIGNIFICANCE AND EFFECT SIZE

In most fields in psychology, the currently accepted practice is for researchers to report whether a given effect is statistically significant, along with an estimate of the magnitude of that effect. As you know, to report that a finding is statistically significant is to say that the probability that the particular finding, or one even more extreme or pronounced, occurred by chance is small. Because that probability is small, the researcher infers that the finding did not occur due to chance; that inference in turn strengthens confidence that the researcher's explanation of the nature of the nonchance effect may be valid. Almost all significance tests used in psychology rely on the null hypothesis of no effect; thus, when an effect is statistically significant, it is significantly different from zero or from no effect.

Of course, when you read empirical reports of clinical findings, you will often be interested not only in whether an effect is greater than zero but also how large and clinically meaningful it is. Questions such as, Does this treatment offer meaningfully better results than another treatment? How accurate would detection of high-risk children be using this risk factor measure? How much improvement does this intervention produce?, or How sensitive to treatment-related changes is a particular measure of depressed mood? are likely to be central to you. Answers to those questions provide empirical guidance for your clinical decision making. It is important to appreciate that statistical significance does not provide direct information on the magnitude of the effect; this is because statistical significance is a function of many variables, in particular the sample size of the study. Thus, the starting point for understanding how large or how meaningful an effect is involves examination of reported effect sizes.

Variability in Psychological Phenomena, the Measures of those Phenomena, and the Meaning of Effect Size

Individuals vary from one another on psychological variables of interest to the clinician. With science-based measurement strategies, that variability is reflected in variability in scores on instruments assessing relevant variables. In essence, effect size statistics provide estimates of how much of the variability among participants can be explained by some effect of interest, such as a treatment effect or the relations between two variables. An effect size is also useful in within-person analyses, such as understanding how much variability in a person's level of pain can be explained by contextual variables (e.g., settings, interpersonal factors, mood).

One way to learn about common effect size estimates is to think in terms of two classic types of clinical research designs. The first is when a treatment group/experimental group is compared to a control group, and there is a need to understand the magnitude of the observed differences between the groups. To assess the magnitude of the experimental or treatment effect, one needs a standardized measure of the mean difference between the two groups. The second is when some criterion of clinical interest is wanted, such as level of psychopathology, likelihood of relapse for addictive behaviors, or marital distress. In this case, a standardized measure of how accurately one can predict (i.e., how accurately one can account for variability among people in the clinical criterion) is needed. Knowing that, for example, a measure of neuroticism significantly predicted subsequent martial adjustment, at the $p < .05$ level, tells little about the size of the relation between the two variables. If the data were taken from an epidemiological survey of tens of thousands of adults, even a small correlation would be statistically significant. If you wish to determine whether it will be clinically useful to obtain a measure of neuroticism as part of your pretreatment assessment for couple therapy, knowing the size of the effect is far more valuable. We next present the most common effect size indicators for each of these two cases.

An Effect Size Estimate for the Difference Between Two Groups

Imagine a clinical research study on a new treatment for depression that includes one group exposed to the new treatment and one control group for which no treatment was provided. At the end of the intervention, the researchers will compare the two groups with respect to their current depression levels. Within each group, there of course will be some variability in depression; not everyone will be the same. The variability in depression within each group is not due to exposure to treatment because everyone within a group was exposed to the same treatment (or the same absence of treatment). One can calculate indices of variability within each group, such as the standard deviation and variance; those values provide an estimate of how much variability there is among people independent of exposure to different treatments and due to errors in measurement.

One can also calculate how much variability there is between groups. If each group is represented with its mean depression score, there are three possible contributors to variability between those two means. The first is the typical differences between people: People exposed to different treatments are likely to vary from one another, just as the people exposed to the same treatment likely vary from one another in important ways that can affect the outcome of treatment. The second is error in research design (i.e., using nonequivalent groups for comparison) or error in measurement. The third possible contributor is the difference between the treatment group and the control group as an effect of the treatment. That is, one possible source of variation in the mean depression levels of the two groups is that the treatment had an impact on depression that was not provided by the no treatment control group. Of course, this source of variation is of most interest.

To evaluate the magnitude of the treatment effect, one must get an index of how much variability there is between the two groups in comparison to how much variability there is within each group (because the latter does not include the treatment effect). The variability between the two groups can be measured by the difference between the mean scores on depression for the two groups. The typical way to assess the variability within groups is to view the standard deviation within each group as an estimate of variability among people not due to treatment effects; most often, one then pools the within-group standard deviations from the two groups to get the best possible estimate of nontreatment variability. One can then compare the mean difference between groups to the nontreatment variability with a simple ratio, which is referred to as Cohen's d or just d (Cohen, 1969):

$$d_{12} = (m_1 - m_2)/s_{12} \qquad (8.1)$$

In this formula, m_1 refers to the posttreatment mean of the control group, and m_2 refers to the posttreatment mean of the treatment group, so the numerator is the difference between the two group means. The term s_{12} refers to the pooled within-group standard deviation. Thus, d reflects the difference between the two means in standard deviation form. For example, suppose s_{12} is 5.0, and $m_1 - m_2$ is 4.0 (the control group mean for depression was 4 points higher than the treatment group mean following the treatment). The value of d, then, is 4/5 = 0.80. This number indicates that the difference between the mean depression scores for the two groups is 0.8 standard deviations on the depression measure.

There are several advantages to the *d* statistic. First, it is easy to understand for anyone familiar with the concepts of means and standard deviations. Second, it is easy to compute even when it is not provided. Third, the statistic is already familiar to virtually all readers of empirical reports: It is a *z* score (i.e., a difference between two means in standard deviation score units).

Before moving on to an effect size estimate for prediction, we would like to mention one additional aspect of how the denominator of the *d* statistic is computed. It makes sense to pool the two within-group standard deviations when one has reason to believe that both are estimates of the population standard deviation on the dependent variable (depression in this case). There are occasions, though, when that may not be true. For example, it sometimes occurs that, following treatment, some people improve a lot, some improve a little, some stay the same, and some get worse. The result is that, after treatment, there is more variability on the dependent variable for the treatment group than for the control group. Under this circumstance, it makes more sense to use the control group standard deviation in the denominator for calculating *d* because it is the only available estimate of variability among persons not influenced by the treatment.

An Effect Size Estimate for Prediction and Correlation

In the preceding section, we discussed means for assessing effect sizes when comparing two groups to each other on a criterion variable. A second set of common clinical research designs involves cases in which both variables are interval scale variables. In this set of designs, clinical scientists typically want to know how strongly the two variables are related to each other. Often, the intent is to predict scores on a criterion of interest; other times, researchers simply seek to determine whether variability among people on some clinical variable is related to variability in another variable. Suppose a researcher wants to examine whether sensation seeking is related to frequency of illegal drug use. To put the researcher's question more precisely, there is a certain amount of variability among people in how frequently they use illegal drugs. How much of that variability is shared with variability in the same people on a measure of sensation seeking? Shared variability means that variability on drug use can be predicted from variability in sensation seeking. To some degree, perhaps, individuals who use drugs frequently tend to be higher than others in sensation seeking. Just as one can estimate variability due to treatment condition in the experimental study we just described, one can estimate what proportion of the overall variability in frequency of drug use is predictable from (or shared with, or overlapping with) variability in sensation seeking. That estimate can be used to predict drug use levels from sensation-seeking scores.

To provide this estimation, one begins with the correlation coefficient. As you know, a correlation coefficient that is statistically significantly greater than zero reflects the finding that individuals who tend to score higher than others on one variable will also tend to score higher than others on the other variable, and individuals who tend to score lower than others on the first variable will tend to score lower on the second variable (a negative correlation that is significantly different from zero indicates that individuals who tend to score high on one variable tend to score low on the other variable and so on). The most commonly used correlation, the Pearson product moment correlation, is standardized in terms of z scores (Cohen, Cohen, West, & Aiken, 2003). In theory, correlation values can range from 0 to 1.0 and from 0 to −1.0. To the degree that measures are not perfectly reliable, actual maximum correlations will be lower than that. Also, when the distributions of the two variables are not precisely the same (as when one is normal and the other is positively skewed), maximum correlations are again lower than 1.0.

If one found a correlation of $r = .30$ between the measures of sensation seeking and frequency of drug use, that value means that a person who scores one standard deviation higher than another in sensation seeking can be expected to score 0.30 standard deviations higher than the other person in a measure of the frequency of drug use. As you can see, the correlation coefficient provides a standardized estimate of the magnitude of the effect, again in standard deviation terms. There are many advantages to the correlation as an estimate of effect size. It is used in many different research contexts, it is commonly reported, it is standardized with respect to the same units as d, and it is readily comprehensible to readers of empirical reports.

Similarities and Differences Between r and d

As just noted, both r and d provide estimates of effect sizes in standard deviation units, and both provide an estimate of how much variability in one variable can be explained by another variable. In fact, in one set of circumstances, r and d can be translated into each other. One version of the correlation coefficient is the point-biserial coefficient, which is an extension of the Pearson correlation to the case in which one variable is measured on an interval scale and the other is dichotomous (Cohen et al., 2003). When that is the case, r provides the same information as does d: It tells how much variability in an interval scale variable is explained by group membership when there are two groups. Here are the formulae for calculating d from r and r from d:

$$d = \frac{r}{\sqrt{pq(1-r^2)}} \tag{8.2}$$

and

$$r = \frac{d}{\sqrt{d^2 + (1/pq)}} \qquad (8.3)$$

where p is the proportion in one group, and q is the proportion in the other group $(1 - p)$. These formulae are presented in numerous articles; we drew from the work of McGrath and Meyer (2006).

Although r and d provide the same information in the case of one dichotomous and one interval scale variable, there is an important way in which the two statistics differ. The d statistic is not influenced by the proportion of individuals that falls in each group, and the point biserial r (r_{pb}) statistic is influenced by group proportions. As you read empirical reports and judge effect sizes, it will be important to understand the impact of this difference between r and d so that you can draw accurate inferences from effect size reports.

Notice that in Formula 8.1, the formula for d, there is no term indicating the proportion of individuals in Group 1 versus Group 2. Therefore, the d statistic does not vary as a function of different proportions of individuals in the two groups. It provides an estimate of effect size that is independent of that factor.

Now, consider r_{pb}. It reflects the degree of variability in an interval scale variable (suppose anxiety) that is explained by variability in a dichotomous variable (suppose the dichotomous variable is sex). Imagine that your sample was all female. In that case, there is no variability on the dichotomous variable of sex, so variability on sex can explain no variance in the interval scale variable. If the sample is all female, the maximum point biserial correlation is 0.00. Next, imagine that your sample was 90% female and 10% male. Obviously, this is a little better in that now there is variability on sex that could conceivably explain variability in anxiety. But, as you can readily see, there is not much variability on sex: 90% of the participants have the same value on that variable (i.e., are women). Nunnally and Bernstein (1994) showed that if the interval scale variable were normally distributed, the maximum point biserial correlation would be .61 in this case. If your sample included 50% women and 50% men, you have the most variability you can have with a dichotomous variable. Thus, there is more variability available on sex, which could, conceivably, explain variability in anxiety. Again assuming a normal distribution for anxiety, the maximum correlation would be .79 (Nunnally & Bernstein, 1994).

As you can see, it makes sense that the maximum r_{pb} varies as a function of the proportion of individuals in each group because that proportion reflects how much variability is present and available to correlate with variability on the other variable. For that reason, actual r_{pb} values vary as a function of this proportion. Accordingly, r_{pb} provides an estimate of effect size that is, in part, a function of the proportion of individuals in each of the two groups. McGrath and Meyer (2006) provided a clear and thorough discussion of this issue.

Whether you want a proportion-dependent (r_{pb}) or proportion-independent (d) effect size estimate depends on your purpose. For many applied purposes, you might want to know how well a variable predicts membership in one of two groups, where the fact that different numbers of people tend to be in the two groups is a real and important clinical reality. If you have a measure of risk for schizophrenia that you are considering using as a general screening tool and the base rate of schizophrenia in your population is 1%, then to evaluate how well your screener works you need an effect size estimate that is sensitive to this extreme base rate situation. You would then test your screener in a population with an estimated 1% base rate of schizophrenia, and r_{pb} would provide you with direct information on how well you can predict schizophrenic status in your sample and hence in the population of interest. The r_{pb} can thus provide a contextually or ecologically valid indicator of the effectiveness of your screener (McGrath & Meyer, 2006).

There are other circumstances for which the base rate of a disorder in your sample is likely to be different from the base rate of the disorder in the population of interest to you clinically. Suppose you had access to the study we just mentioned, in which the base rate of schizophrenia was about 1%, but you hope to use the screening measure in a psychiatric setting, and you believe the base rate of schizophrenia in your setting is about 25%. The r_{pb} from the study would underestimate your ability to predict schizophrenic status in your population because it was based on a sample with less variability in schizophrenia than is present in your population. In such a case, you might prefer d as an estimate of effect size. Because the value of d is not a function of group proportions, it has been described as a more transportable effect size estimate (McGrath & Meyer, 2006). And of course, once you have d, you can estimate what r_{pb} would be in your setting using Formula 8.3.

Text Box 8.1 provides the means to derive r from other statistics that are commonly reported in lieu of r.

So far, we have focused on d and r because those are two of the most commonly reported effect size estimates, they can be easily calculated if they are not provided, and they are readily understood. We next briefly mention three other effect size estimates that are particularly relevant for clinical science because they are cast in terms of treatment success rates. One important task of clinical assessment is to evaluate the success of psychological treatments. Treatment evaluation influences subsequent clinical practice and thus can have a direct impact on the lives of individuals seeking the help of clinical psychologists. It is therefore crucial to measure treatment-based change reliably and validly. Errors in choosing treatments that stem from inadequate measurement of treatment outcomes can harm clients. It is of course the case that the effect size indicators we describe next depend, for their accuracy, on the reliability and validity of the outcome measures used.

TEXT BOX 8.1   WAYS TO DERIVE THE CORRELATION COEFFICIENT FROM OTHER STATISTICS

Rosenthal and Rubin (1982) provided, as have others, procedures for deriving r from statistics such as t, F, and χ^2. These derivations are easy to do:

Test Statistic Provided	Transformation to r
t	$\sqrt{(t^2/t^2 + df)}$
F	$\sqrt{F/F + df_{\text{error}}}$
χ^2	$\sqrt{X^2/N}$

For example, suppose you read a study comparing two groups to assess a treatment for anxiety (perhaps a treatment group and a control group). There are 25 participants per group, so the degrees of freedom are $n_1 + n_2 - 2$, or $25 + 25 - 2 + 48$, and the reported t value is 3.00. Then, $r = \sqrt{9/9 + 48} = \sqrt{9/57} = .40$.

For the moment, let us restrict ourselves to binary treatment outcomes (success/failure). The first of the three effect sizes is the success rate difference (SRD), which is simply the number of successes from the treatment minus the number of successes in the control condition ($S_T - S_C$). The second, closely related, index is the number needed to treat (NNT; Kraemer & Kupfer, 2005). NNT is defined as the number of clients one would expect to treat with a given treatment to have one more success (or one less failure) than if the same number were exposed to a control condition. It is calculated as NNT $= 1/S_T - S_C$ (Kraemer & Kupfer, 2005).

One major source of appeal in these two indices, particularly NNT, is that they have such direct relevance to clinical practice. Kraemer and Kupfer (2005) provided a table showing the values of SRD and NNT for a given value of d and the corresponding r_{pb} (when the group proportions are 50–50). To give you a quick feel for how d and r relate to NNT, they noted that a d of .50, which corresponds to $r_{pb} = .243$ (for a 50–50 group split), is associated with an NNT value of 3.62. Thus, for an effect of this magnitude on a dichotomous, success/failure treatment outcome, you would expect to see 3.6 clients to have one more success in the treatment group than in the control group. For a d value of 1.0, NNT $= 1.92$, you would need to see just fewer than 2 clients to see one improve more than the control condition. Kraemer and Kupfer (2005) show how SRD and NNT can be extended to cases for which the outcome is an interval scale score rather than success or failure.

The third effect size estimate is referred to as the area under the curve or AUC (see Text Box 7.1, p. 164). As noted in Chapter 7, the term is based on a graphical representation of this effect size. For our purpose, you should know that AUC equals the probability that a score (such as on an interval scale measure) drawn at random from one sample (such as the treatment sample) is higher (or lower) than a score drawn at random from another sample (such as the control sample; Rice & Harris, 2005). Suppose we want to know whether individual differences in psychopathy are associated with criminal recidivism (as measured by a second arrest). An AUC of .50 means that there is only a 50–50 chance that the psychopathy score of an arrested person was higher than the psychopathy score of someone not arrested. If that were the case, psychopathy would obviously not have been related to recidivism in our sample; such a finding might have important implications for the prediction of recidivism. Values greater than .50 reflect an increasing magnitude of association between the two variables. An AUC of 1.0 would mean that every arrested person had a higher psychopathy score than every nonarrested person. Kraemer and Kupfer (2005), among others, provided formulae for translating NNT or SRD to AUC values.

Small, Medium, and Large Effects

One of the most commonly used descriptions of effect sizes is that provided by Cohen (1969), who referred to values of d of .2, .5, and .8 as small, medium, and large effects. He translated those values to r_{pb} values, assuming a 50–50 group split, of .10, .24, and .37, respectively, and they were later translated to Pearson r values for correlations between two interval scale scores: Small $r = .10$, medium $r = .30$, and large $r = .50$ (Rice & Harris, 2005). These values have become somewhat reified in the literature, even though Cohen (1969) offered them as tentative guidelines. Rice and Harris (2005) provide an interesting discussion of the source of these values.

We do not think it is wise to routinely use the small, medium, and large descriptive terms in this way for two reasons. The first is that their use can imply a kind of official or empirical conclusion that a given effect is "truly" large, or "truly" small, when Cohen's terms were offered as loose rules of thumb. The second is that clinical scientists should interpret the magnitude of effect sizes in light of the nature of the criterion and the predictive task. For example, $r_{pb} = .10$ could be quite substantial and important if the dichotomous outcome from the treatment is death by suicide versus survival. However, a Pearson r of the same value is likely to be viewed as less substantial, and less important, if the criterion is degree of change on a depression scale. In short, effect sizes must be evaluated along several dimensions, including the importance of the criterion; a blanket conclusion that a given effect is small or large is likely to lack appreciation for the context and the nature of the clinical question.

Be Aware of Factors That Influence Effect Size Estimates

As you read empirical reports, you should also consider whether there are characteristics of the design, the sample, or the measures that would be likely either to exaggerate an effect size or to suppress an effect size. Throughout this book, we discuss many of the factors that can exaggerate or suppress apparent effects. Here, we mention a few of the most important ones briefly. One is shared method variance between a predictor and a criterion (often a problem with convergent validity research). When both the predictor and the criterion are assessed using the same method of assessment and there is evidence for method-based correlations between measures, the resulting association between the predictor and criterion could be larger than it really is in the population (see Chapters 3 and 9). For example, when asked in face-to-face interviews, perhaps people vary in how likely they are to admit (or deny) both past engagement in criminal acts and current substance use. If so, there will be shared variance between interview scores reflecting past criminal acts and interview scores reflecting current substance use that does not involve true shared variance between the two constructs.

The shared variance between the variables in such a study would thus include both the shared method variance and the shared substantive variance, with the result that the effect size overestimates the shared substantive variance. You should read empirical reports with this possibility in mind, and if there is reason to suspect shared method variance (e.g., all measures are derived from self-report questionnaires), you might consider the possibility that the true relations among variables are not as pronounced as it appeared in the study.

The composition of the sample in a study can influence the effect size, and if the sample makeup of the study is substantially different from your specific assessment occasion or the population you, as a clinician, are likely to encounter, you should be aware of the impact of the difference. For example, a validation study of an instrument designed to assess cognitive deficits from head injury might contrast a group of known head-injured individuals with a group of screened, normal, non-injured people. The assessment tool might provide measures with large *d* values, which indicate large differences between the two groups. The large effect sizes do, of course, speak to the validity of the measures. But if, in your clinical practice, you must differentiate between individuals with cognitive deficits due to head injuries and individuals with cognitive deficits due to psychopathology or age-related declines in cognitive abilities, you must appreciate that the success of the measure in achieving your task could be quite different (and quite less) than it was in differentiating head-injured patients from fully normal controls. This is another example of the conditional nature of psychometric evidence discussed in Chapter 7.

A common problem with many studies is that samples with restricted ranges and variability are used. Some samples, such as those comprised entirely of college students, could lead to underestimates of effect sizes because the degree of variation in symptomatology among students may be less than what exists in the population as a whole, resulting in less capacity to predict.

As we discussed in Chapter 2, with each drop in the reliability of a measure there is a drop in the possible correlation of the measure with other measures. Thus, if one's measure of a construct has only adequate internal consistency, say $\alpha = .70$, the magnitude of its possible measurable relation with another variable is lower than if the measure had the excellent internal consistency of $\alpha = .90$. If you observe a lower effect size for a measure with only adequate reliability, you just do not know whether that lower value truly reflects a smaller effect in the population or rather is an artifact of the imprecision of measurement. (Authors of research articles are not always aware of the effects of using instruments with low reliabilities. For that reason, you may find that a researcher interprets one effect size as meaningfully lower than another, not recognizing that the lower effect size was observed between measures with lower reliability and thus not appreciating that low reliability might have caused the apparent effect size difference. This possibility is another example of the need for you to read research reports carefully and in their entirety.)

One factor that may commonly suppress effect sizes is the use of overly brief assessment instruments. Many construct validation or theory-testing studies are multivariate. To measure all construct domains necessary for the study and do so in a reasonable span of time and without fatiguing participants, researchers often rely on brief measures. A research decision to do so may well be the best decision in a given circumstance, but as a reader of such a report you should be aware that a shorter measure may well (a) be less reliable than a longer measure, thus attenuating effect sizes, and (b) not represent the target construct as fully as a longer measure (i.e., have diminished *content validity*), which of course can also lead to an underestimate of the population effect size for the underlying construct. For example, a brief assessment of problem drinking that asks only the number of days per month in which one consumed five or more drinks (this number is defined as heavy drinking for men by the U.S. National Institutes of Health) could easily miss important variation on life problems from consumption and other aspects of drinking that are diagnostically important (e.g., the pattern of drinking, types of alcoholic drinks consumed, the context of drinking). Smith, McCarthy, and Anderson (2000) discussed considerations in the development and validation of brief assessment instruments.

STATISTICAL PROCEDURES: CONVERGENT AND DISCRIMINANT VALIDITY

As you recall from Chapters 1 and 3, in which we discussed construct validity, one builds evidence for the validity of a measure of a construct in part by showing that the measure (a) has associations with measures of other variables as predicted by theory, which we called convergent validity, and (b) fails to associate with measures of other constructs, that, by theory, it should be unrelated to, which we called discriminant validity. What we are going to do next is discuss some of the most common statistical techniques that are used to investigate the validity of theories and the measures of constructs within those theories. The concept of effect size is important in considering validity evidence.

Analysis of Variance and Analysis of Covariance

Often, some form of analysis of variance (ANOVA) is used in validation studies. Recall the basic logic of ANOVA from our discussion of treatment research: One gets an estimate of the variation among people not due to any treatment or manipulation effect (within-group variance), one gets an estimate of the variation among people that also includes variation due to the treatment/manipulation (between-group variance), and one compares the two. If the between-group variation, which includes normal variation among people plus variation introduced by a treatment/manipulation, is much larger than the within-group variation, which includes only normal variation among people (and error), then it may be wise to conclude that the treatment/manipulation was effective (i.e., it produced a significant effect on those persons exposed to it).

ANOVA can be used to investigate the presence of evidence for both convergent and discriminant validity in the same study. For example, Hohlstein, Smith, and Atlas (1998) examined the validity of a measure of the expectancy that eating helps one manage negative affect; that is, eating provides negative reinforcement in the form of relief from subjective distress. According to their theory, women with bulimia nervosa should endorse this expectancy more strongly than normal, control women. The authors also believed that their measure reflected a risk factor specific to eating rather than other disorders. Thus, the authors predicted that women in general psychiatric care would not endorse this expectancy measure more strongly than controls. The authors conducted an ANOVA, with the expectancy measure as the dependent variable, in which they compared three groups: women with bulimia nervosa, normal control women, and women undergoing psychiatric care for noneating disorders. If their theory was correct and the measure was a valid marker for eating expectancy, there should be convergent validity, in that bulimic women should have higher levels of the expectancy than normal control women. There should also be discriminant validity, in that endorsement of the expectancy should not be higher for women with a noneating disorder psychiatric diagnosis than for the control group of women. Using a 7-point measurement scale, they found that bulimic women averaged 5.52 on the expectancy measure, psychiatric control women averaged 2.12, and normal control women averaged 2.03. The *F* statistic indicated that the three groups differed significantly, and additional statistical analysis indicated that the psychiatric and control groups did not differ from each other (expectancy endorsement was unrelated to general psychiatric status), and both groups differed from the bulimic group (expectancy endorsement was related to bulimia nervosa diagnosis). The effect size for this last contrast was $r = .85$. Thus, in one simple ANOVA, Hohlstein and her colleagues (1998) were able to provide evidence speaking to both the convergent and the discriminant validity of their measure and of their theory.

When you read a report of this kind, there are some things for you to consider as you critically evaluate the validity evidence for a measure. As you know, every statistical procedure relies on assumptions, and one of your tasks is to check into whether the assumptions necessary for ANOVA were reasonably met. One assumption is that each score is independent of every other score. This assumption could be violated if some subset of participants in your sample was similar to each other in some way that could influence their responses on the expectancy measures. Suppose Hohlstein et al. (1998) recruited half of their control group from the church one of them attended (they did not do this, by the way). It is possible that members of that church are more likely to have characteristics in common with each other than would two members of the general population drawn at random. If their common characteristics influenced their eating expectancy levels, then their responses to the expectancy scale were not independent of each other (one person's score would be at least somewhat predictable from other people's scores). If this were true, the assumption of independent scores is violated. This problem is common in couples assessment because the scores of wives and husbands are not fully independent. To address it, couples researchers sometimes use only one score from a couple and view the sample size as half the number of participants when both are used.

In Text Box 8.1, we presented the hypothetical case in which the within-group standard deviation was 5.0 and the difference between two means was 4.0, leading to an estimate of the effect size $d = 4/5 = .80$. Now, suppose that we had violated independence of observations in that study, causing individuals within groups to be similar to each other, leading to a lower average within-group standard deviation of 4.0. Had that occurred, our estimate of the effect size would have been $4/4 = 1.0$. Although 1.0 would have been the accurate effect size for the study we did, the effect would have been due both to the treatment and to similarities between people that would presumably not be present in the actual treatment population. Thus, we would have misjudged the magnitude of the treatment effect in the typical context in which the treatment would be provided. As you read reports of effect sizes, consider whether the observed effect size could be due to something other than the variable of interest.

Another assumption that is made for the use of ANOVA in validity studies is that scores on the dependent variable are normally distributed within the population. In their study, Hohlstein et al. (1998) should have examined the distribution of scores on the eating expectancy measure within each of their three groups, and ideally, they should have reported evidence that the assumption was not violated (such as evidence that there was little skew in the data). Unfortunately, they say nothing about this assumption in their report. As a reader, you cannot know whether this occurred because (a) the authors never investigated it; (b) they did investigate it, the assumption was not violated, and either they or the reviewers of the paper decided not to use scarce journal space to mention it; or (c) they did investigate it, the assumption was violated, and they wanted to hide that fact. As we are implying, the inferences that you, as an informed reader, can derive from an empirical study are enhanced by the degree to which the study provides sufficient detail for critical analysis.

A third assumption for ANOVA is what is called homogeneity of variance. This term refers to the assumption that the within-group variance among individuals is about the same for all groups. You can see why it should be: The variance within each group is not due to any treatment effect, so the variance within each group should be an estimate of the same population variance on the dependent variable. If the variances within groups are not equal, there are two things to think about. The first is what impact this difference has on the validity of the significance test (e.g., F). In a nutshell, with substantial violations of homogeneity of variance (i.e., one group has a within-group variance that is 9 times larger than another group), effects that would not otherwise be statistically significant can appear to be significant. Thus, one could erroneously conclude that a predictor is significant when it is not.

The second thing to think about is why there are different within-group variances. If the members of each group are all drawn from the same population (an important assumption in ANOVA research designs), and particularly if they were randomly assigned to groups, why should there be more variability in one group than another? One possibility is that there is a potentially important substantive effect occurring within one of your groups that was not considered in setting up the ANOVA design. Remember our example from earlier in this chapter: If treatment causes some people to improve and others to get worse, there may be a factor moderating treatment effectiveness that is important to know. Another use of ANOVA relevant to clinical assessment is to investigate sensitivity to change. For example, to what degree do scores on a measure of social phobia decline during treatment in which phobic behaviors are declining? A valid measure of social phobia should, presumably, reflect change analogous to what is observed behaviorally. For this purpose, one uses a within-subjects ANOVA, in which one compares scores of the same individuals across time. However, it is difficult to infer sensitivity to change with only one dependent variable. Significant change in a variable across time can be a result of testing effects, fatigue, reactive effects, and so on. For that reason, one can feel more confident that change has occurred when change is noted in more than one measure of the target variable. Convergent evidence for change is important.

To control for variance associated with a variable that is not of primary interest, researchers sometimes use analysis of covariance (ANCOVA). Suppose you want to assess the likelihood of rehospitalization among those patients at your hospital who are being discharged after treatment for psychosis. You might imagine two categories of predictors of rehospitalization: (a) those concerning the patient's mental illness status and the nature of your treatment and (b) those unrelated to characteristics of the patient or your treatment (such as current availability of employment in your community). If the reason for your assessment is to determine what, if anything, your hospital can do differently to reduce rehospitalization rates, you may want to remove the influence of employment availability on rehospitalization so that you can assess the influence of only the factors of interest to you. You can do so by first correlating employment availability with rehospitalization and then statistically removing whatever variance employment availability shares with rehospitalization (this is known as covarying employment availability out of rehospitalization scores). Once you remove that shared variance, you have what is called a residual rehospitalization score (that variance in rehospitalization unrelated to variance in employment availability; see Chapter 4 and the *residual variance* concept in Chapter 6 and the Glossary). You can then run the ANOVA on the residual score. This technique is called ANCOVA; you are determining how well one can predict that variance in rehospitalization that is unrelated to employment availability. ANCOVA is an ANOVA on residual scores.

One thing to consider as you critically evaluate ANCOVA reports is whether it makes sense to remove the variance that was covaried out. In the example, removing the shared variance between employment availability and rehospitalization made sense with respect to the specific reason for your prediction study. However, consider this alternative case: Suppose a researcher wants to predict depression relapse. The researcher wants to study variance in depression that is not confounded by other variables, so the researcher covaries out the variance intelligence shares with depression. But of course, it is possible that variance in intelligence reflects the presence or absence of some causally important contributor to depression relapse. If intelligence is negatively related to depression relapse through a causal process in which high intelligence leads to a greater capacity for cognitive mediation of negative mood states, then removing variance depression shares with intelligence may be to remove variance in depression that is central to the construct of depression relapse. If one's goal is to predict depression relapse, one may not want to study only that part of depression that is unrelated to intelligence, any more than one wants to study that part of risk for Huntington's disease that is unrelated to genetics. Meehl (1971) provided a useful discussion of this general issue. Two implications of this potential problem are (a) the remaining variability in your variable of interest (here, depression) is lower than the actual variability in depression, thus attenuating effect sizes, and more importantly, (b) the meaning of scores reflecting that part of depression unrelated to intelligence is not clear.

Regression, Multiple Regression, and Logistic Regression

Perhaps the other most common set of statistical techniques used in validation studies are those based on the concept of regression. Regression is closely related to correlation. We begin this section with a brief note on terminology. The language of regression relies heavily on the term *prediction*. Statistical authors will describe regression as concerning how well scores on measures of a criterion variable can be predicted from scores on measures of one or more predictors. This language can be understood to imply a research task in which one predicts some outcome, such as diagnostic group membership, and regression can certainly be used for that purpose. However, the statistical procedure of regression does not require any one research design; it uses the same mathematics as correlation and is based on the analysis of shared variance among sets of variables. It can be used for criterion-related validity, and that use is perhaps close to what seems implied in the use of the terms *predictor* and *criterion*. But, it is also frequently used to assess convergent validity. In that case, the clinical assessment researcher might observe a high level of shared variance between the two measures. (Using regression terminology, the same finding might be described as strong prediction of a criterion measure.) Regression can be used to test discriminant validity hypotheses: An absence of a relationship between two variables (alternatively described as a failure to successfully predict a criterion measure) might constitute evidence for discriminant validity. In this chapter, we use the terms *predictor, prediction*, and *criterion* as regression authors use them. When we refer to actual prediction of an outcome, we specify that to be the case.

In your clinical assessment work, there may be circumstances for which you need to predict someone's actual score on a measure of a criterion (examples include level of marital discord, degree of schizophrenic symptomatology, and posttreatment level of depression). When done in a clinical/applied context, it is important that you use raw (not standard) scores on each variable. That is, you use the scores as derived from the measures, so you can make decisions based on the scores you observe in practice. In contrast, in a research context, to get a sense of how important a predictor is in relation to a criterion, it may be useful to use standard scores. With standard scores, the contribution of

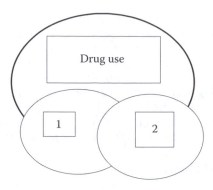

Figure 8.1   Shared and unshared variance among two predictors and a criterion measure of drug use.

each variable can be compared to the contribution of other variables because all variables are on the same scale of measurement. You cannot use standard scores for clinical decision making, but they are useful in helping you determine the most important predictors for a given clinical criterion measure. When you read regression reports, it is important that you (a) know whether your goal in using the information is actual prediction or the assessment of explained variance and (b) use the raw regression scores for the first purpose and the standardized regression scores for the second purpose. A helpful reference for the use and interpretation of regression analyses of this kind is the text by Cohen et al. (2003). You will frequently see reports of multiple regression. Multiple regression refers to the prediction of a criterion using more than one variable simultaneously. Imagine predicting a behavior as complex as drug use. It is likely that many different things contribute to such a behavior, two of which may be a certain personality trait and a certain form of learning. Suppose that the nature of the prediction could be depicted as in Figure 8.1.

The figure includes overlapping circles between each predictor and the criterion of drug use. For example, the clinician may be interested in identifying variables that predict whether a client will resume drug use following treatment. The overlap is meant to indicate shared variance among the three measures or sets of measures. As you can see, the two predictor circles overlap as well, which indicates that the two predictors share variance with each other. One feature of multiple regression is that it corrects each predictor for its overlap with the other. In the figure, the area in which the two predictors overlap with each other and with the criterion reflects criterion variance predicted by both predictors. For accurate prediction, that area of shared prediction is "assigned" to one predictor or divided up between the two predictors (this process results in determining "beta weights" for each predictor; a beta weight indicates the unique influence of that predictor on the criterion measure above and beyond the influence of other predictors). By doing this, multiple regression can estimate how much overall variance in the criterion measure is explained by two or more predictors as a set (the overall explained variance in the criterion measure can be described in correlation terms and is called the multiple correlation). In a clinical assessment context, these data help the clinician decide if additional measures might be helpful in predicting a client's relapse. If the variables suggest an elevated probability of relapse, the clinician can then institute follow-up or booster sessions.

One way in which this technique is used in construct validation studies is to help test the incremental validity of one predictor over prediction that can be made with other predictors. Hunsley and Haynes (2003) provide an excellent source for learning about incremental validity. As discussed in Chapter 4, one important question as you evaluate a new measure is whether its inclusion adds to your ability to predict beyond what can already be accomplished with other measures. Multiple regression can provide a statistical assessment of whether incremental validity is present, thereby helping the clinician know the likelihood that additional measures will improve his or her clinical judgments.

A researcher can enter all established predictors in the first step of the multiple regression and determine how much variance in the criterion measure is explained by the established predictors. Then, at the second step of the process, the researcher can enter a new measure and see whether addition of the new measure increases the amount of criterion measure variance explained. That is, can our ability to predict drug use be significantly enhanced if we add a new predictor? There is a formal significance test to help determine whether the new measure provides a statistically significant improvement in prediction. Such a finding addresses the possible benefits to the assessment task of including the new predictor. Clinicians will then consider those benefits in relation to the costs of adding a new predictor (typical costs are clinician time, client time, and money; see Chapter 5) and make a decision about use of the new measure.

In the example used for Figure 8.1, imagine that a measure of impulsivity is strongly related to the likelihood that a person will use illegal drugs (Circle 1), and a researcher wants to test the hypothesis that learning to expect reinforcement from drug use (Circle 2) explains variance in drug use not explained by personality. The researcher enters a measure of the personality trait in Step 1 and then the measure of learning in Step 2. A finding of a significant increase in variance in measures of drug use explained at Step 2 would provide support for the validity of the researcher's theoretical claim that learning explains additional variance in drug use and the incremental validity of the measure of "reinforcement expectation." The evidence that the learning measure improves prediction from the impulsivity measure will provide information necessary for the clinician's process of choosing measures based on both the benefits (including predictive and incremental validity) and the costs of adding the measure to the assessment task.

There is a way in which predictors are sometimes compared using multiple regression that can lead to inaccurate conclusions. When two variables are entered in the same step of a multiple regression and one is statistically significant and the other is not, researchers sometimes conclude that the first predictor explains more criterion variance than the second predictor. This conclusion is not warranted. Remember that to say something is statistically significant is to say that its effect is greater than zero. Thus, the finding means that one predictor has an effect significantly greater than zero, and the other does not. That conclusion is accurate, but it does not lead to the conclusion that one predictor is more successful than the other. To draw such a conclusion, one would need to test whether the two correlations are significantly different from each other (not from zero). Imagine a situation in which a beta weight of .20 is what is needed to be significantly greater than zero. Imagine that Predictor A has a beta weight of .21, and Predictor B has a beta weight of .19. A is statistically significant, and B is not, but notice that we mentioned no test of whether .21 is significantly higher than .19. Almost surely it is not; indeed, it seems possible that in another sample, Predictor A could have a beta weight of .19, and predictor B could have a beta weight of .21. In fact, there are significance tests that enable one to compare correlations to each other (Meng, Rosenthal, & Rubin, 1992; Olkin & Finn, 1995; Steiger, 1980).

As you read multiple regression reports, be aware of whether the analyses reported permit the conclusions drawn. As you might guess, the same issue is present when comparing correlation coefficients outside the regression context. It will not be uncommon for you to draw different conclusions from those provided in empirical reports.

Another form of regression frequently used in discriminative validity studies is logistic regression. Logistic regression is used when the criterion variable is dichotomous, such as presence/absence of a disorder; persons who have or have not attempted suicide; persons who have or have not experienced domestic violence; or persons who have or have not experienced child abuse. Using the "disorder" example, it is often helpful to get a quantitative index of how well each predictor variable predicts membership in the disordered group (also see our discussion of positive predictive power in Chapter 4, "Predictive Power," p. 88).

We will not go into the underlying statistics of logistic regression. Instead, we note that one helpful value available from logistic regression is that of "odds ratio." The odds ratio indicates by what amount the odds of being in the disordered group are multiplied when the predictor is incremented by a value of 1 unit (Cohen et al., 2003). Suppose we tested the relationship between scores on a schizophrenia risk measure and schizophrenic diagnosis. An odds ratio of 1.50 means that the odds that a case is in the schizophrenic group are multiplied by 1.50 (increased by 50%) for each 1 unit increase on our risk measure. This statistic can provide a useful sense of the practical impact of differences in scores on a psychological measure (Cohen et al., 2003; DeMaris, 1995). Logistic regression can be useful for *discriminative validity*, or the capacity of a measure to discriminate between members of two groups or two classes. Imagine if we were validating our schizophrenia risk measure and we got an odds ratio of 1.00. That finding would mean that the odds of being in the schizophrenic group do not increase with each 1-unit increase on our measure: Schizophrenia is unrelated to variability on our measure. Obviously, the measure has no discriminative validity. Contrast that finding with a finding of an odds ratio of 4.0, that is, the odds of being in the schizophrenic group are multiplied by 4 for each 1-unit increase in the predictor. In this last case, the measure appears useful for discriminating schizophrenic and nonschizophrenic individuals.

There are two primary implications of this set of concepts for the clinician. The first is perhaps obvious: Clinicians should give more credence to risk indicators with odds ratios that depart from zero; the measure with the odds ratio of 4.0 will better relate to schizophrenia diagnosis than will measures with odds ratios closer to 1.0. The second is that, even when there is substantial shared variance between a risk measure and diagnostic status, there can still be considerable error in predicting the diagnostic status of any one individual. Consider an odds ratio of 1.5. On one hand, it reflects a striking degree of covariation that each 1-unit increase in a risk measure increases the probability that a person is in the target group (e.g., diagnostic group) by 50%. On the other hand, a 50% increase in the probability that one is a member of the group speaks to how uncertain is group membership prediction for any individual.

Before finishing our discussion of multiple regression, we would like to mention assumptions underlying the technique about which you should be aware. The first is that the relationship between the predictor and criterion is linear. Regression and correlation are techniques designed to identify linear relationships. If the relationship between a predictor and a criterion is curvilinear, linear multiple regression will provide inaccurate information and may not indicate that a relationship is present. Fortunately, it is possible to test curvilinear relationships using modifications of linear regression. For example, one can test for quadratic effects (these are curves with one bend in them, in contrast to linear effects, in which the curve does not change direction) by entering the square of the predictor one step after the predictor itself is entered. Cohen et al. (2003) provide the necessary details for conducting such analyses.

An example of curvilinear prediction was provided in a longitudinal study of eating (Combs, Smith, Flory, Simmons, & Hill, in press). The authors tested the hypothesis that learned expectancies for life benefits from dieting and thinness predicted increased purging behavior 1 year later among middle school girls. The linear regression was nonsignificant, but as the authors hypothesized, the expectancies had a quadratic relationship to purging behavior (tested by squaring the expectancy scores as indicated by Cohen et al., 2003). At low-to-moderate expectancy levels, there was no relationship to purging (variation in moderate levels of expecting life benefits from thinness was unrelated to purging, $b = -.03$), but variation in high levels of the expectancy (from the mean to the highest possible expectancy endorsement) was significantly related to purging behavior ($b = .36$, $p < .01$). Endorsing extreme levels of expectation for life benefits from dieting and thinness was predictive of purging behavior, even though variation in moderate expectancy levels was not. This distinction, identified through curvilinear regression, is useful for the assessment process. When clinicians use the dieting/thinness expectancy measure, they can focus their attention on the presence or absence of very high scores because only very high scores appear to increase risk for purging.

Another assumption made in multiple regression is that there is no measurement error (Cohen et al., 2003); that is, all variables are measured with perfect reliability. This assumption is, of course, almost always violated, so you should appreciate the implications of the violation. To the degree that measurement error is present, beta weights and the overall multiple correlation will be underestimates or true population values. As we discussed with respect to ANOVA, there are numerous factors that can lead to overestimates and underestimates of effect sizes. Measurement error contributes to underestimates in multiple regression.

In addition to these specific assumptions of multiple regression, there are always basic assumptions one makes and procedures that are necessary when interpreting the result of multiple regression studies relevant for validation evidence for a measure. We mention two of them as we bring this chapter to a close. First, as we referred to when discussing ANOVA, one assumes that the sample is not restricted and is relevant to the target client. Second, it is necessary to recruit a large enough sample that the results are stable and there is sufficient statistical power to detect the presence of an effect, if there is one. The sample size that is necessary varies as a function of the magnitude of the anticipated effect, the statistical power desired, and the statistical procedure employed, among other factors. In general, the larger the sample, the more likely the results are to be stable estimates of population values, and the more statistical power there is to detect an effect that is present. Multiple regression involves the estimation of numerous relationships simultaneously, including the relationship of each predictor with the criterion measure and the relationship of each predictor with every other predictor. Accordingly, larger samples are necessary to produce stable estimates of all those relationships. One common guideline is to recruit 10 participants for each predictor in the analysis (including any interaction or higher-order terms entered into the regression), and this guideline appears to work fairly well, even though it is not based on detailed consideration of power and magnitude of anticipated effects

(Darlington, 1990). When you read multiple regression reports to evaluate assessment instruments, consider the sample size as you decide how much confidence to place in the reported findings.

There are, of course, many other statistical techniques you will encounter in the psychopathology, treatment research, and psychological assessment empirical literatures. In this chapter, we have only focused on some of the most common. But even so, we hope to have communicated a set of basic principles to guide your reading of research findings. We end the chapter by summarizing those principles.

SUMMARY AND RECOMMENDATIONS

1. Clinicians should read empirical reports fully and with a critical eye. Throughout this chapter, we have referred to information you will need to draw your own conclusions about the validity of measures from published data and to determine its applicability to the clinical decisions you make in your own setting for a particular purpose. You may need to do additional calculations before drawing conclusions from a report.

2. It is important to consider not just whether a significant effect is present; one must evaluate the magnitude of the effect. Doing so involves consideration of variables that may have led to either underestimates or overestimates of population effects. To determine whether an effect is meaningful with respect to your clinical decision making, you may need to transform reported data into some other form, such as from t to r.

3. Clinicians should understand that effect sizes are estimates of the proportion of variability in one measure that is explained by another measure, within the context of the research design, the nature of the samples, the specific measures used, and the other predictive variables included or excluded.

4. The statistical procedures used in research reports rely on assumptions for their valid use. Some procedures are robust to some assumptions but not to others. As you draw conclusions from published papers, evaluate carefully whether necessary assumptions have been met in conducting the research (cf. Chapter 7).

RECOMMENDED SOURCES

Haynes, S. N., & Lench, H. C. (2003). Incremental validity of new clinical assessment measures. *Psychological Assessment, 15,* 456–466.

Hunsley, J., & Mash, E. J. (2008). *A guide to assessments that work.* New York: Oxford University Press.

Hunsley, J., & Meyer, G. J. (2003). The incremental validity of psychological testing and assessment: Conceptual, methodological, and statistical issues. *Psychological Assessment, 15*, 446–455.

Kraemer, H. C., & Kupfer, D. J. (2005). Size of treatment effects and their importance to clinical research and practice. *Biological Psychiatry, 59*, 990–996.

McGrath, R. E., & Meyer, G. J. (2006). When effect sizes disagree: The case of *r* and *d*. *Psychological Methods, 11*, 386–401.

9

Using Multiple Sources of Data in Clinical Assessment

INTRODUCTION

In the previous chapters, we emphasized several aspects of a scientific approach to clinical assessment. In particular, we stressed that the validity of the measures acquired during clinical assessment affect the validity of clinical judgments and hence the welfare of individuals seeking psychological services. We discussed the importance of considering psychometric evidence when selecting and applying assessment instruments and when interpreting clinical assessment measures. We reviewed several analytic strategies often used in psychometric evaluations and discussed how the relevance of validity evidence depends on the specific clinical judgments that are to be made, the characteristics of the client, and the context of a particular assessment occasion.

Several chapters reviewed the numerous errors that can occur during the clinical assessment process. Errors in measurement can limit the clinician's ability to identify a client's behavior problems, concerns, treatment goals, and the causal variables affecting them. Errors in measurement also increase the chance of misdiagnosis, under- or overestimating a client's risk of harm or posttreatment relapse, making invalid clinical case formulations, and misestimating treatment effects and side effects. Reliable and valid data on well-specified problems and events, in well-specified contexts, are mandatory for a science-based approach to clinical assessment. This chapter expands on these ideas and examines *multisource clinical assessment*, the use of multiple methods, informants, contexts, or times in clinical assessment to limit the impact of measurement error.

In this chapter, we examine the conceptual and empirical foundations, clinical utility, and costs-benefits of multisource assessment. First, we examine the idiosyncratic sources of error variance associated with specific assessment instruments, informants, methods, and time samples. Then, we examine errors that often accompany monomethod assessment and the convergence and divergence among data across different sources. We also consider time sampling as an assessment strategy to capture dynamic aspects of a client's behavior. Finally, we offer recommendations for multisource clinical assessment.

MULTIPLE SOURCES OF ERROR IN CLINICAL ASSESSMENTS

In our discussions of reliability and validity in Chapters 2 and 3, we noted that each measure in clinical assessment provides an imperfect estimate of the targeted construct and can reflect many sources of error. Some types of errors are especially likely when using a particular assessment instrument and method. Examples of sources of error include (a) a self-report questionnaire that provides insufficient or erroneous coverage of some facets of a construct, leading to a biased estimate of the construct; (b) questionnaire items or behavior observation codes that are ambiguously worded, thereby reducing the reliability of the obtained measures; (c) a rating scale that includes items that are irrelevant to the targeted construct, thereby reducing its discriminant validity; (d) terms in a questionnaire that exceed the cognitive abilities of respondents; (e) a laboratory assessment or self-report questionnaire instrument that is too long and induces fatigue-related errors; (f) errors in the time frame targeted by a rating scale, introducing bias or judgment errors; (g) response formats on a self-monitoring form that are confusing, difficult, or insensitive; (h) technological or data reduction errors that are associated with a psychophysiological assessment instrument; and (i) normative data for a questionnaire scale score that lead to a biased estimate of the targeted construct for some persons.

Table 9.1 outlines examples of sources of measurement error across different assessment instruments and methods.

To illustrate the importance of errors associated with different sources of information, De Los Reyes and Kazdin (2005), in a review article on childhood psychopathology, discussed differences across informants in the measures obtained and some of the reasons for those differences. For example, the authors noted that (a) the apparent relation between a child's cognitive process and depressed mood (i.e., the degree of shared variance, discussed in Chapter 8) depends on whether both are measured by the same or different informants; (b) the likelihood that a parent would identify his or her child as having a conduct disorder depends on the parent's level of depression; (c) the likelihood that a teacher would identify a child as having a conduct disorder depends on the gender of the child and the family income; (d) the most important problem identified for treatment focus depends on whether problem ratings come from the parent, child, or clinician (parents and children disagree 63% of the time; parents, children, and clinicians disagree 76% of the time).* You can see from these data that important clinical judgments about clients, based on clinical assessment data, are strongly affected by the source of the data.

MULTISOURCE ASSESSMENT FOR DECREASING MEASUREMENT ERROR IMPACT

Given that measurement error is unavoidable in clinical assessment, one goal of this book is to help readers to increase the ratio of true variance to error variance in measures they obtain. Because these measures are the basis for important clinical decisions, clinicians should use the best science-based measures—those that most precisely track the behaviors of interest during the times and settings of interest. Measures should inform the clinician about how a parent truly reacts when his or her child misbehaves at home, how much alcohol a client truly drinks during a weekend, and what events are most likely to trigger a client's compulsive rituals at home.

Assuming that all measures include error, what is the best strategy to pursue in clinical assessment to reduce the impact of those errors? The problem of measurement error can be addressed in two ways. First, as we emphasized in all previous chapters, the clinician should apply science-based principles of measurement in the selection, application, and interpretation of assessment instruments. Selecting the most reliable, valid, and sensitive-to-change measures will result in the best data on which to base clinical judgments.

The second strategy to reduce the negative impact of measurement error is to conduct a *multisource assessment*. That is, if the clinician is interested in measuring depressed mood of an adolescent client (or the client's social skills, suicide risk, life stressors), more valid and clinically useful inferences can often be obtained by collecting multiple measures of mood from multiple assessment methods, assessment instruments, informants, settings, and occasions. Given that each measure reflects true variance in the targeted construct and idiosyncratic sources of measurement error,

---

* De Los Reyes and Kazdin (2005) also noted that disagreements among parent, child, and therapist can also impede cooperation and adversely affect treatment outcomes.

the use of more than one measure, when aggregated, can attenuate the impact on clinical judgment of the idiosyncratic error associated with each. To the degree that measures from multiple sources of assessment converge, the clinician can have more confidence in their validity.

Consider the impact of using two self-report questionnaires of depressed mood; one emphasizes cognitive components of depressed mood, and the other emphasizes its behavioral activity components. While bearing in mind inferential limitations because both questionnaires use the same assessment method (i.e., client self-report), the clinician is more likely to make valid and useful clinical judgments about the client's depressed mood by using data from both than by using data from only one (assuming other psychometric evidence is supportive for both). We consider assets and limitations of forming composite measures from multiple sources in a further section of this chapter. Recall also the study by Pelham et al. (2005) discussed in Chapter 4: Reports of attention-deficit/hyperactivity disorder (ADHD) behaviors from both a teacher and a parent were necessary for ruling in a diagnosis of ADHD, but data from only one source were necessary for ruling out the diagnosis.

It is important to note that the relevance of each class of error, such as those listed in Table 9.1, varies across methods. For example "insufficient exposure to the client" is especially relevant to participant rating forms, and "reactive effects of the assessment process" is especially relevant to analog behavioral observation, psychophysiological laboratory assessment, and self-monitoring. Because of the association between particular classes of error and particular assessment methods, the integration of data from more than one assessment method can help to reduce their impact of measurement error on clinical judgments.

Multisource assessment is also consistent with what we know about behavior problems, treatment goals, intervention strategies, and causal variables. As outlined in Chapter 1, we know that behavior problems involve different response modalities, with different causal variables that operate in some contexts more than in others and that can change over time. It is difficult to capture these important sources of variance for a client's problems and goals with only one source of information.

This discussion leads to one of the main recommendations of this chapter: In many clinical assessment contexts, the use of measures from multiple sources can strengthen the validity, specificity, and utility of clinical judgments. This recommendation seems straightforward but actually is deceptively complex. The clinical assessment challenge addressed in multisource assessment is: Which combination of measures, using which assessment methods, from whom, in what settings, and across what times will provide the most valid and clinically useful data? The following sections address several facets of this question.

TABLE 9.1   Examples of Measurement Errors Often Associated With
Various Clinical Assessment Methods

Assessment Methods	Examples	Examples of Potential Sources of Measurement Error
Interview	An interview with a client to establish a diagnosis, identify comorbid problems, and identify events and contexts associated with the behavior problems	Positive or negative bias in self-reports Memory errors in retrospective self-report Imprecise wording of queries Dissimulation Interviewer biases Recall affected by the current emotional state of the respondent
Retrospective self-report questionnaires	A questionnaire to measure a client's symptom severity, exposure to traumatic life events, quality of life, or relationship satisfaction	Imprecise wording of items Random or biased responding Heterogeneous scales and excessively global measures Dissimulation Recall affected by the emotional state of the respondent Imprecise or excessively long time frame for recall
Informant behavior-rating forms and questionnaires	A parent report inventory to identify a child's problem behaviors and strengths A spouse report questionnaire to identify events associated with a patient's trauma-related symptoms (e.g., verbal aggression, startle responses)	Imprecise wording of items Imprecise or excessively long time frames for reporting Rater bias Insufficient exposure to the targeted behavior A greater impact of behaviors most salient to the respondent or more recently occurring

(continued on next page)

TABLE 9.1 (continued)   Examples of Measurement Errors Often Associated
With Various Clinical Assessment Methods

Assessment Methods	Examples	Examples of Potential Sources of Measurement Error
Daily diaries, self-monitoring, ecological momentary assessment	Daily monitoring of physical activity and time on task at school for a child Morning monitoring of a client's previous night's sleep quality and mood	Insufficient adherence to the schedule for self-monitoring Low reliability because of imprecise identification of monitored events Excessive client burden to provide detailed data multiple times each day Sensitivity to social desirability
Ambulatory biomeasurement	Daily measures of blood pressure for a client experiencing labile hypertension Daily activity measures for a client attempting to increase his or her level of aerobic exercise	Reactive effects associated with the intrusiveness of the measures Highly variable responses across time Multiple extraneous events that can affect the obtained measures Technological malfunctions Errors in time or situation sampling
Psychophysiological laboratory assessment	Measuring a client's cardiovascular responses to laboratory trauma-related stressors Electrophysiological monitoring of a child during computerized cognitive tasks	Reactive effects associated with the laboratory setting Technological malfunctions Movement artifacts Insufficient time allowed for establishing baseline or recovery to baseline
Analog behavioral observation	Observing parent-child interactions involving an oppositional child Observing family interactions with a patient released from a psychiatric hospital	Reactive effects associated with the observation process Observer errors Imprecise definitions of behavior codes Insufficient time for observations

TABLE 9.1 (continued)   Examples of Measurement Errors Often Associated With Various Clinical Assessment Methods

Assessment Methods	Examples	Examples of Potential Sources of Measurement Error
Naturalistic observation	Observing the behavior of a child with autistic behaviors while in the classroom Observing the social interactions of a hospitalized psychiatric patient while on a psychiatric unit	Observing in the wrong settings or at the wrong times Observer inattention Reactive effects associated with the observation process Wrong or imprecisely defined behavior codes

USING MULTIPLE INSTRUMENTS FROM ONE ASSESSMENT METHOD

Perhaps the most common approach to dealing with idiosyncratic sources of measurement error is to use more than one assessment instrument within the same assessment method. The most frequent examples are (a) asking a client to complete two different self-report questionnaires that target the same construct (such as two questionnaires on depressed mood or anxiety) and (b) asking two informants to complete the same rating scale (such as a rating form on a child's behavior problems completed by a teacher and parent). These are examples of a *monomethod assessment strategy.*

Monomethod assessment (*monomethod* is sometimes referred to as mono-operation) refers to an assessment strategy that includes multiple assessment instruments or informants but only one assessment method. Monomethod assessment most often involves the use of multiple self-report questionnaires to measure the same construct, but the strategy encompasses all assessment occasions in which the targeted construct is measured by the use of multiple assessment instruments within a single assessment method. A monomethod assessment strategy is often used in the validation of new assessment instruments. For example, a newly developed brief screen for depressed mood might be validated by examining its correlation with measures from the Beck Depression Inventory II. High correlations with the "criterion" measure would be considered supportive of the validity of the new measure.

The problem with monomethod assessment is that psychometric evidence of validity based on estimates of shared variance can be misleading when both measures are derived from the same assessment method (for more details, see discussion in Burns & Haynes, 2006). For example, does a correlation of .7 between two self-report measures of depression provide strong convergent validation for one or both of them? Alternatively, does the correlation reflect a significant amount of *common method variance*—does this correlation reflect the fact that the source of data for both instruments was self-report, with shared sources of error variance associated with the method, items, instrument, and informant? Do both instruments focus on only one facet of depression, have items that overlap in meaning, or include the same irrelevant items? In this example, it is difficult to separate shared variance in the phenomenon that we are attempting to measure—*true variance*—from variance associated with the method, instrument, and informant from which the measures are derived: *method variance*.[*]

A clinical assessment strategy that relies on only one method can increase the chance of biased and inaccurate measures and clinical judgments and overestimation of the shared variance among measured constructs. In the validation of measures, monomethod assessment can inflate obtained correlation coefficients or other measures of functional relations (e.g., conditional probabilities, positive predictive power [PPP]) and can be misleading regarding the validity of a measure. In monomethod assessment strategies, data that are supposed to inform about the degree to which two constructs are related are confounded because they also reflect the degree to which the constructs were measured in the same way and in the degree to which the measures share the same measurement errors.

Multimethod assessment is a common assessment strategy in clinical research (Eid & Diener, 2006; Geiser, Eid, Nussbeck, Courvoisier, & Cole, 2010), and many clinicians rely solely on client self-reports from questionnaires or interviews to make diagnoses, generate case formulations, and estimate treatment effects. There are several reasons why clinicians may confine their assessment strategies to self-report, despite the psychometric evidence arguing against this practice. First, clinicians sometimes reify the measures and may not be sufficiently knowledgeable about the judgment errors that can accompany such a strategy. Second, self-report data are easy to acquire. Books such as that by Fischer and Corcoran (2000) allow scan-friendly and royalty-free access to hundreds of questionnaires. Third, many clinicians have faith in the validity of client reports and assume, for example, that a score on a self-report measure of mood or relationship satisfaction is a true index of the measured construct (i.e., they reify the score).

---

[*] The term method variance is sometimes used as a general term to refer to all nontrait-related sources of variance (e.g., variance that is associated with methods, instruments, and informants).

Understanding Errors Associated
With Monomethod Assessment

What is it about monomethod assessment strategies that lead to these undesirable outcomes? The limitations derive primarily from shared error variance between measures—the errors associated with one measure of a construct are more likely to be associated with the errors of another measure of the same construct to the degree that both measures are derived from the same methods. Shared error variance is a particular cause for concern when using multiple retrospective self-report instruments.

There are several sources of shared error variance in self-report instruments. As Shiffman (2009) discussed, one problem with global self-report (e.g., retrospective estimates by a client of smoking, alcohol use, panic episodes) is that respondents tend to "heap" their estimates around certain values. For example, smokers tend to heap their estimates of smoking around multiples of 20 (the number of cigarettes in a typical pack). To the extent that respondents heap their responses in the same way in response to different self-report questionnaires, the correlation between the measures from the two questionnaires would partially reflect this shared error.

Shared error variance associated with monomethod measures is also a problem when two self-report assessment instruments include semantically similar items. For example, in the validation of a questionnaire on mood, one might want to know if responses to the item "I cry often" truly represent the degree to which a respondent cries often in his or her daily life. A strong correlation between measures from this item and measures from the item "Frequently, I find myself crying" from a different assessment instrument is a weak test of validity. Both are retrospective self-report (meaning the same biased response might occur to both items) and evidence semantic overlap: The two items mean the same thing. These two items simply ask the same question in a slightly different way. The correlation between measures from two self-report questionnaires will be inflated to the degree that they include semantically overlapping items. The correlation between the two items is less an indication of their convergent validity than of their reliability. A similar source of error is *criterion contamination*, which occurs when a predictor and criterion assessment instrument contain the same or semantically similar elements.

Measures from two self-report instruments can also reflect similarities in level of *social desirability*. For example, Logan, Claara, and Scharffa (2008), in a study of over 400 pediatric patients with pain, reported that children who tended to respond in a socially desirable manner reported fewer symptoms of depression and anxiety. Thus, correlations between two self-report measures of distress can also reflect the degree to which respondents are willing to endorse items related to distress on both questionnaires.

A respondent's biases can also inflate the correlation between two measures. Response bias occurs when a response to a question varies in a systematic manner (for example, in a socially desirable manner, as a function of the sex of the respondent, or because the respondent is faking good or bad). Also, as pointed out by Hoyt, Warbasse, and Chu (2006), self-ratings of general traits can reflect recent experiences. For example, ratings of a behavioral "trait" such as extraversion or social anxiety can be influenced by the respondent's recent pertinent experiences. To the degree that those experiences affect two self-report measures of the attributes, correlations between measures will reflect the systematic influence of that bias.

Measures from other assessment methods can also be subject to shared method variance. For example, two ambulatory blood pressure machines or two actigraphs (to measure physical activity) may each provide overestimates of systolic blood pressure and movement (Haynes & Yoshioka, 2007). Data from two trained external observers of the aggressive behavior of children in a classroom may reflect their similar sex biases, expectations, training, and ambiguities in the definitions of behavior codes.

Convergence and Divergence Among Measures From Multiple Methods, Instruments, and Informants

Many studies have examined covariances among data derived on the same constructs from different informants and assessment methods. To give you a better sense of these types of findings, we briefly review studies by Cole, Martin, Powers, and Truglio (1996) on different methods of measuring depression and academic achievement of children; Spangler and Gazelle (2009) on different methods of measuring social anxiety and activity of children; Wienke, Christine, Green, Karver, and Gesten (2009) on differences among informants on measures of bullying; Margraf, Taylor, Ehlers, Roth, and Agras (1987) on different methods of measuring panic episodes; Grimm, Pianta, and Konold (2009) on measuring childhood behavior problems with different informants; and Spangler and Gazelle (2009), Achenbach, McConaughy, and Howell (1987), Wienke and colleagues (2009), and Burns and Haynes (2006) on different methods and different informants for measuring childhood and adult behavior problems. The results from these and many other studies are consistent: There can be significant differences in measures of the same construct, depending on which informant is supplying the data, the setting in which data are acquired, and the instruments and methods used to acquire the data.

Divergence Associated With Informants and Settings

Cole et al. (1996), in a multitrait-multimethod longitudinal study of depression and academic achievement in children, noted that many studies have used both monomethod and heteromethod assessment strategies to measure childhood behavior problems. Correlations between different measures of children's social competence, for example, were about .4 between measures from the same method and about .2 between measures from different methods. Spangler and Gazelle (2009) also used a multitrait-multimethod assessment strategy to examine "anxious solitude," sociability, and peer relations in a sample of young schoolchildren (average age about 9 years). Measures were obtained from parents, teachers, and peers. Although the focus was to examine the convergent and discriminant validity of the constructs, the authors found significant differences between informants, with peers the best at discriminating among the constructs.

In a frequently cited meta-analysis of 119 studies, Achenbach, McConaughy, and Howell (1987) examined the between-informant (e.g., parents, teachers, children, mental health workers, external observers) correlations of measures of child emotional and behavior problems in inpatient and outpatient settings. The correlations between measures of the same behavior from similar informants (e.g., between a father and mother or between two teachers) averaged about .6; the correlations between measures of the same behavior from dissimilar informants (e.g., parent and teacher) averaged about .3; the correlations between the child's and other's ratings ranged between .2 and .27 (see also Grills & Ollendick, 2003, for a discussion of agreements/disagreements between parents and children).

Wienke and colleagues (2009) conducted a study of school bullying for 1,442 middle school students and gathered data from teachers and students. Correlations between peer and self-reports were .2 to .4, and between teacher and self-reports were .4 to .5. The authors found that between-informant Cohen's kappas were .13 for the bullying and .12 for victimization. Grimm et al. (2009), in a longitudinal study of over 1,000 elementary schoolchildren, found that measures of many behaviors, such as social skills and internalizing and externalizing behavior problems, were associated with a significant amount of informant-related variance. The authors reported that, on average, 38% of the variance in measures of child behaviors and behavior problems was related to the informant who completed the form. In contrast, an average of only 28% of the variance was associated with trait-related variance.

Divergence Associated With Assessment Method

The previous studies documented differences among measures mostly as a function of the informant. In many cases, informant variance is confounded with setting variance. That is, different informants often differ in the setting in which they are exposed to the client, a topic discussed in detail by Cone (1979). Other studies have focused on differences in measures associated with different methods of assessment in the same setting. In one of the first studies to use electronic diaries, Margraf et al. (1987) found significant differences between ecological momentary assessment and retrospective interviews and questionnaires in the number and type of panic episodes reported by clients across 6 days. Estimates of the frequency of panic episodes and symptoms were significantly higher for the retrospective reports. For example, the symptom "fear of dying" was more than 20 times as likely to be reported in the retrospective questionnaire than in the electronic diary. Other studies have also reported clinically important differences between daily and retrospective (e.g., through interviews or self-report question-naires) measures of emotions and emotional lability, alcohol and drug use, obsessive and compulsive behavior, smoking, mood, and symptoms associated with borderline personality disorder (see reviews in Ebner-Priemer et al., 2007; Haynes & Yoshioka, 2007; Shiffman, 2009).

Burns and Haynes (2006) reviewed studies that used multimethod-multi-informant confirmatory factor analysis (CFA) strategies to exam-ine trait and "source" variance in measures of child and adult emotional and behavior problems.* With a few exceptions, measures of ADHD, depression, and anxiety in children and measures of many adult behav-ior problems demonstrated consistently stronger informant effects than trait (behavior) effects. For example, CFA results suggested that there is often relatively little trait variance associated with the measures of childhood depression and anxiety. Only one CFA study involved two informants (mothers and fathers) in the same setting; in this case, trait variance was greater than the source variance for measures of children's externalizing problems (e.g., oppositional, aggressive) but not for inter-nalizing problems (e.g., somatic and anxiety measures). In several CFA studies, trait variance was consistently stronger for measures of alcohol use, drug use, and measures associated with developmental disabilities (e.g., cognitive competence, social competence).[†]

De Los Reyes and Kazdin (2005) noted the significant disagree-ments among informants and reviewed the inconsistent findings about the degree to which discrepancies among informants in child

---

* The proportion of trait versus source variance has implications for evaluating conver-gent and discriminant validity of the constructs as well as the measures of those con-structs. For example, if measures of multiple behavior traits such as ADHD and OCD revealed little trait variance, in comparison to source variance, across several sources, then small correlations among the three traits would not be informative about their discriminant validity. However, if the average amount of trait variance in the ratings was high (e.g., 70%), high correlations among the three traits would provide evidence that they may reflect a similar or higher-level construct.

† In noting these results, we must be careful in what is meant by trait. While earlier concepts often invoked the idea that a trait was a relatively stable characteristic of a person, contemporaneous definitions acknowledge important between-setting differ-ences in how people behave. The results discussed in this section are consistent with our understanding that persons can truly behave differently across settings, and that measures of a person's behavior within a setting can be significantly affected by who provides the information.

psychopathology are related to characteristics of the child, parent, and family; the type of problem; the informants' attributions about the behavior; recall and dispositional biases; and the measures used. They proposed an attribution bias context (ABC) model that stresses the importance of assessing contextual factors and informant attributions of the causes of the child's problems.

In summary, many studies have documented that data acquired in clinical assessment are strongly affected by their source. As many clinicians know well, the data the clinician acquires in clinical assessment can vary depending on who the informants are, the settings in which the client and informant interact, and the methods used in assessment. The best assessment sources vary with the targets and goals of assessment. All studies emphasize that the validity and utility of clinical judgments can often be enhanced by the appropriate use of multiple informants, with multiple methods of assessment, and across multiple settings. Clinicians should avoid the common error of reifying any measure—do not presume that a single measure of an important phenomenon is a "true" measure of that phenomenon. Note how these concepts are relevant to the conditional nature of validity evidence. Data from one respondent, or one setting, for example, may be valid for that respondent and setting but not for others. We discuss this further in the next section.

Of course, acquiring data from additional informants or in different settings is helpful only if these data do not increase the amount of source variance. An example of when an additional informant would be unhelpful would be interviewing a substitute teacher with little exposure to the target child or a psychiatric aide with little understanding of a patient's behavior patterns. Clinicians should keep in mind that some informants may not be in a position to provide equally valid information about a client's behavior. A parent may be less exposed to a child's attentional deficits with demanding tasks, a teacher may be less exposed to the child's aggressive interactions with his or her siblings, and neither may fully understand the emotions of a child who reports feeling sad or having troubles interacting with peers. The point is that informants can differ in the validity of data they can provide on a target behavior, and the clinician should consider the degree to which additional data are likely to be valid and useful.

THE CONDITIONAL NATURE OF MULTISOURCE CONVERGENCE AND DIVERGENCE

As with all dimensions of psychometric evidence (see Chapter 7), the degree of convergence of clinical assessment data on the same construct from different informants, instruments, and methods is conditional. For example, Shiffman (2009) reviewed several studies that found good agreement between measures of smoking from time-line follow-back interviews, end-of-day retrospective questionnaire reports, and bio-chemical measures, but only when they were applied within a recent (e.g., past-day) rather than long (e.g., past-week) time frame. Similarly, Ebner-Priemer et al. (2007) noted that the convergence between mea-sures of behavior from retrospective recall and daily monitoring decreases as the time frame for recall increases. They suggested that recall is most accurate (which they defined as being in agreement with daily mea-sures recorded electronically by participants using a handheld computer) within a 1-day time frame and decreases as the time frame increases.

Burns and Haynes (2006) noted that divergence of data on a client across assessment methods can also reflect different time frames in the assessment. For example, low levels of convergence between measures across methods would be expected if the time frame was 6 months for a diagnostic interview, 1 month for a behavior rating scale, and 1 week for behavioral observations.

Broderick et al. (2008) found that the degree of convergence between measures of pain derived from electronic diaries (i.e., ecological momen-tary assessment, EMA) and retrospective recall depended on which aspect of pain was measured. Correlations between different measures of average or typical pain levels ranged from .6 to .8. However, if one is interested in assessing within-person daily variation in pain and the variables affecting it across time (i.e., data that would be particularly helpful in clinical case formulation), correlations between retrospective recall and EMA measures were < .3.

In the meta-analysis by Achenbach, McConaughy, and Howell (1987) of ratings of child behavior problems, correlations between measures from similar and dissimilar informants were higher for younger chil-dren (ages 6–11; average r about .5) than for older children (ages 12–19; average r about .4). He also noted that cross-situational consistency of a child's behavior can vary depending on the severity of behavior prob-lems. Children evidencing very deviant behavior were more likely to demonstrate cross-situational consistency than were those exhibiting less-deviant behavior.

In their multimethod, multi-informant, longitudinal study of adoles-cent suicide ideation and attempts, Connor and Rueter (2009) found that self-report by adolescents and reports by parents were the most useful predictors of future suicide ideation and behaviors (the effects were statistically significant due to the sample size [$N = 559$], but effect sizes and PPP were modest). Sibling reports and observations by inter-viewers (who were not clinicians) were not valid predictors. In Wienke et al.'s (2009) study on school bullying, the degree of agreement between teacher and student self-reports of bullying was greater for stu-dents with more learning problems, and between-informant agreement for bullying victimization was greater for students with lower levels of self-reported "moodiness."

In our discussion of the conditional nature of multisource conver-gence in clinical assessment, we have noted that convergence can be affected by the time frame of the assessment, the age of the person assessed, the settings in which assessment occurs, the type of behavior assessed, and the severity of the behaviors rated. Characteristics of raters also affect the convergence of clinical data. For example, Lakes and Hoyt (2009) noted that bias on the part of raters can be increased (and convergence with alternative measures decreased) when raters receive little training in making their ratings and are asked to make global judgments about behavior (e.g., degree of aggressiveness, anxiety, skills) rather than rate the occurrence or severity of specific behaviors. In line with this finding, in a study of observer ratings, Hoyt and Kerns (1999) found that for rating scales requiring some rater inference, rater bias accounted for 14% of the variance for trained raters and 34% of the variance for untrained raters. As we discussed, augmenting our clinical assessment data by acquiring information from additional informants can enhance the validity of our data and judgments, but only when each informant can provide valid measures. These studies suggest that the degree of convergence among measures depends on several aspects of the assessment occasion. In particular, multimethod convergence can be increased if the idiosyncratic errors associated with an assessment method and the specific instrument are reduced. Considering the sources of error sampled in Table 9.1, multimethod convergence would be increased by (a) using precisely worded items, terms and time frames in self- and participant report questionnaires; (b) ensuring that comparison instruments attend to the same time frame; (c) ensuring that respondents have sufficient exposure to the targeted behaviors when using participant behavior rating forms; and (d) using well-trained and well-supervised observers in behavioral observation. Acknowledging these challenges to the use of multiple sources in clinical assessment, our main tenet remains unchanged: Clinical judgments are more likely to be valid and useful when based on multiple sources of valid information.

SEPARATING TRUE VARIANCE FROM ERROR VARIANCE IN CLINICAL ASSESSMENT DATA

The convergence of data from multiple assessment methods also depends on the degree to which shared variance across sources would be expected, that is, the degree to which differences in measures from different methods, informants, or settings reflect true differences in the measured construct. As we noted, differences between parent and teacher reports of a child's behavior can reflect the fact that parents and teachers are exposed to true differences in the behavior of the child while at home and school, and the child can truly behave differently in these situations. Similarly, differences among psychophysiological measures of anxiety (e.g., heart rate, electrodermal responses, striated muscle tension) or between physiological and cognitive measures of anxiety can reflect true differences in their underlying causal mechanisms.

An important challenge for the clinician raised by the conditional nature of multisource convergence across measures is how to separate true variance from error variance. How does the clinician know if differences between two measures of the same phenomenon reflect true differences in the measured construct or measurement error associated with the informants, methods, or instruments? The challenge to the clinician is often exacerbated because settings, informants, and methods are confounded in clinical assessment (Cone, 1979). The question is relevant to the validity of all measures obtained in clinical assessment: How does the clinician know the degree to which a measure of a child's social anxiety, an adolescent's early signs of schizophrenia, or an older adult's marital interactions truly reflects that client's behavior, thoughts, and emotions?

Separating true variance from error variance in all clinical assessment contexts is challenging and can only occur through multisource assessment strategies—one must have multiple measures of the same phenomenon, often from multiple methods, informants, and sometimes settings, to separate true variance and error variance. If a combination of a teacher, a teacher's aide, and an external observer agree about the behaviors of a child at school, and a combination of father, mother, and external observer agree about the behavior of the child at home, it is likely that disagreements between these sets of observers reflect true differences in the behavior of the child (see Table 9.2). If only one informant is used in each setting, without additional data it is impossible to separate informant variance from true setting variance because they are confounded. In the last case, our ability to identify behavior problems, construct case formulations, and evaluate treatment outcome is compromised, and the client is less likely to receive the best services.

In Table 9.2, measures from the teacher and observer show good agreement but not with data from the teacher's aide and not with data

TABLE 9.2 Correlations Among Multiple Measures of a Child's Communication Abilities, Across Two Settings, Using the Same Assessment Instrument

School	School			Home		
	Teacher	**Aide**	**Observer**	**Father**	**Mother**	**Sibling**
Teacher	x .2 .7	.2 .2 .2				
Teacher aide		x	.2	.2	.2	.2
Observer				.2	.2	.2
Home						
Father				x	.7	.2
Mother					x	.2
Sibling						

from the home. Data from the mother and father show good agreement but not with data from the sibling. The most likely clinical judgments are (a) mother and father, and teacher and observer, are validly measuring the same phenomenon, and (b) therefore the child is behaving differently across the two settings.

THE DYNAMIC NATURE OF BEHAVIOR AND TIME-RELATED SOURCES OF TRUE VARIANCE AND ERROR VARIANCE

The previous sections of this chapter discussed sources of true variance and error variance that are associated with different assessment methods, informants, and settings. "Time" can also be a source of true variances and error variance in measures derived in clinical assessment. First, as we discussed in Chapters 1 and 4, time is an important consideration in clinical assessment because the attributes of a client's behavior problems and the causal variables associated with those problems are dynamic: The dimensions, aspects, and functional relations of behavior can change over time. For example, two people reporting depressed mood may both experience difficulties sleeping and concentrating. However, one could show a reduction while the other shows an increase across time in one or both of these aspects of depression. Or, a client's depressed mood could be triggered by marital conflict at one time and by an accumulation of daily stressors later. The dynamic nature of many behavior problems is also illustrated by daily (or within-day) changes in the frequency and content of a client's obsessive thoughts, blood pressure, pain-related functional impairment, and physical activity. For some clinical assessment purposes, such as identifying variables that trigger manic episodes and tracking the effects of intervention, clinical assessment must involve time-sampling strategies, and samples must be obtained at a rate that is sensitive to the dynamic characteristics (e.g., rate of change) of the targeted phenomena. The problem for the clinician is that data from only one time sample are insufficient to capture the dynamic aspects of the behavior; at that sampling point, the behavior could have been captured at its peak, trough, or an increasing, decreasing, or plateau phase. It is not sufficient to capture the possibly changing nature of precipitants of the behavior, as noted in this chapter.

Second, as we noted in Chapters 1 and 4 and this chapter, the *time frame* of an assessment can also affect the validity of data we obtain. To increase their sensitivity to changes across time, particularly in response to treatment, many commonly used self-report assessment instruments ask respondents to rate behaviors or environmental events within a specific time frame, such as 1 month (e.g., the General Health Questionnaire) or 1 week (e.g., the CES-D). Several studies have found that the validity of retrospective reports often increases as the time frame is more contiguous with the assessment occasion. That is, reports by clients of behavior for the past week are often more valid than their reports for the past month. A longer or less-contiguous time frame often increases many of the informant-related sources of error discussed previously (e.g., positive response bias, effect of recent events; ambient mood, see Shrout et al., 1988; Terry, Stevens, & Lane, 2005). As with all sources of measurement error, those associated with time frame are also conditional. For example, Jacob (1995) noted that the error associated with more distal time frames varied across assessment instruments.

Third, time-related variance in measures is often confounded with setting. For example, self-monitoring measures of fatigue could provide biased estimates of fatigue throughout the day if they were obtained only while the client was at work or only in the afternoons. The data derived from these time-sampling strategies could accurately represent the client's fatigue at those times but would provide a biased measure of the client's typical fatigue in other settings or throughout the day.

There are several strategies for time sampling in clinical assessment, all designed to capture the dynamic aspects of behavior, but each has its own assets and limitations. *Simple random time sampling* is often used in self-monitoring to reduce the biasing effect associated with sampling at restricted times (see special section in *Psychological Assessment*, vol. 11, pp. 411–497, on self-monitoring, edited by John Cone). For example, a programmable wristwatch or cell phone can be set to give random beeps throughout the day for the client to monitor actions, thoughts, emotions, interpersonal interactions, and environmental events and settings. Systematic time sampling strategies can also be implemented. An example would be observation by staff members, at the top of each hour, of the social interactions or delusional speech of a psychiatric inpatient (this specific method of time sampling is referred to as *momentary time sampling.*

Although random and systematic time sampling within a day are sometimes used in clinical assessment, clinicians are often interested in the conditional nature of clinical phenomena (i.e., the fact that problems and particular causal relations are more likely in some settings than in others). That is, clinicians are often interested in measuring behavior and functional relations during particular time frames, settings, or contexts. For example, the clinician may be most interested in gathering data on the mood of a client after a distressing exchange with a partner. Sampling within designated settings or contexts is an example of *stratified random time sampling* (Minke & Haynes, in press).

Perhaps the most frequently used, and most problematic, time-sampling strategy in clinical practice is *convenience time sampling.* For example, in self-monitoring methods, clients are often asked to indicate at night, just before going to bed, their time spent exercising, the number of positive marital interactions, or the frequency of their child's tantrums that day. Or, the client may be asked to rate progress toward treatment goals at the beginning of a weekly therapy session. Although this sampling strategy increases adherence with the assessment task, it can, because of its retrospective nature, provide erroneous measures and can fail to capture important changes in variables that are highly dynamic.

No sampling strategy is without its limitations, and errors are unavoidable no matter what time-sampling strategy is used. For example, momentary time samples of a psychiatric hospital patient may miss important situations or stimuli associated with the patient's aggressive behaviors or delusional speech. Stratified random sampling has the disadvantage of limited generalizability of the findings.

In summary, obtaining measures from time samples of clients' behavior in the natural environment can often provide valid, sensitive-to-change, and useful information that is unavailable through traditional retrospective self-report methods. As with the use of multiple informants, methods, and settings, multiple time samples in clinically relevant settings can reduce measurement and inferential errors associated with only one sample. Time sampling is also necessary to measure changes in a client's behavior across time and within settings and to identify the causal variables associated with changes in the client's behavior. In selecting the best time-sampling strategy in clinical assessment, we refer to the basic tenet of functional assessment: Select the time-sampling strategy that is most consistent with the goals of assessment. Consider whether the data acquired will be relevant to the inferences that you want to derive with this client.

MULTIMETHOD ASSESSMENT IS CONGRUENT WITH THE MULTIMODAL NATURE OF BEHAVIOR PROBLEMS

We noted in Chapter 1 that behavior problems have multiple response modes and multiple dimensions, and that methods of assessment, and often assessment instruments within a method, differ in their applicability across response modes and dimensions. For example, ambulatory biosensor measurement can often contribute to clinical assessment because many behavioral health problems and their moderators (e.g., exercise, sleep, and responses to traumatic life events) have important motor and physiological aspects (see Weyandt, 2006, for an overview of the physiological bases of behavior disorders).

Multimodal assessment can be important in case formulation and treatment outcome evaluation because response systems can differ in their time course, response to interventions, and their associated causal variables. For example, some persons with anxiety disorders experience hypothalamic-pituitary-adrenocortical (HPA) activation during an anxiety episode (e.g., increased heart rate, rapid breathing) that can be triggered by an environmental stressor. In contrast, cognitive responses during an anxiety episode (e.g., "I am having a heart attack") are more likely to be triggered by physiologically based sensations. Treatment components such as exposure, learning to reinterpret anxiety symptoms,

education, response contingency manipulations, and aerobic condition-
ing can differ in their magnitude, latency, and duration of effects across
response systems.

Research on individual differences in the multimodal aspects of
behavior problems support an idiographic and multisource approach to
clinical assessment (see Text Box 5.3). That is, persons with the same
behavior problem can differ in the importance of different response
systems associated with that behavior problem, which in turn affects
the utility of different assessment methods. For example, persons with
anxiety or other Axis I disorders can differ in the degree to which they
exhibit physiological, subjective, cognitive, or overt behavioral responses
when exposed to environmental stressors (see overviews in Andrasek,
2006). Matching assessment method to the most important response
modality can enhance the clinician's ability to identify important causal
factors and measure change in response to intervention.

INTEGRATING DISCREPANT DATA FROM MULTIPLE SOURCES

We have encouraged clinicians to adopt a multisource approach to
assessment but also observed how data from an informant or other
source can reflect both true variance and error variance in the measured construct. When measures from different informants or different
assessment instruments do not agree, how can the clinician determine
the "true" value of the measured construct (remembering that true is
always an estimate that can vary across setting, etc.)? Consider several assessment outcomes: (a) disagreement among multiple self-report
measures regarding a client's level of generalized anxiety; (b) disagreement among parents, teachers, and a child regarding a child's social
anxiety and peer interactions; (c) differences between a client's self-
monitored and weekly retrospective measures of sleep problems; and
(d) differences between questionnaire and observation measures of how
a parent responds to a child's disobedience. It is our impression that
assessment outcomes such as these tend to be the rule, rather than the
exception, across most clinical settings.

Four principles guide integration of discrepant data. First, consider if
the discordant measures have a similar focus in time, setting, response
mode, and context. If differences cannot be attributable to different
assessment contexts, for example, at least one measure reflects considerable measurement error. Second, examine convergent validity for the
measures used in the assessment. This requires that there be at least
three measures of a construct, such as measures from a teacher, teacher's
aide, and child, about the child's social functioning in one setting, as
illustrated in Table 9.2. High correlations between two suggests that the
third may be measuring a different construct or may be unduly influenced by reporting biases. Third, in assessment contexts in which two

TEXT BOX 9.1   FORMING COMPOSITE MEASURES
AND Z-SCORE TRANSFORMATION

In multisource clinical assessment, a z-score transformation is often used to form a single composite measure from multiple measures of the same construct that differ in their metric or normal distribution. A z score (standard score) is the number of standard deviations an observation or datum is above or below the mean of the sample. It is derived by subtracting the population mean from a client's raw score and then dividing the difference by the sample/population standard deviation. This process converts all measures to the same metric and allows the clinician to combine measures with different metrics and normal distributions and attenuates the measurement error uniquely associated with each.

The formula for a z score is

$$z = \frac{x - \mu}{\sigma}$$

where x is a raw score to be standardized, μ is the mean of the population or sample, and σ is the standard deviation of the population or sample.

When two valid measures of a construct are combined with a z-score transformation, the resulting composite measure should provide a more valid measure of the construct. It is important that the combined measures be homogeneous, that is, they measure the same construct or facet of a construct. It is also important that they not have correlated errors. In time series measurement with a client (e.g., tracking a client's mood states over time), the sample mean is composed of all time samples of the targeted variable.

or more measures have a reasonable level of validity but are in modest disagreement, construct an aggregate of the measures by using a z-score (standard score) transformation and summing (see Text Box 9.1). This aggregate score typically provides a better estimate of the construct of interest because it reduces the idiosyncratic error associated with each measure. Fourth, avoid the use of assessment instruments with overlapping sources of error (e.g., two retrospective self-report questionnaires of generalized anxiety that both fail to measure a client's ability to control his or her worry). As we discussed, forming a composite from measures that have the same sources of error would fail to attenuate those errors.[*]

---

[*] As De Los Reyes and Kazdin (2005) noted, confronting informants with discrepancies between their and other's data may be counterproductive. Such a strategy may force an informant to provide concordant data that does not reflect the informant's judgments or observations.

De Los Reyes and Kazdin (2005) addressed the same question in reference to evaluating the outcome of evidence-based treatment studies: "What if the measures do not all lead to the same conclusion?" (p. 47). They noted that there is no model for integrating inconsistent results, and that such results may reflect true differences in behavior across assessment contexts. The authors advanced a range of possible changes (RPC) model, a classification system to address discrepant results in evidence-based treatments, based on the degree of consistency in outcome of multiple or specific outcome assessment methods.[*]

SUMMARY AND RECOMMENDATIONS

A wide range of issues has been presented in this chapter, all of which bear directly on the validity and potential utility of commonly collected assessment data. There are several recommendations for clinical assessment derived from this chapter on multisource assessment:

1. The clinician should first identify the most important facets (e.g., symptoms, response modes, dimensions) of a client's behavior problems or treatment goals and select the assessment strategies that best measure those facets.
2. Match the assessment strategy to the goals of assessment (e.g., case formulation, treatment outcome evaluation). This suggests at least partial use of an idiographic assessment strategy (i.e., supplement a standard battery of measures with additional measures).
3. Whenever measuring a clinically important construct, use multiple, well-validated assessment methods and instruments, without overlapping sources of error, to reduce measurement error uniquely associated with each method and instrument.
4. Use multisource assessment strategies to estimate the degree to which differences in data from different sources reflect true variance versus error variance.
5. Avoid the use of multiple instruments with overlapping sources of error.

---

[*] Addressing mostly discrepant measures from controlled treatment trials, the authors (De Los Reyes and Kazdin, 2005, p. 49) proposed six categories of outcome evidence. For example, a study would be categorized as "best evidence for change" if at least 80% of the findings from three or more informants, measures, and analytic methods showed differences, and at least three findings were gleaned from each of the informants, measures, and methods. A study would be categorized as "limited evidence for change" if either 50% or less of the findings from three or more informants, measures, and analytic methods showed differences or less than the grand majority (less than 80%) of findings from specific informant's ratings, measures, or methods showed differences.

6. Specify the time frame for measurement that is most useful for the clinical judgments to be made (e.g., daily variation or aggregated over weeks) and avoid excessively retrospective measures.
7. Be cautious about deriving clinical judgments from only one assessment source.
8. Do not add additional sources of data unless they will incrementally contribute to the validity of clinical inferences.
9. When integrating discrepant data, look for evidence of convergent validity and consider whether discrepancies are likely to reflect measurement error or true differences in a client's behavior across time or settings.

RECOMMENDED SOURCES

Burns, G. L., & Haynes, S. N. (2006). Clinical psychology: Construct validation with multiple sources of information and multiple settings. In M. Eid & E. Diener (Eds.), *Handbook of multimethod measurement in psychology* (pp. 401–418). Washington, DC: American Psychological Association.

Campbell, D. T., & Fiske, D. W. (1959). Convergent and discriminant validation by the multi-trait multi-method matrix. *Psychological Bulletin, 56,* 81–105.

Eid, M., & Diener, E. (Eds.). (2006). *Handbook of multimethod measurement in psychology.* Washington, DC: American Psychological Association.

Grimm, K. J., Pianta, R. C., & Konold, T (2009). Longitudinal multitrait-multimethod models for developmental research. *Multivariate Behavioral Research, 44,* 233–258.

Haynes, S. N., & Heiby, E. H (Eds.). (2004). *Comprehensive handbook of psychological assessment, Volume 3, Behavioral assessment.* Hoboken, NJ: Wiley.

GLOSSARY OF TERMS AND CONCEPTS IN THE SCIENTIFIC FOUNDATIONS OF CLINICAL ASSESSMENT

Some terms have more than one definition. In these cases, the first definition is closest to how the term is used in this book.

accuracy: The extent to which obtained measures approximate the "true" state of the targeted variable (often requires a comparison with a "gold standard" measure of the targeted variable).

acquiescence: A **response set** in which the degree to which a measure derived from an assessment instrument reflects the respondent's tendency to answer "yes" or "true" to instrument items.

agreement: (1) The degree of overlap, agreement, or congruence between two more independently obtained measures. (2) The degree of correspondence between the outputs of two or more assessment instruments.

aggregate measure (score): A measure that is formed by combining multiple measures. Similar to a **composite measure**.

alternate forms (of an assessment instrument): Two assessment instruments are considered alternate if their true score, error variance, reliability coefficients, and correlations with other measures are similar but not necessarily equivalent.

analog assessment: (1) The observation of clients (e.g., individual children and adults, families, couples) in an environment that is designed to increase the chance that the assessor can observe clinically important behavior and interactions. (2) An assessment method in which the subject is systematically exposed to one or more hypothesized causal variables while measures of dependent variables (usually the target behavior) are obtained. (3) Direct measurement of behavior in situations different from the participant's natural environment (e.g., role-play assessment of social skills in a clinic setting; observation of parent-child interactions in clinic playroom). (4) Assessment under conditions different from the situation to which one wishes to generalize.

analog assessment, behavior: Direct measurement of behavior in situations different from the participant's natural environment and in which the behavior measured is assumed to be analogous to, or a marker of, the primary behavior of interest (e.g., measuring bar presses of a client to estimate how the subject would respond to various classes of reinforcers; responses on a Stroop test to estimate information-processing bias).

analog behavioral observation (ABO): A method of assessment in which the assessment situation is designed, manipulated, or constrained to increase the occurrence of a behavior or functional relation of interest (for example, observing parent-child interactions in a clinic playroom as the parent is instructed to have the child put away the toys; asking a distressed couple in a clinic setting to discuss a topic about which they disagree).

assessment instrument: A specific tool for deriving measures of (a) the actions, thoughts, emotions of a person; (b) aspects of the environment; or (c) functional relations among variables (e.g., a specific self-report depression questionnaire; a specific marital interaction observation and coding system).

assessment method: A class of procedures or tools for deriving measures on the behavior of a person, aspects of the environment, or functional relations among variables (e.g., self-report questionnaires; analog behavioral observations).

assessment strategy: The overall plan of action for deriving assessment measures. It involves a particular set of assessment methods, instruments, instructions to client, time-sampling parameters, and the context of assessment (e.g., in the clinic, home, or school).

attenuation: A reduction in estimates of true covariance between measured constructs, usually as a result of measurement error, low reliability of measures, or a restricted range of obtained measures.

autocorrelation (serial correlation; serial dependency): (1) The correlation between scores from the same instrument at two different time points. (2) The extent to which values in one part of a time series for a measure predict values in subsequent parts of the time series for that measure.

baseline condition: (1) A phase of data acquisition prior to intervention. (2) A condition or phase of an experiment in which the independent variable is not present.

base rate: The unconditional probability (**marginal probability**) of an event or category for a specified time, condition, or place (e.g., the rate of persons coming to a mental health center who report family violence or are members of a specific ethnic group or the rate of a client's panic episodes prior to treatment).

behavior avoidance test (BAT): An assessment method in which a person is requested to approach a feared object or produce a feared behavior. Obtained measures during the BAT often involve physical proximity to the feared object, anxious behaviors, thoughts, psychophysiological responses, and degree of subjective distress.

behavior disorder: A formalized syndrome composed of several clinically recognizable signs and symptoms (e.g., defined in the *Diagnostic and Statistical Manual of Mental Disorders, Fourth Edition, Text Revision [DSM-IV-TR]* as a "clinically significant behavioral or psychological syndrome or pattern that occurs in an individual and is associated with present distress [e.g., painful symptom] or disability [e.g., impairment in one or more important areas of functioning, such as work, household responsibilities, school] or with a significantly increased risk of suffering death, pain, disability or an important loss of freedom"; American Psychiatric Association, 2000).

behavior problem: Any behavior (i.e., thought, action, emotion, physiological response) that is associated with harm, distress, impairment, or concern, whether or not it meets criteria for a formal diagnosis (e.g., nightmares, depressed mood, threats of violence, marital conflict, binge eating, elevated blood pressure, chronic pain, oppositional behavior, and repetitive unwanted thoughts).

believability: The extent to which judges believe that a measure from an assessment instrument represents the phenomenon it is intended to represent and therefore warrants interpretation (Johnson & Pennypacker, 1993; e.g., the degree to which a measure from a depression scale represents the degree of depression of the respondent).

bias, clinical judgment: A systematic, nonrandom error in clinical judgment. Sources of bias may be age, sex, sexual orientation, appearance, and ethnicity of the client or a priori assumptions of the clinician on any dimension of individual differences.

bias, of a measure or assessment instrument: The degree to which scores from an assessment instrument reflect error in a systematic manner (e.g., the degree to which a measure of anxiety overestimates the level of anxiety).

bias, response: When responses to a question or other assessment element (e.g., responses during analog behavioral observation) vary in a systematic manner as a function of the respondents' prior expectations, intent to affect the assessor, desire to exhibit a socially desirable answer, or tendency to over- or underrate a phenomenon.

bootstrapping: (1) In psychological assessment, a metaphor referring to the iterative process of repeated sampling from within the original sample to provide a closer approximation to, and often refinement of, a measured construct or criterion. (2) As a strategy for refining constructs and their measurement, an ongoing process of building a knowledge base by developing hypotheses, testing them, using those results both to improve the hypotheses and to improve the ability to measure the target constructs.

calibration: A method of establishing the scales, and their meaning, of an assessment instrument by comparing obtained scores with the scores obtained from a "gold standard" instrument (e.g., calibrating measures of blood pressure from an arm occlusion cuff with measures of blood pressure from direct cannulation).

categorical variable: A variable (nominal) that distinguishes among participants by placing them into categories.

causal model (of behavior disorders): A qualitative or quantitative simplified description of the variables hypothesized to control or explain variance in a behavior disorder or problem for an individual or a group of persons.

ceiling effect: (1) The degree to which a measure fails to reflect true changes in the measured construct when the value of the construct exceeds a certain high level. Often, this occurs because a measure lacks the items or tasks necessary to differentiate among individuals at the highest levels of the target construct. (2) Lower magnitudes of shared variance between two measures when one or both variables approach or exceed a certain high level.

classical test theory: An approach to psychometry in which an obtained measure or score in psychological assessment is assumed to be composed of a person's true score for the measured construct and measurement error.

clinical applicability (of an assessment instrument): The degree of **clinical utility** of an assessment instrument across clinical populations, settings, contexts, ages, and other sources of individual differences.

clinical case formulation: (1) An integrated system of clinical judgments and hypotheses about the characteristics of, and functional relations among, a patient's behavior problems and treatment goals and the variables affecting those behavior problems and the likelihood of attaining those goals. (2) An integration of data and inferences from clinical assessment information about the client, with empirical research in psychopathology and therapy, to guide the clinician in making the best intervention decision.

clinical judgment: A prediction, decision, or judgment regarding a client. Clinical judgments include diagnosis, problem identification, clinical case formulation, the prediction of behavior, risk and harm assessment, treatment selection and design, and treatment process and outcome evaluation.

clinical significance/substantive significance: (1) The extent to which an obtained measure or effect (e.g., intervention effect, estimate of shared variance between variables) is important, has practical value, or can guide clinical judgments. (2) The degree to which measures contribute meaningful information and aid clinical judgment.

clinical utility (of a measure or an assessment instrument): The degree to which the results of an assessment instrument assist the clinician in making judgments about a client or enhance the validity of those judgments.

coefficient alpha: An approach to evaluating internal consistency that reflects interitem correlations for scores involving multiple items that have a continuous response format. The formula

$$\alpha = nr_M/[1 + r_M(n - 1)]$$

where n is the number of items and r_M is the mean intercorrelation among all the items.

An alternative formula is

$$\alpha = [n/(n - 1)][1 - \{(\Sigma SD^2_i)/SD^2_T\}]$$

where n is the number of items, SD^2_i is the variance for each item, and SD^2_T is the variance for the total score.

coefficient of determination: The square of the correlation between two measures (r^2); an index of how much variance is shared between the two measures.

coefficient of equivalence: *See* **internal consistency**

coefficient of stability: *See* **temporal stability**

collaborative (therapeutic) assessment strategy: The process of discussing the plans for a clinical assessment and the results of assessment with clients. Usually done as part of case formulation, treatment selection, and the monitoring of treatment effects.

common method variance: Covariance between measures (e.g., correlations) that are attributable to common measurement strategies (e.g., the same respondent or assessment method) rather than to true covariance between the constructs that are being measured.

composite measure (score): A measure that is formed by combining multiple measures. Similar to **aggregate measure**.

conditional probability: The chance that an event will occur given that some other event has occurred. It is the probability of some event A given the occurrence of some other event B, written $P(A|B)$—the (conditional) probability of A given B.

conditional probability fallacy: The assumption that the probability of A, given B, is the same as the probability of B, given A.

confidence interval: A range of values of a measure from a sample that is likely to include the true value for that measure for the population, at a designated confidence level, or probability (typically, 99% or 95%).

confidence limits: The upper and lower boundaries of a confidence interval.

confounding (in measurement): The reliable, systematic variance in measures that is irrelevant to the measured construct and associated with the effects of another variable.

construct: A synthetic variable, usually composed of multiple systematically related elements that are inferred but cannot be directly observed. Similar to a latent variable.

construct homogeneity: (1) The degree to which the elements or facets of a construct are similar in meaning. (2) The degree to which a measure derived from an assessment instrument represents a homogeneous facet or dimension of a psychological construct.

construct-irrelevant test variance: Variance in a measure due to variance in dimensions and facets that is irrelevant to the targeted construct.

construct representation: (1) The degree to which variation in a measure is related to variation in the construct it is presumed to measure. (2) The degree to which a construct is represented validly by a measure from an assessment task (*see also* **validity**).

construct underrepresentation: The degree to which a measure fails to include important dimensions or facets of the targeted construct. Similar to degree of representativeness in **content validity**.

context (of assessment): The conditions surrounding the measurement of a person. Contexts can include naturally occurring settings (such as a classroom or clinic); social factors (such as the presence of strangers or a spouse); states of the person (such as medication state, fatigue, or current stress level); and recent history (such as recent trauma or history of eating or social interactions).

continuous measurement: Measurement in which all possible occurrences of the targeted variable can be detected or measurement that continually tracks changes in the targeted variable.

continuous variable: A variable that can be measured on an interval or ratio scale across a large range of values (in contrast to a **categorical variable**).

convenience time sampling: A time-sampling strategy in which measures are obtained at times that are convenient for the observer (e.g., before mealtimes for a psychiatric nurse, at the end of each class period for a teacher).

cost-benefits (or cost-outcomes, of an assessment instrument, method, or strategy): The cost (e.g., time, treatment delay, financial) of deriving information with an assessment instrument, method, or strategy relative to the contribution of that information to clinical judgments (e.g., enhanced treatment outcome, the identification of behavior problems or causal relations).

criterion: A measure that is to be explained or predicted from another measure. Criteria can be immediate, intermediate, or ultimate.

criterion contamination: When a predictor and criterion assessment instruments contain the same or semantically similar elements; the estimate of shared variance between measures from the two instruments (the predictive relation between the two constructs) is inflated because of the shared elements. *See also* **item contamination**.

criterion keying: A strategy for the construction and validation of an assessment instrument in which the elements of an instrument (e.g., the items on a questionnaire) are selected entirely on the basis of whether they predict a designated criterion.

criterion referenced test (assessment instrument): An assessment instrument whose measures are interpreted in reference to an established criterion or a specified performance standard.

criterion variance: Disagreement between judges or observers (e.g., diagnosticians, observers in the natural environment) that is attributable to insufficiently precise criteria on which the judgment is based (Spitzer, Endicott, & Robins, 1975).

critical event sampling: An assessment strategy in which the most important behaviors, contexts, or causal events are selected for measurement (e.g., assessment on a client only during his or her panic episodes or at only at bedtime for an oppositional child).

critical multiplism (in psychological assessment): A philosophy of science that acknowledges that psychological constructs can be defined and measured in different ways (i.e., multiple operationalism), and that every method of measuring a construct is fallible. Consequently, the validity of a construct must be established through multiple operations and measured in multiple ways. Similarly, the validity of a measure of a construct must be established through multiple evaluations.

cut score: The use of a specific score on a measure to divide the distribution of scores into two (or more) categories.

dependent variable: The variable that may change depending on the value (e.g., occurrence, magnitude) of the independent variable.

deviation (a response set): The degree to which a measure reflects the respondent's tendency to provide uncommon responses.

diagnosis (in clinical assessment): The process of assigning a psychiatric label to a person based on the degree to which the person's **signs** and symptoms conform to standardized inclusion and exclusion criteria.

differential item functioning: Respondents from different groups respond differentially to an item even though they are equal on the trait, construct, behavior, or event that the item measures.

dimension, of measurement, assessment, or event: (1) Quantitative attribute of an event (such as the frequency, duration, magnitude, cyclicity, or rate of an event of interest, for example, the rate, intensity, or duration of headaches or panic episodes). (2) A fundamental quantity, on which psychological/behavioral phenomena can be measured. (3) A homogeneous facet of a construct, such as a "unidimensional" measure of fear. A multidimensional variable has several facets or aspects.

dissimulation (a response set): The degree to which measures derived from an assessment instrument reflect the respondent's intent to affect the derived inferences in a particular direction (e.g., an intent to appear healthy or disturbed on a questionnaire measure of psychopathology). Also known as faking.

dissimulation, negative: When a respondent responds in a way to purposefully appear "bad," "disordered," or "distressed" or to exaggerate symptoms on an assessment instrument. Simply put, it is known as faking bad on an assessment instrument. *See also* **malingering**.

dissimulation, positive: When a respondent responds in a way to purposefully appear "good," "healthy," or "nondistressed" or to minimize symptoms on an assessment instrument. Also known as faking good on an assessment instrument.

domain (of clinical judgment): The conditions, contexts, and limits associated with the validity of a clinical inference (e.g., the validity of a measure of social anxiety may be limited to persons of a certain age or who are at a certain level of severity of anxiety).

ecological validity: Similar to external validity. (1) The degree to which findings from an assessment instrument are generalizable to the setting or context of primary interest (e.g., the degree to which measures from an analog observation assessment of a psychiatric inpatient's social behaviors are indicative of that patient's social behavior while on the psychiatric unit or living at home). (2) The degree to which changes on a standardized measure (e.g., a 3-point change in a measure of mood or anxiety) translate to changes in functioning in everyday life (e.g., the rate or valence of social interactions).

effect indicator model: A measurement model in which responses to assessment instrument items are a function of the amount of the latent trait or construct possessed by the respondent (Bollen & Lennox, 1991).

effect size: A coefficient of the statistical relation between two variables designed to indicate how well variability in one measure can account for variability in another measure. In correlational research, the correlation coefficient r is often used to indicate effect size. In treatment outcome research, d is a way of expressing the difference between two groups in a metric that can be applied across studies (e.g., difference between means divided by pooled standard deviation). Specifically, the mean difference between the control group and the treatment group [($mean_1$ − $mean_2$)/SD of control group] or [($mean_1$ − $mean_2$)/pooled SD], which can then be adjusted to take into account instrument reliability. *See also* **magnitude of effect**.

empiricism: In the behavioral sciences, an epistemology that emphasizes the use of observation and systematic experimentation.

epistemology: A branch of philosophy and philosophy of science that addresses the theory and methods of acquiring knowledge. This includes the methods and criteria used to determine when something is "known" and the sources of error in the acquisition of knowledge (Blackburn, 1994).

equivalence: (1) The degree of congruence between measures from the same instrument, or measures from two different instruments, derived from different groups, within different assessment contexts, or using different assessment methods or strategies. (2) The degree of congruence between measures derived from two assessment instruments that are presumed to be identical measures of the same construct. (3) In cross-cultural psychology, the degree to which a behavior, concept, or measurement procedure shares common meanings and relevance for culturally different groups (Chin & Kameoka, 2006) (*see also* **measurement invariance**).

equivalence, conceptual or functional: The degree to which a measure or indicator (e.g., an item on a questionnaire) has the same meaning across groups.

equivalence, operational: The degree to which the same set of behaviors is used and combined to generate meaning for a construct across groups.

equivalence, scalar: The degree to which the same scores or measures from an assessment instrument mean the same thing for different groups (similar to **equivalence, conceptual** or **functional**).

exportability: The degree to which an assessment instrument developed in one setting can be used in another setting (e.g., the degree to which an analog observation measure of childhood social anxiety developed at a university research clinic can be adopted by clinicians at a community-based clinic).

facets: Components that contribute to an overall whole, as in facets of a construct or variable (e.g., there are behavioral, cognitive, and physiological facets of the construct of depression).

factor: (1) A group of correlated variables that are presumed to affect, or be related to, a higher-order variable. (2) In factor analysis, a cluster of highly correlated variables within a larger group of variables. In mathematics and physiology, the term has multiple meanings.

factor analysis:

> **eigenvalue:** The amount of variance explained by a factor, it is the sum of the squared factor loadings of a factor.
>
> **communality:** The proportion of the total variance of a variable that is explained by the factors. It is the sum of the squared loadings for a variable on each factor.
>
> **oblique rotation:** A procedure for rotating factors geometrically so that each factor is maximally associated with a distinct

cluster of variables that does not require factors to be unrelated to each other.

orthogonal rotation: A procedure for rotating factors geometrically so that each factor is maximally associated with a distinct cluster of variables and unrelated to all other factors.

false negative: A specific outcome is predicted to not occur on the basis of data, and the outcome does occur.

false positive: A specific outcome is predicted to occur on the basis of data, and the outcome does not occur.

floor effect: (1) The degree to which a measure fails to reflect true changes in the measured construct when the value of the construct falls below a certain low level. Often, this occurs because a measure lacks the items or tasks necessary to differentiate among individuals at the lowest levels of the target construct. (2) Lower magnitudes of shared variance between two measures when one or both variables approach or fall below a certain level.

functional analysis: (1) The identification of important, controllable, causal, and noncausal functional relations relevant to specified behaviors for an individual (Haynes & O'Brien, 2000). (2) The experimental manipulation of hypothesized controlling variables as a method of identifying functional relations between the manipulated variable and one or more dependent variables.

functional approach to assessment: An approach to clinical assessment in which the instruments, methods, and strategies used in an assessment occasion are selected on the basis of the goals and contexts of the assessment.

functional assessment: (1) The identification of the antecedent and consequent events that are temporally contiguous to the target response and that occasion and maintain it; often refers to indirect methods of assessment, such as interviews and questionnaires. (2) In rehabilitation psychology and neuropsychology, this terms often refers to the assessment of functional capabilities (e.g., self-help skills, work skills).

functional relation: A functional relation exists when two or more measures or variables have shared variance: Some dimension (e.g., rate, magnitude, length, age) of one variable is associated with some dimension of another. Variables are functionally related when they demonstrate a mathematical relation. Functional relations can be causal or noncausal.

funneling (funnel assessment strategy): A strategy for assessment in which responses to more generally focused instruments or elements are used to subsequently select more specifically focused instruments and elements (e.g., first broadly surveying behavior problems in an interview and then following up with more focused assessment of the specific behavior problems reported by the client).

generalizability: The degree to which data or inferences derived from one sample, setting, context, or behavior are representative of data or inferences from another sample, setting context, or behavior (e.g., the degree to which data derived from a client's responses to a laboratory stressor are generalizable to how the client responds to other stressors in the natural environment).

generalizability theory (G theory): An alternative measurement framework to classical test theory for conceptualizing and investigating the degree to which one can presume that measures from a sample can be generalized across multiple facets, such as time, observers or raters, items, settings, samples, and alternative measures. Uses an analysis-of-variance strategy to study or identify sources of true variation and error variation.

heuristic (in clinical judgment; shortcuts): A decision-making strategy in clinical assessment in which the clinician arrives at judgments about a client on the basis of a limited amount of information or selective weighting of some types of information. Heuristic judgments can be derived quickly but are unlikely to be optimally valid.

homogeneity: The conceptual integrity of a set of elements in an assessment instrument (e.g., the conceptual integrity of items in a questionnaire scale or a set of behavior codes designed to measure a latent construct). Sometimes confused with **internal consistency**.

index of reliability: The square root of the reliability coefficient (assuming that true scores and error scores can be assumed to be independent). Provides the best estimate of the maximum validity of an instrument (e.g., a reliability coefficient of .89 means that the index of reliability is .89; therefore, the maximum validity coefficient possible with the sample is .89).

idiographic assessment: (1) The measurement of variables and functional relations that have been individually selected, or derived from assessment stimuli or contexts that have been individually tailored, to maximize their relevance for the particular individual. (2) The assessment of psychological or behavioral attributes of a person in relation to other aspects of the person (in contrast to **nomothetic assessment**, which compares a person's attributes to those of a reference group).

informant: The person (such as a client, partner, parent, staff member, teacher, clinician, or observer) who supplies data.

informant measures: Measures obtained on a subject from other persons in the natural environment of the subject (e.g., parents, teachers, partners, staff members).

internal consistency: A statistical term referring to the degree of consistency of the items or elements within an assessment instrument when they are used to form a composite measure. Can be reflected by split-half reliability, Kuder-Richardson 20 formula, coefficient alpha (Kazdin, 2002). Sometimes referred to as **coefficients of equivalence**.

internal validity: The degree to which observed changes in a dependent variable are attributable to changes in the independent variable.

interobserver, interrater, interscorer agreement: The degree of agreement between scores (or ratings, diagnoses, behavior rates) obtained from different sources (observers, instruments, and clinicians). Can be indicated by percentage agreement, kappa, or correlation (for estimating linear relations).

intraclass correlation (ICC): In clinical assessment, the ICC is most often used to assess the consistency of measures obtained from multiple observers of the same phenomenon (i.e., the generalizability of a measure across observers or raters); it can also be used to examine temporal stability. There are six models of ICC that can be calculated, depending on whether all or subsets of judges measure all or a subset of subjects and behaviors. ICC models can be sensitive to both the rank order differences in observations and the mean differences in the use of a rating scale.

item characteristic curve (ICC) or response characteristic curve: In item response theory, the ICC is a curve that reflects the probability that, across the range of severities or other dimensions of a construct, a respondent will endorse a response option (estimated by means of measuring the area under the curve).

item contamination: When two assessment instruments contain the same or semantically similar elements. The magnitude of shared variance between the two instruments can overestimate the relation between the two constructs because of the overlapping items. *See also* **criterion contamination**.

item discrimination: The degree to which an item or other element of an assessment instrument (e.g., behavior code, physiological marker) discriminates among subjects who differ on the measured construct.

item response theory (IRT): A measurement model in which item difficulty and discrimination are assumed to determine the probability of a response of an individual who is at a given level on the targeted construct or trait. This model is an alternative to classic test theory.

kappa: A measure of interrater reliability or agreement that adjusts for the level of chance agreement between raters. For dichotomous measures:

$$k = P_o - P_e/1 - P_e$$

P_o = obtained proportion of agreement (agreements/ agreements + disagreements)

P_e = expected proportion of agreement by chance ($P_e =$ $p_1p_2 + q_1q_2$). This is a product of the marginals in a contingency table (note that this number becomes higher as the proportion of either occurrences or nonoccurrences deviates from .5)

Numerator = difference between obtained and expected agreement by chance

Denominator = total possible difference between obtained agreement and expected chance agreement

latent variable: A variable that cannot be directly observed but is inferred from observable measures or operations.

level of inference (specificity): The number of elements, facets, or components subsumed by a variable label. Behavior problems, goals, and causal variables can be at higher or lower levels (sometimes termed *molar* or *molecular, higher order* or *lower order*). A higher-level behavior problem is illustrated by *depression*, which can refer to multiple lower-level facets, such as motor slowness, negative affect, insomnia, and eating disturbances.

likelihood ratio: The degree to which the odds of a correct classification are increased by the use of the assessment data.

LR^+ = Sensitivity/(1 − Specificity) = True Positive Rate/ True Negative Rate.

The odds that a person with a positive test result (i.e., a score above a selected cut score) actually has the characteristic, condition, or diagnosis of interest, and

LR^- = Specificity/(1 − Sensitivity) = True Negative Rate/ True Positive Rate.

The odds that a negative test result (i.e., a score below a selected cut score) does not have the characteristic, condition, or diagnosis of interest.

longitudinal assessment: An assessment strategy that involves repeated measures of participants over time. Longitudinal assessment can, but need not, be **time series assessment**.

magnitude of effect: A measure of the strength of relation between variables, the magnitude of change across time, or the magnitude of difference between groups. The degree to which change in one variable is associated with change in another variable or the proportion of variance accounted for in a dependent variable by variance in an independent variable. Indices of the magnitude of effect include r, R^2, d, η^2, ω^2, and conditional probabilities.

marginal probability: The unconditional probability of A $P(A)$, that is, the probability of A independent of the occurrence or nonoccurrence of B.

marker variable: A variable whose value is correlated with another variable of primary interest or the magnitude of covariance between two variables (e.g., a parental history of hypertension may serve as a marker variable for an increased probability that a client will develop hypertension, the variable of primary interest).

measure (or score): (1) A number that represents the value of a variable being measured. The data obtained from a measurement process or an assessment instrument (e.g., a blood pressure reading obtained from a sphygmomanometer, a scale score obtained from the Minnesota Multiphasic Personality Inventory (MMPI)) (note that some assessment instruments provide multiple measures). (2) In psychological assessment literature, *measure* sometimes refers to the tool used to collect data.

measurement: (1) The process of assigning a numerical value to a variable dimension so that relations of the numbers reflect true relations among the measured variables (e.g., the process of obtaining measures of a child's rate of aggressive behaviors in a classroom or clinic setting). (2) The process of assigning numbers to properties or attributes of people, objects, or events using a set of rules (Stevens, 1968).

measurement equivalence: *See* **measurement invariance** and **equivalence**

measurement/assessment strategy: (1) The overall plan of assessment; it involves a particular set of assessment methods, instruments, instructions to the client, the timing of assessments, and the settings and contexts of assessment.

measurement invariance (equivalence): (1) The degree of congruence between measures from the same instrument derived from different groups, assessment contexts, or strategies. (2) The equivalence of a measured construct in two or more groups or contexts (e.g., between young and old participants or between persons from different ethnic backgrounds). *See also* **equivalence**.

mediating variable (mediator): (1) A variable that accounts for, or explains, the relation between two other variables; similar to a causal mechanism. (2) The mechanism through which the independent variable influences the dependent variable.

method variance: Variance in measures attributable to the measurement method (or instrument of respondent) rather than to the constructs that the measures represent.

model: A generalized, simplified, and hypothetical description of a complex phenomenon.

momentary time sampling: (1) An observation procedure in which the observer records the status of selected behaviors and events at the end of preset intervals. (2) Measuring a variable at a single instant in time or at preset times; sometimes referred to as "flashpoint" sampling (e.g., observing the occurrence or non-occurrence of a patient's "aggressive" behaviors on a psychiatric unit every 2 hours or before lunch).

monomethod assessment: An assessment strategy that includes only one method of gathering information, such as using only self-report questionnaires in the assessment of a client.

monosource assessment: A general term referring to an assessment that includes only one source of information, such as one respondent (client, parent, teacher, or spouse), one method of assessment, or one assessment instrument.

monotonic functional relation: (1) The degree to which a measure accurately tracks, in linear or nonlinear fashion, changes in the target phenomenon. (2) When scores on a measure consistently increase with increases in the level of the target phenomenon and consistently decrease with decreases in the level of the target phenomenon.

multicollinearity: When two or more variables are highly correlated. In multiple regression, multicollinearity makes it difficult to separate the independent effects of variables, and in psychological assessment it implies that two measures are tapping the same facets of the same variable.

multi-informant assessment: An assessment strategy that involves the collection of data from more than one informant (e.g., client, parents, teachers, spouse, and staff members).

multimethod assessment: An assessment strategy that involves more than one method of gathering information (e.g., observation, self-monitoring, psychophysiological assessment, and interviews).

multisource assessment: An assessment strategy that involves the use of multiple methods, informants, contexts, or times in clinical assessment.

nomothetic assessment: The assessment process in which judgments about a person are based on comparison of data from the person with data from other persons who completed the same assessment instrument administered in a standardized manner (e.g., inferences about persons from Minnesota Multiphasic Personality Inventory [MMPI] scale scores or Wechsler Adult Intelligence Scale [WAIS] scores are often based on norms derived from large samples).

negative predictive power: (1) True negative rate/true negative + false negative rate; the proportion of individuals indicated on the basis of a measure as not having a disorder or behavior who truly do not. (2) The probability that an individual does not have a characteristic, condition, or diagnosis when the classification criterion indicates that the person does not have it. Sometimes confused with **specificity**.

norm-referenced test (assessment instrument): An assessment instrument whose measures are interpreted in reference to data derived from others using the same assessment instrument.

odds ratio: (1) By what amount the odds of being in a target group are multiplied when the predictor is incremented by a value of

1 unit (Cohen et al., 2003). (2) The ratio of the odds of an event occurring in one group to the odds of it occurring in another group or to a sample-based estimate of that ratio. For example, the ratio of the odds that a person with no parental history of schizophrenia will develop schizophrenia compared to the odds that a person with one or two parents with a history of schizophrenia will develop schizophrenia.

obtrusive measurement: An assessment instrument that affects the behavior of the participant or others in the participant's environment; an assessment instrument that the participant is aware of and that produces **reactive effects**.

operational definition (operationalization): The procedures or measurements that give meaning to a construct or theoretical term. It includes a precise definition of the concept and how it is to be measured. One concept can have multiple operational definitions. Validity of an operational definition is the degree to which its values predict theoretically related external phenomena (e.g., measures derived from an operational definition of intelligence must predict other important related phenomena) (Johnston & Pennypacker, 1993).

paradigm: The principles, beliefs, values, hypotheses and methods advocated in a discipline or by its adherents. A clinical assessment paradigm includes beliefs and hypotheses about the relative importance of behavior problems, the causal variables that affect behavior, the mechanisms of causal action, the importance of assessment, and the best methods of obtaining data and gathering psychometric evidence. It also includes guidelines for deductive and inductive problem solving, decision-making strategies, and data interpretation.

parallel forms (of a test): Within classical test theory, two tests are considered parallel if their true score and error variance, reliability coefficients, and correlations with other measures are equivalent. If these criteria are not met or only approximated, the tests are considered **alternate forms** instead; that is, they are considered similar but do not meet the strict criteria associated with parallel forms.

parameter: (1) Sometimes used to refer to a "domain": a quantifiable dimension of a variable, sample or population (e.g., behavior problem, causal variable, or group). Examples of parameters include magnitude, duration, level, latency, frequency, recovery rate, intensity, mean, and standard deviation. (2) In statistics, a numerical characteristic of an attribute (e.g., mean, standard deviation) in a population that is estimated by a sample. (3) Limit or boundary.

parsimony: (1) The degree to which the ratio of predictor/explanatory elements that provide a particular outcome is maximized. (2) Economy of measurement and prediction. Given equal outcomes (e.g., a valid clinical judgment), the strategy that includes the least measures and variables without reducing predictive efficacy.

participant observation: (1) Observation by a person who is normally part of the client's natural environment (e.g., teachers, staff, parents). (2) In ethnographic research, observation, usually qualitative, by an observer who is not normally part of the client's natural environment. In this research strategy, the observer typically joins and participates in the natural environment to derive subjective judgments about the environment.

positive predictive power: (1) The positive "hit rate" for an assessment instrument score; true positive rate/(true positive + false positive rate). (2) The probability that an individual has a characteristic, condition, or diagnosis when the classification criterion indicates that the person has it. For example, the degree to which a person identified on the basis of a measure as having an eating disorder truly has the disorder. Sometimes confused with **sensitivity**.

power (of an assessment instrument or measure): (1) The predictive accuracy of measures from an assessment instrument. Usually estimated by (a) the proportion of persons identified as having and not having a disorder or attribute who truly do and do not have the disorder or attribute or (b) the proportion of persons a measure accurately identifies with (**sensitivity**) an attribute (such as a diagnosis). (2) For individuals who have a target attribute, the probability that a measure will reflect the presence of the attribute (note that there are different meanings for the term in statistics and mathematics).

precision, of a measure: (1) The accuracy, specificity, repeatability, and sensitivity to change of a measure. (2) The degree to which a measure approximates the "true" value of the selected variable and is estimated through coefficients of internal consistency, temporal stability, and dispersion (Marriott, 1990).

predictive efficacy (predictive validity): The degree to which a measure can predict another measure, usually taken at a later time, although the time frame can be implied rather than real (e.g., the degree to which an IQ measure predicts grades).

psychological assessment: The systematic measurement of a person's behavior, variables associated with variance in behaviors, and the inferences and judgments based on those measurements. It incorporates measurement instruments, methods, strategies, and targets (e.g., behavior problems, causal and correlated variables) and the inferences and clinical judgments (e.g., functional analysis, diagnosis, estimates of treatment outcome) based on the obtained measures.

psychometrics: The evaluative processes applied to psychological assessment. Psychometrics is concerned with the evaluation of data from assessment instruments and the judgments based on those data; it is the science of psychological measurement.

psychometric continuity: The degree to which scores on elements of an assessment instrument (such as items on a questionnaire) differentiate individuals with varying degrees of a construct or behavior problem (e.g., the degree to which items on a questionnaire on depression differentiate persons throughout the continuum of depression severity or the degree to which a measure demonstrates a monotonic functional relation with the measured variable). An important focus in IRT in terms of differential item functioning.

random responding: Responding to items on a measurement instrument in an unpredictable manner and unrelated to the content of the item.

Range of Possible Changes (RPC) Model: A classification system proposed by De Los Reyes and Kazdin (2005) to address discrepant results from multiple measures in evidence-based treatments; based on examining the degree of consistency in outcome of multiple or specific outcome assessment methods.

reactive effects (of assessment): The degree to which an assessment process modifies the behavior of the target person or the behavior of others in the target person's environment.

receiver operating characteristics (ROCs): A strategy to evaluate the predictive efficacy of a measure across a range of cut scores by constructing an ROC curve that plots positive rates against true negative rates. Values can range from .5 (chance discrimination) to 1.0 (perfect discrimination).

Reliable Change Index: An approach to estimating the clinical significance of treatment effects, based on the degree of pre-to-posttreatment change in a measure, the standard deviation of that measure for the client's sample, and the internal consistency of the measure,

$$\text{RCI} = (X_{post} - X_{pre})/\text{sqrt}\{2[SD_{pre} * \text{sqrt}(1 - r_{xx})]^2\}$$

where X_{post} is the posttreatment score, X_{pre} is the pretreatment score, SD_{pre} is the standard deviation of the client sample scores at pretreatment, and r_{xx} is the reliability (coefficient alpha) of the measure. The RCI value must be at least ±1.96 to be considered significant.

reliability: (1) The part of a test result that is due to permanent, systematic effects and therefore persists across time and settings. (2) The stability of data yielded by an assessment instrument under constant conditions. (3) The degree to which measures of individuals taken by similar or parallel instruments, by different observers, or at different points in time yield the same or similar results.

reliability, alternative form: The correlation between measures from different forms of the same assessment instrument when all items are presumed to tap the same construct or to be drawn from the same pool.

reliability generalization: The degree to which indices of reliability of a measure can be generalized across samples or measurement settings or contexts. Often estimated through meta-analyses of reliability data obtained from multiple studies.

reliability, interrater: The degree to which different observers or raters agree on the dimensions (e.g., occurrence, magnitude) of an event or behavior of a person being measured. Often estimated with kappa or intraclass correlation coefficients.

reliability, test-retest: *See* **temporal stability**

reliability coefficient: A coefficient that represents the true, as distinct from error, variance in a measure.

residual variance (unexplained variance): (1) Variance that remains after shared or explained variance (R^2) between two variables has been removed. (2) That part of variance in a variable that is not attributable to a specific other variable. Residual variance can be a function of random or systematic variation.

response set: Systematic or unsystematic variance in responses to an assessment instrument that are a function of variables other than the assessment instrument content. Can include **dissimulation, random responding,** and **social desirability**.

sample (in measurement theory): An event or measure of an event that is presumed to be an element of a criterion, or the criterion itself, and therefore of interest itself rather than as a sign of a latent variable or inferred construct. Examples include measures of aggressive behavior, blood pressure, short-term memory, and response contingencies (*see also* **sign**). This use of sample is different from the use of sample in research design to denote a group of individuals who are a subset of a population of interest and represent that population for research purposes.

scale: A set of graduations and figures that calibrate a measurement instrument or obtained measure (Darton & Clark, 1994).

scale, interval: When numbers are assigned to persons or objects that are rank ordered on an attribute and the differences between the numbers can be meaningfully interpreted. Involves the use of constant units of measurement and a presumption equality of intervals or differences (Nunnally & Bernstein, 1994).

scale, log interval: Persons or objects are assigned numbers such that ratios between the numbers reflect ratios of the attribute.

scale, nominal: When numbers are assigned to unordered classes of objects.

scale, ordinal: When numbers are assigned to persons or objects on the basis of their rank order on an attribute without implying equal differences between ranks.

scale, ratio: When numbers are assigned to persons or objects on an interval scale that also has a true 0 point (Pedhazur & Schmelkin, 1991). A scale that allows the determination of equality, order, the quality of intervals among data values, and the equality of ratios among values (Nunnally & Bernstein, 1994).

score: In this book, used interchangeably with **measure**. A number that represents the variable measured. The data obtained from a measurement process or assessment instrument.

sensitivity: (1) The proportion of positive cases so identified on the basis of a measure from a particular assessment instrument. (2) The probability that a person with a particular attribute will manifest a particular behavior. *See also* **positive predictive power**.

sensitivity to change: The degree to which measures from an instrument reflect true changes across time in the targeted construct.

shared-method variance (common method variance): The similarity in the procedures used to acquire data, which can contribute to the magnitude of correlation between data from different assessment instruments (e.g., both instruments are self-report; both instruments use the same informant; two instruments include semantically similar items).

sign (in measurement): An event or measure of an event that is significantly related to a phenomenon of interest. A referent, which may or may not be of interest itself, that demonstrates a functional relation to, or is an indicator of, a criterion or latent variable. Examples include a score on a questionnaire that represents a higher-order construct such as depressed mood; a biological marker for alcohol or drug use. *See also* **marker variable**.

simple random time sampling: A time sampling assessment strategy in which measures are obtained randomly throughout a specified period (e.g., throughout a day).

skewness: The degree of asymmetry in the distribution of scores. A positive skew indicates a disproportionate number of low scores.

slope: A coefficient of rate and direction of change in one variable in relation to change in another variable. It sometimes refers to the rate and direction of change of a variable over time.

social desirability (characteristic an assessment instrument): A response set. The degree to which measures derived from an assessment instrument reflect the respondent's tendency to provide socially approved or accepted responses.

specificity, of an assessment instrument: The probability that a person without a particular attribute will be so identified on the basis of a measure from a particular assessment instrument. The proportion of negative cases so identified by an assessment instrument.

specificity, of a measure or variable: The degree of molarity or precision of a measure. Can refer to (a) the diversity and number of elements subsumed by a measure (**level of inference**); (b) the degree to which the dimensions or parameters of a variable are specified (e.g., a measure that provides an overall score for "depression" vs. one that provides separate scores for the duration or intensity of depression episodes); (c) the degree to which situational and temporal conditions relevant for the target variable are specified (e.g., a measure that provides an overall score for a child's aggressive behavior vs. one that provides a score for the child's aggressive behavior in different settings); and (d) the level of specificity of clinical judgments based on obtained measures.

standard error of measurement (standard error of a score): In classical test theory, the standard deviation of the errors in measurement. It is calculated as the positive square root of the reliability of a test r_{tt} multiplied by the standard deviation of test scores SD_t:

$$SD_t(1 - r_{tt})^{1/2}$$

or

$$SEM = SD_T \text{sqrt}(1 - r_{xx})]$$

where SD_T is the standard deviation of the total score for the sample on which the reliability was determined, and r_{xx} is the reliability (alpha) of the instrument.

standard score: A measure of the relative standing of a subject among a group, usually derived by transforming raw scores into a z score (reflecting a person's standing in relation to the mean and standard deviation of the group).

stratified random time sampling: A time-sampling strategy in which measures are obtained randomly within designated settings, times, or contexts (e.g., obtaining random measures of a child's behavior during a particular classroom activity).

syndrome: Several signs or symptoms that often occur together, are typically thought to have a common cause, and serve as indicators of a behavior disorder, behavior problem, disease, or underlying pathology. Examples include SARS (severe acute respiratory syndrome), Korsakoff's syndrome, and sleep apnea syndrome.

temporal stability (test-retest reliability): The degree of linear relation of a measure obtained across occasions from the same instrument, individuals, and assessment conditions. The correlation of scores, from the same instrument obtained from the same individuals, at two different points in time. Measures of temporal stability are sometimes termed **coefficients of stability**.

time course: (1) The values of a variable dimension as a function of time. (2) The temporally related dimensions of a variable, such as cyclicity, latency, duration, and rate. The time courses of variables are frequently presented in graphical form, with time on the horizontal axis and the value of the variable on the vertical axis.

time-frame, of assessment/measurement: (1) The period of time to which a measurement refers (e.g., past month or past day). (2) The period of time within which measures are obtained (e.g., within a particular hour of the day).

time series assessment: Includes a diverse set of assessment strategies to describe and analyze the time courses and interrelations of multiple variables. With time series assessment, behavior problems or hypothesized causal variables are measured frequently (e.g., 30 or more measurements) across time. Measurement occurs at a sufficient rate to detect serial correlations and rapid changes in the time series.

treatment mechanism: The process or mechanism of action through which an intervention affects a behavior.

true negative: A specific outcome is predicted to not occur on the basis of data, and the outcome does not occur.

true positive: A specific outcome is predicted to occur on the basis of data, and the outcome does occur.

validity: (1) The degree to which changes on a dimension of an attribute produce changes in a measure of that attribute dimension (e.g., Borsboom et al., 2004). (2) How well a measure from an instrument measures what it purports to measure (Nunnally & Bernstein, 1994). (3) An overall judgment of the degree to which empirical evidence and theoretical rationales support the adequacy and appropriateness of inferences based on the data acquired from an assessment instrument (Messick, 1995). (4) The meaning of scores from an assessment instrument (Cronbach & Meehl, 1955). Closest in meaning to **construct validity**.

validity, concurrent: The degree to which multiple measures of the same construct obtained on the same assessment occasion are correlated.

validity, consequential: The validity of the implications and applications of measures (Messick, 1995; e.g., the appropriate use of data from educational testing to design an individualized educational plan for a child).

validity, construct: (1) Comprises the evidence and rationales supporting the trustworthiness of assessment instrument data interpretation in terms of explanatory concepts that account for both the obtained data and relations with other variables (Messick, 1995). (2) The degree of validity of inferences about unobserved variables (constructs) based on observed indicators (Pedhazur & Schmelkin, 1991). (3) The degree to which the measure assesses the domain, trait, or characteristic of interest;

refers broadly to the evidence bearing on the measure and encompasses all types of validity (Kazdin, 2002).

validity, content: The degree to which elements of an assessment instrument are relevant to and representative of the targeted construct for a particular assessment purpose (Haynes et al., 1995).

validity, convergent: (1) The degree to which the data from an assessment instrument are coherently related to other measures of the same construct as well as to other variables that it is expected, on theoretical grounds, to be related (Messick, 1995). (2) The degree of covariance between scores from two assessment instruments that measure the same or related constructs.

validity, criterion referenced (criterion-related validity; criterion validity): (1) The degree to which measures from an assessment instrument correlate with scores from previously validated instruments that measure the phenomena of interest or with nontest criteria of practical value. (2) Correlation of a measure with some other (validated) criteria.

validity, discriminant (divergent): (1) The degree to which data from an assessment instrument are not unduly related to other exemplars of other constructs. (2) The degree to which data from an assessment instrument are distinct from measures of dissimilar constructs. Discriminant validity of an instrument is suggested by small or no significant correlation with data from instruments that tap dissimilar but potentially related constructs. Discriminant validation evidence is most useful when applied to constructs that should not, but could, account for variance in the primary measure of interest.

validity, discriminative: The degree to which measures from an assessment instrument can differentiate individuals in groups, formed from independent criteria, known to vary on the measured construct (e.g., the ability of a score from a marital inventory to differentiate individuals who are and who are not seeking marital counseling).

validity, ecological: The generalizability of measures, and judgments from measures, to the populations, contexts, purposes, or situations that are of primary interest of the assessment (e.g., the degree to which data derived from "depressed" college students are generalizable to persons seeking assistance for "depression" at an outpatient mental health center; the degree to which samples of couple interactions in a clinic setting are representative of how they interact at home).

validity, face: A component of content validity. The degree that respondents or users judge that the items of an assessment instrument are appropriate to the targeted construct and assessment objectives (Anastasi & Urbina, 1997). It is commonly thought to measure the "acceptability" of the assessment instrument to users and administrators.

validity, incremental: The degree to which a measure explains or predicts; some phenomena of interest, relative to another measure.

validity predictive (predictive efficacy): The degree to which a measure can predict another measure, usually taken at a later time.

validity, social (in clinical assessment): The degree to which users of assessment data (e.g., parents, teachers, clients, clinicians, administrators) believe the assessment methods, strategies, instruments, and measures are valuable and socially acceptable.

variance: The sum of the deviations of individual scores from the mean, divided by N; variance $= \Sigma x^2/N$, where $x^2 =$ the deviation of a score, squared.

REFERENCES

Abramowitz, J. S., Tolin, D. F., & Diefenbach, G. J. (2005). Measuring change in OCD: Sensitivity of the Obsessive-Compulsive Inventory-Revised. *Journal of Psychopathology and Behavioral Assessment, 27,* 317–324.

Achenbach, T. M., & Edelbrock, C. S. (1978). The classification of child psychopathology: A review and analysis of empirical efforts. *Psychological Bulletin, 85,* 1275–1301.

Achenbach, T. M., McConaughy, S. H., & Howell, C. T. (1987). Child/adolescent behavioral and emotional problems: Implications of crossinformant correlations for situational specificity. *Psychological Bulletin, 101,* 213–232.

Ægisdóttir, S., White, M. J., Spengler, P. M., Maugherman, A. S., Anderson, L. A., Cook, R. S., et al. (2006). The meta-analysis of clinical judgment project: Fifty-six years of accumulated research on clinical versus statistical prediction. *The Counseling Psychologist, 34,* 341–382.

American Educational Research Association, American Psychological Association, National Council on Measurement in Education. (1999). *Standards for educational and psychological testing.* Washington, DC: American Educational Research Association.

American Psychiatric Association. (1994). *Diagnostic and statistical manual of mental disorders* (4th ed.). Washington, DC: Author.

American Psychiatric Association. (2000). *Diagnostic and statistical manual of mental disorders* (4th ed., text revision). Washington, DC: Author.

American Psychological Association Presidential Task Force on Evidence-Based Practice. (2006). Evidence-based practice in psychology. *American Psychologist, 61,* 271–285.

Ames, H., Hendrickse, W. A., Bakshi, R. S., Lepage, J. P., & Keefe, C. (2009). Utility of the Neurobehavioral Cognitive Status Examination (Cognistat) with geriatric mental health outpatients. *Clinical Gerontologist: The Journal of Aging and Mental Health, 32,* 198–210.

Anastasi, A. (1950). The concept of validity in the interpretation of test scores. *Educational and Psychological Measurement, 10,* 67–78.

Anastasi, A., & Urbina, S. (1997). *Psychological testing* (7th ed.). Upper Saddle River, NJ: Prentice-Hall.

Andrasek, F. (2006). *Adult psychopathology.* New York: Wiley.

Antony, M. M., & Barlow, D. H. (Eds.). (2010). *Handbook of assessment and treatment planning for psychological disorders* (2nd ed.). New York: Guilford Press.

Antony, M. M., Orsillo, S. M., & Roemer, L. (Eds.). (2001). *Practitioner's guide to empirically based measures of anxiety.* New York: Plenum.

Aschenbrand, S. G., Angelosante, A. G., & Kendall, P. C. (2005). Discriminant validity and clinical utility of the CBCL with anxiety-disordered youth. *Journal of Clinical Child and Adolescent Psychology, 34,* 735–746.

Atkins, D. C., Bedics, J. D., McGlinchey, J. B., & Beauchaine, T. P. (2005). Assessing clinical significance: Does it matter which method we use? *Journal of Consulting and Clinical Psychology, 73,* 982–989.

Bagby, R. M., Marshall, M. B., & Bacchiochi, J. R. (2005). The validity and clinical utility of the MMPI-2 malingering depression scale. *Journal of Personality Assessment, 85,* 304–311.

Bartko, J. J., & Carpenter, W. T. (1976). On the methods and theory of reliability. *Journal of Nervous and Mental Disease, 163,* 307–317.

Bartley, W. W., III. (1987). Philosophy of biology versus philosophy of physics. In G. Radnitzky and W. W. Bartley III (Eds.), *Evolutionary epistemology, rationality, and the sociology of knowledge* (pp. 7–46). La Salle, IL: Open Court.

Bechtoldt, H. P. (1951). Selection. In S. S. Stevens (Ed.), *Handbook of experimental psychology* (pp. 1237–1266). Oxford, UK: Wiley.

Beiling, P. J., & Kuyken, W. (2003). Is cognitive case formulation science or science fiction? *Clinical Psychology: Science and Practice, 10,* 52–69.

Bellack, A. S., Mueser, K. T., Gingerich, S., & Agresta, J. (1997). *Social skills training for schizophrenia—A step-by-step guide.* New York: Guilford Press.

Beutler, L. E., & Harwood, T. M. (2000). *Prescriptive therapy: A practical guide to systematic treatment selection.* New York: Oxford University Press.

Beutler, L. E., Malik, M., Talebi, H., Fleming, J., & Moleiro, C. (2004). Use of psychological tests/instruments for treatment planning. In M. E. Maruish (Ed.), *The use of psychological testing for treatment planning and outcomes assessment. Volume 1, General considerations* (3rd ed., pp. 111–145). Mahwah, NJ: Erlbaum.

Bingenheimer, J. B., Raudenbush, S. W. Leventhal, T., & Brooks-Gunn, J. (2005). Differential item functioning in family psychology. *Journal of Family Psychology, 19,* 441–455.

Blackburn, S. (1994). *The Oxford dictionary of philosophy.* New York: Oxford University Press.

Blanton, H., & Jaccard, J. (2006). Arbitrary metrics in psychology. *American Psychologist, 61,* 27–41.

Blumberg, A. E., & Feigl, H. (1931). Logical positivism. *Journal of Philosophy, 28,* 281–296.

Bollen, K., & Lennox, R. (1991). Conventional wisdom on measurement: A structural equation perspective. *Psychological Bulletin, 110,* 305–314.

Borsboom, D., Mellenbergh, G. J., & van Heerden, J. (2004). The concept of validity. *Psychological Review, 111,* 1061–1072.

Bossuyt, P. M., Reitsma, J. B., Bruns, D. E., Gatsonis, C. A., Glasziou, P. P., Irwig, L. M., et al. for the STARD Group. (2003). Towards complete and accurate reporting of students of diagnostic accuracy: The STARD initiative. *Clinical Chemistry, 49,* 1–6.

Broderick, J. E., Schwartz, J. E., Vikingstad, G., Pribbernow, M., Grossman, S., & Stone, A. A. (2008). The accuracy of pain and fatigue items across different reporting periods. *Pain, 139,* 146–157.

Brooks, B. L., Strauss, E., Sherman, E. M. S., Iverson, G. L., & Slick, D. J. (2009). Developments in neuropsychological assessment: Refining psychometric and clinical interpretive methods. *Canadian Psychology, 50,* 2196–2209.

Brown, T. A. & Barlow, D. H. (2009). A proposal for a dimensional classification system based on the shared features of the DSM-IV anxiety and mood disorders: Implications for assessment and treatment. *Psychological Assessment, 21,* 256–271.

Brown, T. A., Campbell, L. A., Lehman, C. L., Grisham, J. R., & Mancill, R. B. (2001). Current and lifetime comorbidity of the DSM-IV anxiety and mood disorders in a large clinical sample. *Journal of Abnormal Psychology, 110,* 585–589.

Browne, M. W., & Cudeck, R. (1993). Alternative ways of assessing model fit. In K. A. Bollen & J. S. Long (Eds.), *Testing structural equation models* (pp. 136–162). Newbury Park, CA: Sage.

Burns, G. L., & Haynes, S. N. (2006). Clinical psychology: Construct validation with multiple sources of information and multiple settings. In M. Eid & E. Diener (Eds.), *Handbook of multimethod measurement in psychology* (pp. 401–418). Washington, DC: American Psychological Association.

Burlingame, G. M., Mosier, J. I., Wells, M. G., Atkin, Q. G., Lambert, M. J., Whoolery, M., et al. (2001). Tracking the influence of mental health treatment: The development of the Youth Outcome Questionnaire. *Clinical Psychology and Psychotherapy, 8,* 361–379.

Butcher, J. N. (1990). *Use of the MMPI-2 in treatment planning.* New York: Oxford University Press.

Butcher, J. N. (1995). *Clinical personality assessment: Practical approaches,* 2nd edition. New York: Oxford University Press.

Butcher, J. N. (2009). *Clinical personality assessment: Practical approaches.* New York: Oxford University Press.

Butcher, J. N., Graham, J. R., & Ben-Porath, Y. S. (1995). Methodological problems and issues in MMPI, MMPI-2, and MMPI-A research. *Psychological Assessment, 7,* 320–329.

Butcher, J., & Perry, J. (2008). *Personality assessment in treatment planning: Use of the MMPI-2 and BTPI.* New York: Oxford University Press.

Cacciola, J. S., Pecoraro, A., & Alterman, A. I. (2008). Development of ASI psychiatric severity cut-off scores to identify co-occurring psychiatric disorders. *International Journal of Mental Health and Addiction, 6,* 77–92.

Campbell, D. T., & Fiske, D. W. (1959). Convergent and discriminant validation by the multi-trait multi-method matrix. *Psychological Bulletin, 56,* 81–105.

Charles, E. P. (2005). The correction for attenuation due to measurement error: Clarifying concepts and creating confidence sets. *Psychological Methods, 10,* 206–226.

Chen, F. F. (2008). What happens if we compare chopsticks with forks? The impact of making inappropriate comparisons in cross-cultural research. *Journal of Personality and Social Psychology, 95,* 1005–1018.

Chin, D., & Kameoka, V. (2006). Sociocultural influences. In F. Andrasek (Ed.), *Comprehensive handbook of personality and psychopathology* (pp. 67–84). Hoboken, NJ: Wiley.

Chmielewski, M., & Watson, D. (2009). What is being assessed and why it matters: The impact of transient error on trait research. *Journal of Personality and Social Psychology, 97,* 186–202.

Christensen, A., & Hazzard, A. (1983). Reactive effects during naturalistic observation of families. *Behavioral Assessment, 5,* 349–362.

Clark, L. A., & Watson, D. (1991). Tripartite model of anxiety and depression: Psychometric evidence and taxonomic implications. *Journal of Abnormal Psychology, 100,* 316–336.

Cohen, J. A. (1960). A coefficient of agreement for nominal scales. *Educational and Psychological Measurement, 20,* 37–46.

Cohen, J. (1969). *Statistical power analysis for the behavioral sciences.* New York: Academic Press.

Cohen, J., Cohen, P., West, S.G., & Aiken, L.S. (2003). *Applied multiple regression/correlation analysis for the behavioral sciences* (3rd edition). Mahwah, NJ: Lawrence Erlbaum Associates.

Cole, D. A., Martin, J. M., Powers, B., & Truglio, R. (1996). Modeling causal relations between academic and social competence and depression: A multitrait-multimethod longitudinal study of children. *Journal of Abnormal Psychology, 105,* 258–270.

Combs, J., Smith, G. T., Flory, K., Simmons, J. R., & Hill, K. K. (2010). The acquired preparedness model of eating disorder risk. *Psychology of Addictive Behaviors, 24,* 475–486.

Cone, J. D. (1979). Confounded comparisons in triple response mode assessment research. *Behavioral Assessment, 11,* 85–95.

Connell, J., Barkham, M., Stiles, W. B., Twigg, E., Singleton, N., Evans, O., et al. (2007). Distribution of CORE-OM scores in a general population, clinical cut-off points and comparison with the CIS-R. *British Journal of Psychiatry, 190,* 69–74.

Connor, J., & Rueter, M. (2009). Predicting adolescent suicidality: Comparing multiple informants and assessment techniques. *Journal of Adolescence, 32,* 619–631.

Conway, J. M., Lombardo, K., & Sanders, K. C. (2001). A meta-analysis of incremental validity and nomological networks for subordinate and peer ratings. *Human Performance, 14,* 267–303.

Costa, P. T., Jr., & McCrae, R. R. (1992). *Revised NEO Personality Inventory (NEO PI-R) and NEO Five-Factor Inventory (NEO-FFI) professional manual.* Odessa, FL: Psychological Assessment Resources.

Costello, A. B., & Osborne, J. W. (2005). Best practices in exploratory factor analysis: Four recommendations for getting the most from your analysis. *Practial Assessment, Research and Evaluation, 10,* 1–9.

Cronbach, L. J. (1951). Coefficient alpha and the internal structure of tests. *Psychometrika, 16,* 297–334.

Cronbach, L. J. (1988). Five perspectives on validation argument. In H. Wainer & H. Braun (Eds.), *Test validity* (pp. 3–17). Hillsdale, NJ: Erlbaum.

Cronbach, L. J., Gleser, G. C., Nanda, H., & Rajaratnum, N. (1972). *The dependability of behavioral measures: Theory of generalizability for scores and profiles.* New York: Wiley.

Cronbach, L. J., & Meehl, P. E. (1955). Construct validity in psychological tests. *Psychological Bulletin, 52,* 281–302.

Curtis, K. L., Greve, K. W., & Bianchini, K. J. (2009). The Wechsler Adult Intelligence Scale-III and malingering in traumatic brain injury. *Assessment, 16,* 401–414.

Darlington, R. B. (1990). *Regression and linear models.* New York: McGraw-Hill.

Darton, M., & Clark, J. (1994). *The Macmillan dictionary of measurement.* New York: Macmillan.

De Los Reyes, A., & Kazdin, A. E. (2005). Informant discrepancies in the assessment of childhood psychopathology: A critical review, theoretical framework, and recommendations for further study. *Psychological Bulletin, 131,* 483–509.

DeMaris, A. (1995). A tutorial in logistic regression. *Journal of Marriage and the Family, 57,* 956–968.

Dickson, D. H., & Kelly, I. W. (1985). The "Barnum effect" in personality assessment: A review of the literature. *Psychological Reports, 57,* 367–382.

Dimidjian, S., Hollon, S. D., Dobson, K. S., Schmaling, K. B., Kohlenberg, R. J., Addis, M. E., et al. (2006). Randomized trial of behavioral activation, cognitive therapy and antidepressant medication in the acute treatment of adults with major depression. *Journal of Consulting and Clinical Psychology, 74,* 658–670.

Dougherty, L., Klein, D. K., Olino, T. M., & Laptook, R. S. (2008). Depression in children and adolescents. In J. Hunsley & E. J. Mash (Eds.), *A guide to assessments that work* (pp. 69–95). New York: Oxford University Press.

Doust, J. (2009). Using probabilistic reasoning. *British Medical Journal, 339,* b3823.

Draguns, J. G., & Tanaka-Matsumi, J. (2003). Assessment of psychopathology across and within cultures: Issues and findings. *Behaviour Research and Therapy, 41,* 755–776.

Dwyer, C. A. (1996). Cut scores and testing: Statistics, judgment, truth, and error. *Psychological Assessment, 8,* 360–362.

Ebner-Priemer, U. W., Kuo, J., Kleindienst, N., Welch, S. S., Reisch, T., Reinhard, I., et al. (2007). Assessing state affective instability in borderline personality disorder using an ambulatory monitoring approach. *Psychological Medicine, 37,* 961–970.

Eells, T. (2007). *Handbook of psychotherapy case formulation* (2nd edition). New York: Guilford Press.

Eid, M., & Diener, E. (Eds.). (2006). *Handbook of multimethod measurement in psychology.* Washington, DC: American Psychological Association.

Elliott, A. N., O'Donohue, W. T. O., & Nickerson, M. A. (1993). The use of sexually anatomically detailed dolls in the assessment of sexual abuse. *Clinical Psychology Review, 13,* 207–221.

Embretson, S. E. (1996). The new rules of measurement. *Psychological Assessment, 8,* 341–349.

Fava, M. (2006). Pharmacological approaches to the treatment of residual symptoms. *Journal of Psychopharmacology, 20*(3, Suppl.), 29–34.

Feldt, L. S., & Charter, R. A. (2003). Estimating the reliability of a test split into two parts of equal or unequal length. *Psychological Methods, 8,* 102–109.

Feldt, L. S., & Kim, S. (2006). Testing the difference between two alpha coefficients with small samples of subjects and raters. *Educational and Psychological Measurement, 66,* 589–600.

Fernandez, K., Boccaccini, M. T., & Noland, R. M. (2007). Professionally responsible test selection for Spanish-speaking clients: A four-step approach for identifying and selecting translated tests. *Professional Psychology: Research and Practice, 38*, 363–374.

Fernandez-Ballésteros, R., & Botella, J. (2008). Self-report measures. In A. M. Nezu and C. Nezu (Eds.), *Evidenced-based outcome research: A practical guide to conducting randomized controlled trials for psychosocial interventions* (pp. 95–122). New York: Oxford University Press.

Finn, S. E., & Kamphuis, J. H. (1995). What a clinician needs to know about base rates. In J. N. Butcher (Ed.) *Clinical personality assessment: Practical approaches* (pp. 224–235). New York: Oxford University Press.

First, M. B., Pincus, H. A., Levine, J. B., Williams, J. B. W., Ustun, B., & Peele, R. (2004). Clinical utility as a criterion for revising psychiatric diagnoses. *American Journal of Psychiatry, 161*, 946–954.

Fischer, J., & Corcoran, K. (2000). *Measures for clinical practice* (3rd ed.). New York: Free Press.

Flemming, E. G., & Flemming, C. W. (1929). The validity of the Mathews' revision of the woodworth personal data questionnaire. *Journal of Abnormal and Social Psychology, 23*, 500–506.

Floyd, F. J., & Widaman, K. F. (1995). Factor analysis in the development and refinement of clinical assessment instruments. *Psychological Assessment, 7*, 286–299.

Forkmann, T., Vehren, T., Boecker, M., Norra, C., Wirtz, M., & Gauggel, S. (2009). Sensitivity and specificity of the Beck Depression Inventory in cardiologic inpatients: How useful is the conventional cut-off score? *Journal of Psychosomatic Research, 67*, 347–352.

Foster, S. L., & Mash, E. J. (1999). Assessing social validity in clinical treatment research: Issues and procedures. *Journal of Consulting and Clinical Psychology, 67*, 308–319.

Frederick, R. I., & Bowden, S. C. (2009). The test validation summary. *Assessment, 16*, 215–236.

Froyd, J. E., Lambert, M. J., & Froyd, J. D. (1996). A survey and critique of psychotherapy outcome measurement. *Journal of Mental Health, 5*, 11–15.

Furr, R. M., & Bacharach, V. R. (2008). *Psychometrics, an introduction.* London: Sage.

Garb, H. N. (1998). *Studying the clinician—Judgment research and psychological assessment.* Washington, DC: American Psychological Association.

Garb, H. N. (2003). Incremental validity and the assessment of psychopathology in adults. *Psychological Assessment, 15*, 508–520.

Garb, H. N. (2005). Clinical judgment and decision making. *Annual Review of Clinical Psychology, 1*, 67–89.

Garb, H. N., Lilienfeld, S. O., & Fowler, K. A. (2008). Psychological assessment and clinical judgment. In J. E. Maddux & B. A. Winstead (Eds.), *Psychopathology: Foundations for a contemporary understanding* (2nd ed., pp. 103–124). New York: Routledge.

Garb, H. N., Wood, J. M., Lilienfeld, S. O., & Nezworski, M. T. (2002). Effective use of projective techniques in clinical practice: Let the data help with selection and interpretation. *Professional Psychology: Research and Practice, 33*, 454–463.

Garland, A. F., Kruse, M., & Aarons, G. A. (2003). Clinicians and outcome measurement: What's the use? *Journal of Behavioral Health Services and Research, 30,* 393–405.

Garrett, H. E., & Schneck, M. R. (1928). A study of the discriminate value of the Woodworth Personal Data Sheet. *Journal of General Psychology, 1,* 459–471.

Geiser, C., Eid, M., Nussbeck, F. W., Courvoisier, D. S., & Cole, D. A. (2010). Analyzing true change in longitudinal multitrait-multimethod studies: Application of a multimethod change model to depression and anxiety in children. *Developmental Psychology, 46,* 29–45.

Gigerenzer, G., Gaissmaier, W., Kurz-Milcke, E., Schwartz, L. M., & Woloshin, S. (2008). Helping doctors and patients make sense of health statistics. *Psychological Science in the Public Interest, 8,* 53–96.

Gilbody, S. M., House, A. O., & Sheldon, T. A. (2002). Psychiatrists in the UK do not use outcomes measures: National survey. *British Journal of Psychiatry, 180,* 101–103.

Gorin, J. S., & Embretson, S. E. (2008). Item response theory and Rasch models. In D. McKay (Ed.). *Handbook of research methods in abnormal and clinical psychology* (pp. 271–292). Los Angeles: Sage.

Gotham, H. J. (2004). Diffusion of mental health and substance abuse treatments: Development, dissemination, and implementation. *Clinical Psychology: Science and Practice, 11,* 160–176.

Gough, H. G. (1996). *CPI manual.* Palo Alto, CA: Consulting Psychologists Press.

Green, S. B. (2003). A coefficient alpha for test-retest data. *Psychological Methods, 8,* 88–101.

Greene, R. L. (2006). Use of the MMPI-2 in outpatient mental health settings. In J. Butcher (Ed.), *MMPI-2: A practitioner's guide* (pp. 253–272). Washington, DC: American Psychological Association.

Grills, A. E., & Ollendick, T. H. 2003. Issues in parent–child agreement: The case of structured diagnostic interviews. *Clinical Child and Family Psychology Review, 5,* 57–83.

Grimm, K. J., Pianta, R. C., & Konold, T. (2009). Longitudinal multitrait-multimethod models for developmental research. *Multivariate Behavioral Research, 44,* 233–258.

Gross, D., Fogg, L., Young, M., Ridge, A., Cowell, J. M., Richardson, R., et al. (2006). The equivalence of the Child Behavior Checklist/1 1/2–5 across parent race/ethnicity, income level, and language. *Psychological Assessment, 18,* 313–323.

Grove, W. M., Zald, D. H., Lebow, B. S., Snitz, B. E., & Nelson, C. (2000). Clinical versus mechanical prediction: A meta-analysis. *Psychological Assessment, 12,* 19–30.

Gutierrez, P. M., & Osman, A. (2009). Getting the best return on your screening investment: An analysis of the Suicidal Ideation Questionnaire and Reynolds Adolescent Depression Scale. *School Psychology Review, 38,* 200–217.

Harding, T. P. (2007). Clinical decision-making: How prepared are we? *Training and Education in Professional Psychology, 1,* 95–104.

Hatfield, D. R., & Ogles, B. M. (2007). Why some clinicians use outcome measures and others do not. *Administration and Policy in Mental Health and Mental Health Services Research, 34,* 283–291.

Hayes, S. C., Nelson, R. O., & Jarrett, R. B. (1987). The treatment utility of assessment: A functional approach to evaluating assessment quality. *American Psychologist, 42,* 963–974.

Haynes, S. N. (1992). *Causal models in psychopathology.* New York: Kluwer.

Haynes, S. N. (2001). Clinical applications of analogue observation: dimensions of psychometric evaluation. *Psychological assessment, 13,* 73–85.

Haynes, S. N., & Kaholokula, J. K. (2007). Behavioral assessment. In M. Hersen and A. M. Gross (Eds.), *Handbook of clinical psychology.* New York: Wiley.

Haynes, S. N., Kaholokula, J. K., and Yoshioka, D. (2008). Behavioral assessment in treatment research. In A. M. Nezu & C. Nezu (Eds.), *Evidenced-based outcome research: A practical guide to conducting RCTs for psychosocial interventions* (pp. 67–94). New York: Oxford University Press.

Haynes, S. N., Leisen, M. B., & Blaine, D. D. (1997). Design of individualized behavioural treatment programs using functional analytic clinical case models. *Psychological Assessment, 9,* 332–348.

Haynes, S. N., & Lench, H. (2003). Incremental validity of new clinical assessment measures. *Psychological Assessment, 15,* 456–466.

Haynes, S. N., Mumma, G. H., & Pinson, C. (2009). Idiographic assessment: Conceptual and psychometric foundations of individualized behavioral assessment. *Clinical Psychology Review, 29,* 179–191.

Haynes, S. N., & O'Brien, W. O. (2000). *Principles of behavioral assessment: A functional approach to psychological assessment.* New York: Plenum Press.

Haynes, S. N., O'Brien, W. O., & Kaholokula, J. K. (in press). *Behavioral assessment and case formulation.* Hoboken, NJ: John Wiley & Sons.

Haynes, S. N., Richard, D. C. S., & Kubany, E. S. (1995). Content validity in psychological assessment: A functional approach to concepts and methods. *Psychological Assessment, 7,* 238–247.

Haynes, S. N., & Yoshioka, D. T. (2007). Clinical assessment applications of ambulatory biosensors. *Psychological Assessment, 19,* 44–57.

Hersen, M. (2004). *Comprehensive handbook of psychological assessment.* Hoboken, NJ: John Wiley & Sons.

Heyman, R. E., Chaudhry, B. R., Treboux, D., Crowell, J., Lord, C., Vivian, D., et al. (2001). How much observational data is enough? An empirical test using marital interaction coding. *Behavior Therapy, 32,* 107–123.

Hogan, T. P. (2007). *Psychological testing: A practical introduction* (2nd ed.). New York: Wiley.

Hogan, T. P., Benjamin, A., & Brezinski, K. L. (2000). Reliability methods: A note on the frequency of use of various types. *Educational and Psychological Measurement, 60,* 523–531.

Hohlstein, L. A., Smith, G. T., & Atlas, J. G. (1998). An application of expectancy theory to eating disorders: Development and validation of measures of eating and dieting expectancies. *Psychological Assessment, 10,* 49–58.

Holmbeck G. N., & Devine, K. A. (2009). Editorial: An author's checklist for measure development and validation manuscripts. *Journal of Pediatric Psychology, 34,* 691–696.

Hoyt, W. T., Warbasse, R. E., & Chu, E. Y. (2006). Construct validation in counseling psychology research. *Counseling Psychologist, 34,* 769–805.

Hoyt, W. T., & Kerns, M. D. (1999). Magnitude and moderators of bias in observer ratings: A meta-analysis. *Psychological Methods, 4,* 403–424.

Hsu, L. M. (2002). Diagnostic validity statistics and the MCMI-III. *Psychological Assessment, 14,* 410–422.

Hu, L., & Bentler, P. M. (1995). Evaluating model fit. In R. H. Hoyle (Ed.), *Structural equation modeling* (pp. 76–99). Thousand Oaks, CA: Sage.

Hu, L., & Bentler, P. M. (1999). Cutoff criteria for fit indexes in covariance structure analysis: Conventional criteria versus new alternatives. *Structural Equation Modeling, 6,* 1–55.

Huffcutt, A. I., Roth, P. L., & McDaniel, M. A. (1996). A meta-analytic investigation of cognitive ability in employment interview evaluations: Moderating characteristics and implications for incremental validity. *Journal of Applied Psychology, 81,* 459–473.

Hunsley, J. (2003). Cost-effectiveness and cost offset considerations in psychological service provision. *Canadian Psychology, 44,* 61–73.

Hunsley, J., & Bailey, J. M. (1999). The clinical utility of the Rorschach: Unfulfilled promises and an uncertain future. *Psychological Assessment, 11,* 266–277.

Hunsley, J., & Bailey, J. M. (2001). Whither the Rorschach? An analysis of the evidence. *Psychological Assessment, 13,* 472–485.

Hunsley, J., & Haynes, S. N. (Special Section Eds.). (2003). Incremental validity and utility in clinical assessment. *Psychological Assessment, 15,* 450.

Hunsley, J., Lee, C. M., & Wood, J. M. (2003). Controversial and questionable assessment techniques. In S. O. Lilienfeld, S. J. Lynn, & J. M. Lohr (Eds.), *Science and pseudoscience in clinical psychology* (pp. 39–76). New York: Guilford.

Hunsley, J., & Mash, E. J. (2007). Evidence-based assessment. *Annual Review of Clinical Psychology, 3,* 29–51.

Hunsley, J., & Mash, E. J. (2008a). Developing criteria for evidence-based assessment: An introduction to assessments that work. In J. Hunsley & E. J. Mash (Eds.), *A guide to assessments that work* (pp. 3–14). New York: Oxford University Press.

Hunsley, J., & Mash, E. J. (Eds.). (2008b). *A guide to assessments that work.* New York: Oxford University Press.

Hunsley, J., & Meyer, G. J. (2003). The incremental validity of psychological testing and assessment: Conceptual, methodological, and statistical issues. *Psychological Assessment, 15,* 446–455.

Jacob, T. (1995). The role of time frame in the assessment of family functioning. *Journal of Marital and Family Therapy, 21,* 281–288.

Jacobson, N. S., Follette, W. C., & Revenstorf, D. (1984). Toward a standard definition of clinically significant change. *Behavior Therapy, 17,* 308–311.

Jacobson, N. S., & Truax, P. (1991). Clinical significance: A statistical approach to defining meaningful change in psychotherapy research. *Journal of Consulting and Clinical Psychology, 59,* 12–19.

Jarrett, R. B., Kraft, D., Doyle, J., Foster, B. M., Eaves, G. G., & Silver, P. C. (2001). Preventing recurrent depression using cognitive therapy with and without a continuation phase: a randomized clinical trial. *Archives of General Psychiatry, 58,* 381–388.

Jarrett, R. B., Vittengl, J. R., & Clark, L. A. (2008). How much cognitive therapy, for which patients, will prevent depressive relapse? *Journal of Affective Disorders, 111,* 185–192.

Jensen-Doss, A., Hawley, K. M., Lopez, M., & Osterberg, L. D. (2009). Using evidence-based treatments: The experiences of youth providers working under a mandate. *Professional Psychology: Research and Practice, 40,* 417–424.

Johnston, C., & Murray, C. (2003). Incremental validity in the psychological assessment of children and adolescents. *Psychological Assessment, 15,* 496–507.

Johnston, J. M., & Pennypacker, H. S. (1993). *Strategies and tactics of behavioral research,* (2nd edition). Hillsdale, NJ: Lawrence Erlbaum Associates.

Kaholokula, J. K., Bello, I. Nacapoy, A. H., & Haynes, S. (2009). Behavioral assessment and functional analysis. In D. Richard & S. Huprich (Eds.), *Clinical psychology: Assessment, treatment, and research* (pp. 113–142). Burllington, MA: Elsevier Academic Press.

Kamphuis, J. H., & Noorhof, A. (2009). On categorical diagnoses in *DSM-V*: Cutting dimensions at useful points? *Psychological Assessment, 21,* 294–301.

Kane, M. T. (2001). Current concerns in validity theory. *Journal of Educational Measurement, 38,* 319–342.

Kazdin, A. E. (1993). Evaluation in clinical practice: Clinically sensitive and systematic methods of treatment delivery. *Behavior Therapy, 24,* 11–45.

Kazdin, A. E. (2002). *Research designs in clinical psychology* (4th ed.). Boston: Allyn & Bacon.

Kazdin, A. E. (2008) Evidence-based treatment and practice: New opportunities to bridge clinical research and practice, enhance the knowledge base, and improve patient care. *American Psychologist, 63,* 146-159.

Keane, T. M., Silberbogen, A. K., & Seierich, M. R. (2008). Post-traumatic stress disorder. In J. Hunsley & E. J. Mash (Eds.), *A guide to assessments that work* (pp. 293–318). New York: Oxford University Press.

Keller, M. L., & Craske, M. G. (2008). Panic disorder and agoraphobia. In J. Hunsley & E. J. Mash (Eds.), *A guide to assessments that work* (pp. 229–253). New York: Oxford University Press.

Kendell, R., & Jablensky, A. (2003). Distinguishing between the validity and utility of psychiatric diagnoses. *American Journal of Psychiatry, 160,* 4–12.

Kihlstrom, J. F. (2006). What qualifies as evidence of effective practice? Scientific research. In J. C. Norcross, L. E. Beutler, & R. F. Levant (Eds.). *Evidence-based practices in mental health: Debate and dialogue on the fundamental questions* (pp. 23–31). Washington, DC: American Psychological Association.

Kline, R. B. (2005). *Principles and practice of structural equation modeling.* New York: Guilford Press.

Kline, T. J. B. (2005). *Psychological testing: A practical approach to design and evaluation.* Thousand Oaks, CA: Sage.

Knight, G. P., Roosa, M. W., & Umaña-Taylor, A. J. (2009). Measurement and measurement equivalence issues. In G. P. Knight, M. W. Roosa, & A. J. Umaña-Taylor (Eds.). *Studying ethnic minority and economically disadvantaged populations: Methodological challenges and best practices* (pp. 97–134). Washington, DC: American Psychological Association.

Kraemer, H. C., & Kupfer, D. J. (2005). Size of treatment effects and their importance to clinical research and practice. *Biological Psychiatry, 59,* 990–996.

Krueger, R. F., & Markon, K. E. (2006). Reinterpreting comorbidity: A model-based approach to understanding and classifying psychopathology. *Annual Review of Clinical Psychology, 2,* 111–133.

Kuder, G. F., & Richardson, M. W. (1937). The theory of the estimation of test reliability. *Psychometrika, 2,* 151–160.

Laird, D. A. (1925). A mental hygiene and vocational test. *Journal of Educational Psychology, 16,* 419–422.

Lakatos, I. (1968). Criticism and the methodology of scientific research programs. *Proceedings of the Aristotelian Society, 69,* 149–186.

Lakes, K. D., & Hoyt, W. T. (2009). Applications of generalizability theory to clinical child and adolescent psychology research. *Journal of Clinical Child and Adolescent Psychology, 38,* 144–165.

Lambert, M. J., Hansen, N. B., & Finch, A. E. (2001). Patient-focused research: Using patient outcome data to enhance treatment effects. *Journal of Consulting and Clinical Psychology, 69,* 159–172.

Lambert, M. J., & Hawkins, E. J. (2004). Measuring outcome in professional practice: Considerations in selecting and using brief outcome instruments. *Professional Psychology: Research and Practice, 35,* 492–499.

Lambert, M. J., Whipple, J. L., Hawkings, E. J., Vermeersch, D., Nielsen, S. L., & Smart, D. W. (2003). Is it time to track patient outcome on a routine basis? A meta-analysis. *Clinical Psychology: Science and Practice, 10,* 288–301.

Lichtenberger, E. O., & Kaufman, A. S. (2009). *Essentials of WAIS-IV assessment (essentials of psychological assessment).* Hoboken, NJ: Wiley.

Lilienfield, S. O., Lynn, S. J., & Lohr, J. M. (2003). *Science and pseudoscience in clinical psychology.* New York: Guilford Press.

Lilienfeld, S. O., Waldman, I. D., & Israel, A. C. (1994). A critical examination of the use of the term and concept of *comorbidity* in psychopathology research. *Clinical Psychology Science and Practice, 1,* 71–103.

Lima, E. N., Stanley, S., Kaboski, B., Reitzel, L. R., Richey, J. A., Castro, Y., et al. (2005). The incremental validity of the MMPI-2: When does therapist access not enhance treatment outcome? *Psychological Assessment, 17,* 462–468.

Loevinger, J. (1957). Objective tests as instruments of psychological theory. *Psychological Reports, Monograph Supplement 3,* 635–694.

Loewenstein, D. A., Acevdeo, A., Ownby, R., Agron, J., Barker, W. W., Isaacson, R., et al. (2006). Using different memory cutoffs to assess mild cognitive impairment. *American Journal of Geriatric Psychiatry, 14,* 911–919.

Logan, D. E., Claara, R. L., and Scharffa, L. (2008). Social desirability response bias and self-report of psychological distress in pediatric chronic pain patients. *Pain, 136,* 366–372.

Longwell, B. T., & Truax, P. (2005). The differential effects of weekly, monthly, and bimonthly administration of the Beck Depression Inventory-II: Psychometric properties and clinical implications. *Behavior Therapy, 36,* 265–275.

Lynam, D. R., & Widiger, T. A. (2007). Using a general model of personality to identify the basic elements of psychopathy. *Journal of Personality Disorders, 21,* 160–178.

MacCallum, R. C., Roznowski, M., & Necowitz, L. B. (1992). Model modifications in covariance structure analysis: The problem of capitalization on chance. *Psychological Bulletin, 111,* 490–504.

MacCorquodale, K., & Meehl, P. E. (1948). On a distinction between hypothetical constructs and intervening variables. *Psychological Review, 55*, 95–107.

Malda, M., van de Vijver, F. J. R., Srinivasan, K., Sukumar, P., Rao, K., & Transler,
C. (2008). Adapting a cognitive test for a different culture: An illustration
of qualitative procedures. *Psychology Science, 50*, 451–468.

Margraf, J., Taylor, C. B., Ehlers, A., Roth, W. T., & Agras, W. S. (1987). Panic
attacks in the natural environment. *Journal of Nervous and Mental Disease,
175*, 558–565.

Marriott, F. H. C. (1990). *A dictionary of statistical terms* (5th ed.). New York:
Longman Scientific and Technical.

Marshall, M. B., & Bagby, R. M. (2006). The incremental validity and clinical
utility of the MMPI-2 Infrequency Posttraumatic Stress Disorder scale.
Assessment, 13, 417–429.

Mash, E. J., & Hunsley, J. (1993). Assessment considerations in the identification of failing psychotherapy: Bringing the negatives out of the darkroom.
Psychological Assessment, 5, 292–301.

McFall, R. M. (2005). Theory and utility—key themes in evidence-based
assessment comment on the special section. *Psychological Assessment, 17*,
312–323.

McFall, R. M., & Treat, T. A. (1999). Quantifying the information value of clinical
assessments with signal detection theory. *Annual Review of Psychology, 50*,
215–241.

McGrath, R. E. (2001). Toward more clinically relevant assessment research.
Journal of Personality Assessment, 77, 307–332.

McGrath, R. E. (2005). Conceptual complexity and construct validity. *Journal of
Personality Assessment, 85*, 112–124.

McGrath, R. E., & Meyer, G. J. (2006). When effect sizes disagree: The case of
r and *d*. *Psychological Methods, 11*, 386–401.

Meehl, P. E. (1971). High school yearbooks: A reply to Schwarz. *Journal of
Abnormal Psychology, 77*, 143–148.

Meehl, P. E., & Rosen, A. (1955). Antecedent probability and the efficiency of
psychometric signs, patterns, or cutting scores. *Psychological Bulletin, 52*,
194–216.

Megargee, E. (2009). The California Psychological Inventory. In J. N. Butcher
(Ed.), *Oxford handbook of personality assessment* (pp. 323–335). New York:
Oxford University Press.

Meier, S. T., & Davis, S. R. (1990). Trends in reporting psychometric properties
of scales used in counseling psychology research. *Journal of Counseling
Psychology, 37*, 113–115.

Meng, X., Rosenthal, R., & Rubin, D. B. (1992). Comparing correlated correlation coefficients. *Psychological Bulletin, 111*, 172–175.

Messick, S. (1995). Validity of psychological assessment: Validation of inferences
from persons' response and performances as scientific inquiry into score
meaning. *American Psychologist, 50*, 741–749.

Messick, S. (1998). Test validity: A matter of consequence. *Social Indicators
Research, 45*, 35–44.

Minke, K., & Haynes, S. N. (in press). Sampling issues. In J. C. Thomas & M.
Hersen (Eds.). *Understanding research in clinical and counseling psychology*
(2nd edition). New York: Taylor & Francis.

Mizrahi, R., Kiang, M., Mamo, D. C., Arenovich, T., Bagby, R. M., Zipursky, R. B., et al. (2006). The selective effect of antipsychotics on the different dimensions of the experience of psychosis in schizophrenia spectrum disorders. *Schizophrenia Research, 88,* 111–118.

Moskowitz, D. S., Russell, J. J., Sadikaj, G., & Sutton, R. (2009). Measuring people intensively. *Canadian Psychology, 50,* 131–140.

Mueser, K. T., & Glynn, S. M. (2008). Schizophrenia. In J. Hunsley & E. J. Mash (Eds.), *A guide to assessments that work* (pp. 391–412). New York: Oxford University Press.

Mullins-Sweatt, S. N., & Widiger, T. A. (2009). Clinical utility and *DSM-V*. *Psychological Assessment, 21,* 302–312.

Murphy, K. R., & Davidshofer, C. O. (2005). *Psychological testing. Principles and applications* (6th ed.). Upper Saddle River, NJ: Pearson Education.

Nair, R. L., White, R. M. B., Knight, G. P., & Roosa, M. W. (2009). Cross-language measurement equivalence of parenting measures for use with Mexican American populations. *Journal of Family Psychology, 23,* 680–689.

National Council on Measurement in Education. (1999). *Standards for educational and psychological assessment.* Washington, DC: Author.

Nelson-Gray, R. O. (2003). Treatment utility of psychological assessment. *Psychological Assessment, 15,* 521–531.

Nezu, A. M., & Nezu, C. M. (Eds.). (1989). *Clinical decision making in behavior therapy—A problem-solving perspective.* Champaign, IL: Research Press.

Nezu, A. M., & Nezu, C. (Eds.). (2008). *Evidenced-based outcome research: A practical guide to conducting randomized controlled trials for psychosocial interventions.* New York: Oxford University Press.

Nezu, A. M., Nezu, C. M., & Lombardo, E. (2004). *Cognitive-behavioral case formulation and treatment design: A problem solving approach.* New York: Springer.

Nichols, D. S., & Crowhurst, B. (2006). Use of the MMPI-2 in inpatient mental health settings. In J. Butcher (Ed.), *MMPI-2: A practitioner's guide* (pp. 195–252). Washington, DC: American Psychological Association.

Nunnally, J. C., & Bernstein, I. H. (1994). *Psychometric theory.* New York: McGraw-Hill.

Olkin, I., & Finn, J. D. (1995). Correlations redux. *Psychological Bulletin, 118,* 155–164.

Osburn, H. G. (2000). Coefficient alpha and related internal consistency reliability coefficients. *Psychological Methods, 5,* 343–355.

Palmiter, D. J., Jr. (2004). A survey of the assessment practices of child and adolescent clinicians. *American Journal of Orthopsychiatry, 74,* 122–128.

Pedhauzer, E. J., & Schmelkin, L. P. (1991). *Measurement, design, and analysis: An integrated approach.* Hillsdale, NJ: Erlbaum.

Pelham, W. E., Fabiano, G. A., & Massetti, G. M. (2005). Evidence-based assessment of attention deficit hyperactivity disorder in children and adolescents. *Journal of Clinical Child and Adolescent Psychology, 34,* 449–476.

Persons, J. B. (2008). *The case formulation approach to cognitive-behavior therapy.* New York: Guilford Press.

Persons, J. B., & Mikami, A. Y. (2002). Strategies for handling treatment failure successfully. *Psychotherapy: Theory, Research, Practice, Training, 39,* 139–151.

Poston, J. M., & Hanson, W. E. (2010). Meta-analysis of psychological assessment as a therapeutic intervention. *Psychological Assessment, 22,* 203–212.

Prigatano, G. P., & Pliskin, N. H. (Eds.). (2003). *Clinical neuropsychology and cost outcome research: A beginning.* New York: Psychology Press.

Rattan, R. B., & Chapman, L. J. (1973). Associative intrusions in schizophrenic verbal behavior. *Journal of Abnormal Psychology, 85,* 151–155.

Reyna, V. F., Nelson, W. L., Han, P. K., & Dieckmann, N. F. (2009). How numeracy influences risk comprehension and medical decision making. *Psychological Bulletin, 135,* 943–973.

Rhule, D. M., McMahon, R. J., & Vando, J. (2009). The acceptability and representativeness of standardized parent-child interaction tasks. *Behavior Therapy, 40,* 393–402.

Rice, M. E., & Harris, G. T. (2005). Comparing effect sizes in follow-up studies: ROC area, Cohen's *d*, and *r. Law and Human Behavior, 29,* 615–620.

Rodriquez, M. C., & Maeda, Y. (2006). Meta-analysis of coefficient alpha. *Psychological Methods, 11,* 306–322.

Rosenthal, R. (1991). *Meta-analytic procedures for social research.* Newbury Park, CA: Sage.

Rosenthal, R., & Rubin, D. B. (1982). A simple, general-purpose display of magnitude of experimental effect. *Journal of Educational Psychology, 74,* 166–169.

Ross, R. G., Heinlein, S., & Tregellas, H. (2006). High rates of comorbidity are found in childhood-onset schizophrenia. *Schizophrenia Research, 88,* 90–95.

Rowa, K., McCabe, R., & Antony, M. M. (2008). Specific phobia and social phobia. In J. Hunsley & E. J. Mash (Eds.), *A guide to assessments that work* (pp. 207–228). New York: Oxford University Press.

Rummel, R. J. (1988). *Applied factor analysis.* Evanston, IL: Northwestern University Press.

Santor, D. A., Debrota, D., Engelhardt, N., & Gelwicks, S. (2008). Optimizing the ability of the Hamilton Depression Rating Scale to discriminate across levels of severity and between antidepressants and placebos. *Depression and Anxiety, 25,* 774–786.

Sattler, J. M. (2001). *Assessment of children.* San Diego, CA: Sattler.

Schmidt, F. L., & Hunter, J. E. (1998). The validity and utility of selection methods in personnel psychology: Practical and theoretical implications of 85 years of research findings. *Psychological Bulletin, 124,* 262–274.

Schmidt, F. L., Le, H., & Ilies, R. (2003). Beyond alpha: An empirical examination of the effects of different sources of measurement error on reliability estimates for measures of individual differences constructs. *Psychological Methods, 8,* 206–224.

Sechrest, L. (1963). Incremental validity: A recommendation. *Educational and Psychological Measurement, 23,* 153–158.

Sechrest, L. (2005). Validity of measures is no simple matter. *Health Research and Educational Trust, 40,* 1584–1604.

Sharpe, J. P., & Gilbert, D. G. (1998). Effects of repeated administration of the Beck Depression Inventory and other measures of negative mood states. *Personality and Individual Differences, 24,* 457–463.

Shiffman, S. (2009). How many cigarettes did you smoke? Assessing cigarette consumption by global report, time-line follow-back, and ecological momentary assessment. *Health Psychology, 28,* 519–526.

Shrout, P. E., & Fleiss, J. L. (1979). Intraclass correlations: Uses in assessing rater reliability. *Psychological Bulletin, 86,* 420–428.

Shrout, P. E., Lyons, M., Dohrenwend, B. P., Skodol, A. E., Murray, S., & Kass, F. (1988). Changing time frames on symptom inventories: Effects on the psychiatric epidemiology research interview. *Journal of Consulting and Clinical Psychology, 56*, 267–272.

Simms, L., Watson, D., & Doebbeling, B. (2002). Confirmatory factor analyses of posttraumatic stress symptoms in deployed and nondeployed veterans of the Gulf War. *Journal of Abnormal Psychology, 111*, 637–647.

Smart, A. (2006). A multi-dimensional model of clinical utility. *International Journal for Quality in Health Care, 18*, 377–382.

Smith, G. T. (2005). On construct validity: Issues of method and measurement. *Psychological Assessment, 17*, 396–408.

Smith, G. T., & Combs, J. (2010). Issues of construct validity in psychological diagnoses. In T. Millon, R. F. Krueger, & E. Simonsen (Eds.), *Contemporary directions in psychopathology: Toward the DSM-V and ICD-11* (pp. 205–222). New York: Guilford Press.

Smith, G. T., McCarthy, D. M., & Anderson, K. (2000). On the sins of short form development. *Psychological Assessment, 10*, 49–58.

Smith, G. T., McCarthy, D. M., & Zapolski, T. C. B. (2009). On the value of homogeneous constructs for construct validation, theory testing, and the description of psychopathology. *Psychological Assessment, 21*, 272–284.

Smith, G. T., Spillane, N. S., & Annus, A. M. (2006). Implications of an emerging integration of universal and culturally-specific psychologies. *Perspectives on Psychological Science, 1*, 211–233.

Snyder, D., Heyman, R., & Haynes, S. N. (2008). Couple assessment. In J. Hunsley & E. J. Mash (Eds.), *A guide to assessments that work* (pp. 439–463). Oxford, UK: Oxford University Press.

Spangler, T., & Gazelle, H. (2009), Anxious solitude, unsociability, and peer exclusion in middle childhood: A multitrait–multimethod matrix. *Social Development, 18*, 833–856.

Spitzer, R. L., Endicott, J., & Robins, E. (1975). Clinical criteria for psychiatric diagnosis and *DSM-III. American Journal of Psychiatry, 132*, 1187–1192.

Steiger, J. H. (1980). Tests for comparing elements of a correlation matrix. *Psychological Bulletin, 87*, 245–251.

Stevens, S. S. (1968). Measurement, statistics, and the schemapiric view. *Science, 161*, 849–856.

Strauss, M. E. (2001). Demonstrating specific cognitive deficits: A psychometric perspective. *Journal of Abnormal Psychology, 110*, 6–14.

Strauss, M. E., & Smith, G. T. (2009). Construct validity: Advances in theory and methodology. *Annual Review of Clinical Psychology, 5*, 89–113.

Streiner, D. L. (2003a). Being inconsistent about consistency: When coefficient alpha does and doesn't matter. *Journal of Personality Assessment, 80*, 217–222.

Streiner, D. L. (2003b). Diagnosing tests: Using and misusing diagnostic and screening tests. *Journal of Personality Assessment, 81*, 209–219.

Streiner, D. L. (2003c). Starting at the beginning: An introduction to coefficient alpha and internal consistency. *Journal of Personality Assessment, 80*, 99–103.

Streiner, D. L., & Norman, G. R. (2008). *Health measurement scales: A practical guide to their development and use* (4th ed.). New York: Oxford University Press.

Sturmey, P. (Ed.) (2009). *Clinical case formulation, varieties of approaches.* Chichester, UK: Wiley-Blackwell.

Suen, H. K., & Ary, D. (1989). *Analyzing quantitative behavioral data.* Hillsdale, NJ: Erlbaum.

Suen, H. K., & Rzasa, S. E. (2004). Psychometric foundations of behavioral assessment. In S. N. Haynes & E. M. Heiby (Eds.), M. Hersen (Series Ed.), *Comprehensive handbook of psychological assessment, Volume 3, Behavioral assessment* (pp. 37–56). Hoboken, NJ: Wiley.

Sullivan, K. (2005). Alternate forms of prose packages for the assessment of auditory-verbal memory. *Archives of clinical neuropsychology, 20,* 745–753.

Takegami, M., Hayashino, Y., Chin, K., Sokejima, S., Kadotani, H., Akashiba, T., et al. (2009). Simple four-variable screening tool for identification of patients with sleep-disordered breathing. *Sleep: Journal of Sleep and Sleep Disorders Research, 32,* 939–948.

Tanaka-Matsumi, J. (2004). Individual differences and behavioral assessment. In S. N. Haynes & E. M. Heiby (Eds.), *Comprehensive handbook of psychological assessment (Vol. 3): Behavioral assessment* (pp. 128–139). Hoboken, NJ: Wiley.

Taylor, H. C., & Russell, J. T. (1939). The relationship of validity coefficients to the practical effectiveness of tests in selection. *Journal of Applied Psychology, 23,* 565–578.

Terbizan, D. J., Dolezal, B. A., & Albano, C. (2002). Validity of seven commercially available heart rate monitors. *Measurement in Physical Education and Exercise Science, 6,* 243–247.

Terry, P. C., Stevens, M. J., & Lane, A. M. (2005). Influence of response time frame on mood assessment. *Anxiety, Stress and Coping: An International Journal, 18,* 279–285.

Thompson, B. (1994). Guidelines for authors. *Educational and Psychological Measurement, 54,* 837–847.

Turk, D.C., & Melzack, R. (Eds.) (2001). *Handbook of Pain Assessment* (2nd edition). New York: Guilford Press.

Twenge, J. M., & Nolen-Hoeksema, S. (2002). Age, gender, race, socioeconomic status, and birth cohort differences on the Children's Depression Inventory: A meta-analysis. *Journal of Abnormal Psychology, 111,* 578–588.

Vacha-Haase, T. (1998). Reliability generalization: Exploring variance in measurement error affecting score reliability across studies. *Educational and Psychological Measurement, 58,* 6–20.

van de Vijver, F., & Tanaka-Matsumi, J. (2007). Multicultural research. In D. McKay (Ed.), *Handbook of research methods in abnormal and clinical psychology* (pp. 463–482). Los Angeles: Sage Publications.

Vermeersch, D. A., Lambert, M. J., & Burlingame, G. M. (2000). Outcome Questionnaire: Item sensitivity to change. *Journal of Personality Assessment, 74,* 242–261.

Vermeersch, D. A., Whipple, J. L., Lambert, M. J., Hawkins, E. J., Burchfield, C. M., & Okiishi, J. C. (2004). Outcome Questionnaire: Is it sensitive to changes in counseling center clients? *Journal of Counseling Psychology, 51,* 38–49.

von Baeyer, C. L. (1994). Reactive effects of measurement of pain. *Clinical Journal of Pain, 10*, 18-21.

Vrieze, S. I., & Grove, W. M. (2009). Survey on the use of clinical and mechanical prediction methods in clinical psychology. *Professional Psychology: Research and Practice, 40*, 525–531.

Warren, C. S., Cepeda-Benito, A., Gleaves, D. H., Rodriguez, S., Fingeret, M. C., Pearson, C. A., et al. (2008). English and Spanish versions of the Body Shape Questionnaire: Measurement equivalence across ethnicity and clinical status. *International Journal of Eating Disorders, 41*, 265–272.

Watkins, M. W., & Glutting, J. J. (2000). Incremental validity of WISC-III profile elevation, scatter, and shape information for predicting reading and math achievement. *Psychological Assessment, 12*, 402–408.

Weimer, W. B. (1979). *Notes on the methodology of scientific research.* Hillsdale, NJ: Erlbaum.

Weyandt, L. L. (2006). *The physiological bases of cognitive and behavioral disorders.* Mahwah, NJ: Erlbaum.

Whisman, M. A., Snyder, D. K., & Beach, S. R. H. (2009). Screening for marital and relationship discord. *Journal of Family Psychology, 23*, 247–254.

Whittington, D. (1998). How well do researchers report their measures?: An evaluation of measurement in published educational research. *Educational and Psychological Measurement, 58*, 21–37.

Widiger, T. A. (2008). Personality disorders. In J. Hunsley & E. J. Mash (Eds.), *A guide to assessments that work* (pp. 413–435). New York: Oxford University Press.

Wienke, T., Christine, M., Green, A. E., Karver, M. S., & Gesten, E. L. (2009). Multiple informants in the assessment of psychological, behavioral, and academic correlates of bullying and victimization in middle school. *Journal of Adolescence, 32*, 193–211.

Wiggins, J. S. (1973). *Personality and prediction: Principles of personality assessment.* Menlo Park, CA: Addison-Wesley.

Wilder, D. A., Chen, L., Atwell, J., Pritchard, J., & Weinstein, P. (2006). Brief functional analysis and treatment of tantrums associated with transitions in preschool children. *Journal of Applied Behavior Analysis, 39*, 103–107.

Williams, R. H., & Zimmerman, D. W. (1966). Some conjectures concerning the index of reliability and related quantities when true scores and error scores on mental tests are not independent. *Journal of Experimental Education, 35*, 76–79.

Wolf, E. J., Miller, M. W., Orazem, R. J., Weicrich, M. R., Castillo, D. T., Milford, J., et al. (2008). The MMPI-2 Restructured Clinical Scales in the assessment of posttraumatic stress disorder and comorbid disorders. *Psychological Assessment, 20*, 327–340.

Wood, J. M. (2007, October 3). Understanding and computing Cohen's kappa: A tutorial. *WebPsychEmpiricist.* Retrieved September 11, 2009, from http://www.wpe.info/papers_table

Wu, L. T., & Howard, M. O. (2007). Psychiatric disorders in inhalant users: Results from the National Epidemiologic Survey on Alcohol and Related Conditions. *Drug and Alcohol Dependence, 88*, 146–155.

Yates, B. T., & Taub, J. (2003). Assessing the costs, benefits, cost-effectiveness, and cost-benefit of psychological assessment: We should, we can, and here's how. *Psychological Assessment, 15,* 478–495.

Yin, P., & Fan, X. (2000). Assessing the reliability of Beck Depression Scores: Reliability generalization across studies. *Educational and Psychological Measurement, 60,* 201–223.

Youden, W. J. (1950). Index for rating diagnostic tests. *Cancer, 3,* 32–35.

Youngstrom, E. A., Findling, R. L., Calabrese, J. R., Gracious, B. L., Demeter, C., Bedoya, D. D., et al. (2004). Comparing the diagnostic accuracy of six potential screening instruments for bipolar disorder in youths ages 5 to 17 years. *Journal of the American Academy of Child and Adolescent Psychiatry, 43,* 847–858.

Zeldow, P. B. (2009). In defense of clinical judgment, credentialed clinicians, and reflective practice. *Psychotherapy: Research, Practice, Training, 46,* 1–10.

Zink, T., Klesges, L. M., Levin, L., & Putnam, F. (2007). Abuse Behavior Inventory: Cutpoint, validity, and characterization of discrepancies. *Journal of Interpersonal Violence, 22,* 921–931.

AUTHOR INDEX

A

B

SUBJECT INDEX

A

Accuracy, 217
Acquiescence, 217
Agreement, 217
Aggregate measure, 217
Alternate forms, 32, 217
Analog assessment, 217–218
Analysis of variance and covariance,
    181–185
  assumptions underlying, 182–184
Area under the curve, 163–164
Assessment instrument
  alternate forms of, 33
  brief form of, 180
  clinical utility of, 107-123
  content validity of, 15, 56, 167-168
  definition of, 7, 218
  factor structure of, 127-150
  errors in construction of, 14, 58, 86
  feasibility of, 123-125
  idiographic assessment with, 115
  incremental validity and utility of,
    151-154
  interpretation of measures from, 6
  measures from, 18-19, 60-61, 69,
    161-166
  selecting the best to use in clinical
    assessment, 28, 52, 76-86, 10,
    193-195
  sensitivity to change of measures
    from, 97
Assessment method
  acceptability of, 124-125
  definition of, 7, 218

divergence associated with, 203-204
errors associated with, 28, 195-199
multiple, 207-213
Assessment strategy
  collaborative, 221
  definition of, 7, 218, 230
  funneling, 226
  errors associated with, 6
  importance of, 15
  individualized, 4, 214
  longitudinal, 229
  monomethod, 199-202, 231
  multi-informant, 231
  multimethod, 231
  sequential, 94
Attenuation, 218
Autocorrelation, 218

B

Baseline condition, 218
Base rate, 218
Behavior avoidance test, 218
Behavior disorder/problems,
  base rates of, 27
  causal models of, 11, 220
  characteristics of, 8–10
  comorbidity of, 11
  definition, 219
  dynamic nature of, 209-210
  effects of on assessment strategies, 9
  diagnosis and identification of, 5
  dimensions of, 10, 12
  idiographic assessment and, 115, 212
  multimodal nature of, 211-212